D1483247

STUDIES IN HISTORY, ECONOMICS AND PUBLIC LAW

Edited by the
FACULTY OF POLITICAL SCIENCE
OF COLUMBIA UNIVERSITY

———

NUMBER 122

BRITISH RADICALISM, 1791–1797

BY

WALTER PHELPS HALL

BRITISH RADICALISM

1791-1797

BY

WALTER PHELPS HALL

OCTAGON BOOKS

A DIVISION OF FARRAR, STRAUS AND GIROUX

New York   1976

Reprinted 1976
by special arrangement with Columbia University Press

OCTAGON BOOKS
A DIVISION OF FARRAR, STRAUS & GIROUX, INC.
19 Union Square West
New York, N.Y. 10003

Library of Congress Cataloging in Publication Data

Hall, Walter Phelps, 1884-1962.
    British radicalism, 1791-1797.

    Reprint of the ed. published by Columbia University, New York,
which was issued as v. 49, no. 1, whole no. 122 of Studies in
history, economics, and public law.

    Originally presented as the author's thesis, Columbia University.

    Bibliography: p.
    1. Great Britain—Politics and government—1789-1820. 2. Radi-
cal Party (Gt. Brit.) I. Title. II. Series: Columbia studies in
the social sciences; no. 122.

JN1129.R3   1791b   320.9′41′073   76-18289
ISBN 0-374-93383-9

Manufactured by Braun-Brumfield, Inc.
Ann Arbor, Michigan
Printed in the United States of America

10

WILLIAM MARTIN RICHARDS

PREFACE

TODAY, with *Kulturgeschichte* almost orthodox, and radicalism made respectable,[1] it is unnecessary to apologize for the subject of this dissertation. Concerning its treatment, however, the author feels no such assurance. His original endeavor was to describe the political organization of radicalism which, by the constituent nature of the House of Commons, existed perforce beyond the pale of that body. But upon further study, organized radicalism, when compared with theoretical, appeared in significance inconsequential and abortive. Therefore, the emphasis has been shifted to an analysis of radical theory. That analysis is far from complete. To trace with accuracy the influence of either Paine or Godwin alone, would be no small task. This treatise does not pretend to treat the radicalism of the period comprehensively or exhaustively. Its aim is to construct a just and well-proportioned synthesis of radical opinion.

In the introduction, the framework of British society within which radicalism operated, has been briefly summarized in its more characteristic features. Therein the changes of the economic structure of society at the end of the eighteenth century are deemed worthy of first consideration, and second only to them in importance is a catalog of those cumbersome and antiquated statutes which so clogged the wheels of British progress.

In the preparation of this dissertation the author has

---

[1] J. H. Robinson, *The New History*, p. 236.

been assisted by Dr. Austin B. Keep, of the College of the City of New York; Dr. A. Z. Reed, and Mr. W. C. Gerrish. Acknowledgments are due also to several members of the Columbia University Faculty: to Professor William M. Sloane, under whose general supervision this thesis has been written; to Professor James T. Shotwell, for keen criticism and suggestion; to Professor Carlton H. Hayes, for the sacrifice of many hours in proof-reading; and in a special sense to Professor James H. Robinson, whose point of view, always fresh and stimulating, has been a paramount influence in the author's graduate work.

CONTENTS

PAGE

SECTION II RADICALISM IN PRACTICE

INTRODUCTION

I⊤ is an obvious, indisputable and salient fact that the cost of living, toward the close of the eighteenth century, increased with great rapidity. The rise in value of wheat was particularly noticeable, as is demonstrated by the audit books of Eton College and Prince's "Prices Current."[1] From the latter source we also learn of a corresponding rise in value of other food commodities of staple use. Nor was this rise confined to foodstuffs. Raw wool, tobacco, soap, lumber and other articles registered an advance; and, though certain wares, such as rice, cotton and tea, decreased somewhat in value, the unusually high average of prices was thereby but little affected.

In addition to "Prices Current" and the Eton tables, exact and minute information upon the subject is contained in Sir John Sinclair's "Statistical Account of Scotland." This book, or series of books, was compiled from letters written by the Scottish clergy. In them the clergymen described as they saw fit the noteworthy features of their own parishes; and it is significant that almost all took cognizance of their increased living expenses. Their estimate for a period of some twenty

[1] Wheat advanced from 43s. 1¼d. in 1780, to 48s. in 1785; to 56s. 2½d. in 1790; to 81s. 6d. in 1795; to 127s. in 1800. Beef, which in 1787 cost per tierce (304 lbs.) 76s., in 1797 sold for 110s. Butter, valued in 1787 at 47s. per hundredweight, brought, in 1797, 85s. Sugar, at 24s. per hundredweight in 1787, was quoted at 52s. in 1797. Tooke, *History of Prices, Appendix* to Volumes I and II, *passim*.

years varied from thirty to fifty per cent.[1]   One more instance will suffice.   Arthur Young tells us, in 1801, that he knew a person then living who formerly could have bought a bushel of wheat, a bushel of malt, a pound of butter, a pound of cheese, and a pennyworth of tobacco for five shillings.   These same commodities cost, in 1801, no less than one pound, six shillings and five pence.[2]

There was no relative advance in wages to offset this rise of prices.   The buying power of wages in 1800 has been compared with that of 1790.   In accordance with Porter's estimate the laborer could buy fifty-three pints of wheat with a week's wages in 1800.   In 1790 he could have bought eighty-two pints.   The skilled artisan, who could buy only eighty-three pints of wheat in 1800 could in 1790 have procured one hundred and sixty-nine.[3]   A slight increase did take place during the last decade of the century.   Especially was this true in 1795, 1796 and 1800, but it was piteously inadequate, as the records of the journeymen tailors of London and of the Greenwich hospital prove.[4]

Poverty, suffering and discontent accompanied this

[1] Sinclair, *Statistical Account, passim.*

[2] Young, *Annals of Agriculture and other Useful Arts*, xxxvii, 265.

[3] Porter, *State of the Nation.* p. 478.

[4] " The wages of the tailors had been, from 1775 to 1795, one pound, one shilling and nine pence per week, which, at the price of 7¼d. per quartern loaf would purchase thirty-six loaves, while the utmost advance in wages which, in 1795, was to twenty-five shillings, and in 1810 twenty-seven shillings, would purchase in the latter year only eighteen and one-half loaves."   The increase at the hospital was: Carpenters from 2/7 per day to 3/2.   Bricklayers from 2/4 per day to 3/.   Masons from 3/ per day to 3/3.   Plumbers from 3/ per day to 3/3.   Tooke, *History of Prices*, i, 227.   J. E. and Barbara Hammond, *The Village Laborer*, p. 111, give a careful résumé from many contemporary sources of the slight increase in wages during the last quarter of the century.

rise of prices. To the wage earner it meant sharp distress; to the middle-class Englishmen on a fixed income it was a heavy grievance, especially since, as Malthus later indicated, the growing pauperism of the laborers was reacting directly upon the middle class, owing to the vicious poor-law system then in operation.[1] Indeed, this rise in prices was responsible, more than any other factor, for the social unrest which is the subject of our study. It is our intention to approach that unrest later from many different perspectives. For the present let us concede its existence, and confine our attention to the attitude of the government toward the laboring poor.

The Tory government was not greatly perturbed by high prices. To be sure Parliament in October, 1795, was urged to take some action by the speech from the throne, and a brisk word-skirmish ensued, but judged by its results, the debate was both trifling and desultory. High prices did not ruffle the equanimity of the lords. On the day Parliament opened, somewhat over a hun-

[1] Malthus, *Essay on Population* (1798), pp. 71 *et seq.* This idea is further treated by Malthus in 1800, *vide*, *Investigation of the High Price of Living*. Specific figures are given by Tooke, i, *op. cit.*, 228:

	1773.			1793.			1797.		
	£.	s.	d.	£.	s.	d.	£.	s.	d.
Coomb of mart	—	12	—	1	3	—	1	3	—
A caldron of coals. . . .	1	11	6	2	—	6	2	6	—
A coomb of oats.	—	5	—	—	13	—	—	16	—
A load of hay	2	2	—	4	10	—	5	5	—
Meat	—	—	4	—	—	5	—	—	7
Butter.	—	—	6	—	—	11	—	—	11
Sugar.	—	—	8	—	1	—	—	1	3
Soap	—	—	6	—	—	8	—	—	—
Light.	3	10	6	7	10	8	12	12	9½
Poor rates per quarter	—	1	—	—	2	6	—	3	9½
	8	4	0	16	2	8	22	9	4

dred peers spiritual and temporal were present. The
next day there were fourteen, and throughout this
session and the next the attendance averaged perhaps
ten.[1]   The lords did, however. pass a resolution binding
themselves not to consume more than two-thirds of
their accustomed quantity of flour.[2]   Conscious then of
duty well performed, they rested from their labors.

In the House of Commons, though no one knew why
prices had risen, there were many ready with the reason.
The Tories censured nature, and forsooth with perfect
propriety, for had not crops been unusually poor?[3] Fox,
the Whig leader, denounced the war,[4] and others held
the mechanism of distribution responsible, for the government refrained from regulating the corn market.
Indeed, one Lechmere stated that his study of the sub-

---

[1] *Journal of the House of Lords* for 1795. The lowest number at
any meeting was three. At the time of the attack on the king nearly a
full house assembled.

[2] On debating this resolution, some animation was displayed. The
Earl of Lauderdale protested that ''such a palpable catch at popularity should be disclaimed. He would not have his name trumpeted
forth in the public ear while he was conscious that he afforded no real
mitigation to the pressure of public calamity.'' *Parliamentary Register*,
xlv, 180.

[3] There were no good crops in England between 1791 and 1796.
The year 1792 was stated in the annals of agriculture to have been
remarkable for an extremely wet summer, by which the crop of wheat
was much injured everywhere. In 1793 the crop was moderate. The
years 1794–1795 were marked by very bad harvests. The winter of
1794-1795 was unusually severe, the spring following unusually late,
and the following harvest being both late and poor. Similar conditions
existed in North America and in Northern Europe. Tooke, *op. cit.*, i,
179.

[4] *Parliamentary Register*, xliii, 71. Tooke, *History of Prices*, p. 115.
Tooke, by an ingenious comparison of the Eton Tables, demonstrated
that from 1688 to 1792 prices in England were as high in times of
peace as in times of war. *Op. cit.*, p. 81.

ject had brought him to conclude that monopoly was the root of the evil. He knew of two kinds of monopolies. First, there was a monopoly of farms. All the government could do in this instance was to prevent the evil from growing worse. Second, there was a monopoly in corn. The jobbers were responsible for this, and he would bring the career of these gentlemen to a close. Lechmere proposed that a number of state granaries be erected, and that existing distinctions between wholesale and retail prices be abolished. [1]

These opinions heard in Parliament were reflected and amplified in committee reports.[2] To meet the emergency there were three recommendations : a system of bounties ; a reduced consumption of wheat (diet reform); and regulation of the Corn Exchange by the government. The bounty on the importation of wheat was to be determined by a scale graduated in accordance with the current prices in England. This bounty was to be given to both American and European wheat, but at a higher rate to the latter, because ships for the Mediterranean sailed in ballast and were heavily insured.[3] On the other hand the consumption of grain was to be lessened. His Majesty was requested to issue a proclamation to this effect, which should be circulated by the clergy and magistrates of the realm; and yet more definite than the general advice of economy were proposed substitutes for wheat. Rice and potatoes were especially favored. The

---

[1] *Parliamentary Register*, xliii, 70.

[2] The committee appointed to inquire into the high price of corn made three reports in 1795, and two in 1796. Another committee on the high price of provisions, made six reports in 1800. A third committee, appointed to report on the assize of bread, made two reports in the same year.

[3] First report of the committee on the high price of corn, Nov, 24, 1793. *Reports of Committees,* ix, 45.

director of a London foundling asylum testified that since 1795 he had exclusively used rice for the dinner of his charges, in place of a suet flour pudding. Thereby was the treasury of the foundling asylum greatly benefited and no difference in the health of the children was noted, save possibly in the case of a few, who were given wheaten bread by special dispensation.[1] A Rev. Mr. Smith, from Wendover, Bucks, in 1795 changed his method of bread making. "In the course of that year," he said, "I made many experiments in the mixture of potatoes, barley and oats, together with wheaten flour; which articles, though they are moderate in price, did not answer as cheap substitutes." Mr. Smith discovered that by adding two pounds of rice to eleven pounds of flour he could obtain a satisfactory loaf of bread weighing eighteen pounds.[2]

These efforts were virtually useless. The diet of the laborer was confined largely to bread. He objected vigorously to substitutes of an inferior nutritive quality.[3] The attempt to introduce oatmeal in the south of England met with signal failure. This was inevitable. The cooking of oats was a slow process and firewood was expensive. Furthermore, oatmeal without milk was regarded as unpalatable, and milk toward the end of the century was a luxury to the poor.

Some well-meaning philanthropists were pained by the

[1] *Report of the Committee on the High Price of Provisions*, ix, 93.

[2] Such substitutes of cheaper foodstuffs for flour were frequently used, *vide* numerous letters in the *Annals*. A popular combination seems to have been one-fourth ground potato to three-quarters flour. Twelve pounds of ground potato baked with twenty pounds of flour made forty-two pounds of bread. Young, *Annals*, xxvii, 57. In some localities the idea of mixing wheat flour with cheaper substitutes was not known. Young, *Annals*, xxiv, 45, 62.

[3] Young, *Annals*, xxiv, 131.

laborers' refusal to use cheaper forms of bread. Indeed, much to the distress of the donor, free tickets for a coarsened bread supply were refused in one locality,[1] and this despite the proof that coarser food would do nicely. Said one writer: "Suppose the peasant's family to be well supplied with barley, oats, peas, beans and potatoes. Will it be said either that his necessities require so large a supply of wheat as they otherwise would, or that his discontents would not be allayed by his acquiescence purchased by other compensatory comforts? The acidity of the barley-loaf would be sheathed by having the indigestable lumpiness of it softened by the mild beverage that flows from the same grain, and dried in the kiln and decocted in the furnace. The water pot herb would become hearty and nutritious; the oat cake be rendered unctuous and savory by the oily fatness of the barley corn after it had been animalized in the stye, and smoke-dried in the chimney. These various combinations of the four, corrected in the stomach by its own acid, the indigestable dissolved by its attendant menstruum, and more palatable to the taste, may perhaps be convertible by the concoctive powers into a wholesomer and stronger nutriment than the whitest wheaten bread."[2]

Two propositions were brought forward for the regulation of the manufacture and sale of flour. In the first place, the substitution of either standard or household flour for pure wheat flour was advocated. (Household flour was much coarser than wheaten flour, and standard flour was even more so.) Testimony regarding this proposal was detailed. Physicians summoned as wit-

---

[1] J. E. and Barbara Hammond, *Village Laborer, 1760-1832*, p. 124.

[2] Henry Gabell, *On the Expediency of Offering and Amending the Regulation Recommended by Parliament for Reducing the High Price of Provisions*, 1796.

nesses could not agree on the physical effect of a coarser
quality of flour. Bakers, on the other hand, were unanimously of opinion that it would not be acceptable to
customers. When confronted with this question, " Do
you concede that, if the legislature was to order any
particular sort of flour to be ground, and that the bread
to be made of it should be of coarser sort from that
which is at present used, it would be acceptable to your
customers?" the bakers all answered in the negative.[1]
A number of millers and corn factors declared that even
if the coarser bread was baked, no more nourishment
could be obtained from a given quantity of wheat. Only
one witness held a contrary opinion. Alderman Watson,
an army contractor, spoke in defence of "camp bread,"
which, though admittedly of coarser flour, he declared
highly desirable.[2] The testimony of Arthur Young ended
the evidence before the committee. He acknowledged
that brown bread would be a very slight remédy, and
probably not as nourishing for laborers as wheaten
loaves. In fact, Young saw no escape from the situation, save in the substitution of soups for bread.[3]

Finally the government sought in yet one other way
to improve the situation. Criticism of those old-time
public enemies, the corn-engrosser and forestaller, was
rife, and in consequence a somewhat strict inquiry was
set on foot into the working of the Corn Exchange. In
London it was private property, owned by some eighty
shareholders. These persons rented selling-stands to
privileged dealers, who controlled the London market.

[1] *First Report of the Committee on the Assize of Bread, Reports of
Committees*, ix, 69, 70.

[2] *Ibid.*, ix, 73.

[3] In this opinion Arthur Young was sustained by a clerical witness.
Ibid., ix, 76.

It was true that any man might, if he could, or would, buy in the Exchange from those who owned no stands. But this was not feasible, for, among other practices and manipulations, the dealers contrived to keep the opening of the Exchange as to day and hour a secret.[1] To modernize the methods of the Exchange it was recommended: (1) that every seller be licensed; (2) that registration be kept of every sale; (3) that inspectors regularly be present; (4) that every grower of wheat state, under compulsion, the amount he was ready to sell; (5) that a new market be opened under the management of the Board of Aldermen.

Parliamentary committees, by all of these measures— by the giving of bounties, by economy in consumption, by reform in diet, by the coarsening of the wheaten loaf, and, finally, by the regulation of the Corn Exchange, suggested governmental assistance. More was suggested, however, than was accomplished. The authorities did, in a special emergency, secure grain from the Baltic, and a tax was imposed on those who wore hair powder. Little else was done.

The rise in prices was but the outward and visible sign of a new dispensation, which thoroughly and rapidly transformed the economic and industrial life of Great Britain. Its advent was marked by changes in the forms, standards and character of the entire social fabric. Methods in both agriculture and manufacturing were revolutionized. The new agriculture was characterized by great improvements in technique; a sudden rise in rental value; a consolidation of the smaller farms of the

---

[1] *Report of the Committee on the High Cost of Provisions,* June 24, 1801. *Reports of Committees,* ix, 146 *et seq.*

country into large estates; and a rapid enclosure of the public domain.

Improvements in the technique of agriculture were varied in character: some had to do with a more thorough knowledge of the nature and composition of soils, others involved experimentation in the various uses to which manure might be applied, and an intimate knowledge of the several qualities and adaptations of different kinds of fertilizers.[1] "Artificial grasses" were also much improved; and the use of root crops, such as turnips, in place of fallow, made great headway, for the farmer quickly appreciated the additional quantity of winter feed which these root crops afforded. Enthusiastic inquiries were made into the problem of land drainage;[2] and the irrigation of dry districts was carefully studied. Various ways and means were found for the enrichment of the soil, and encouraged by all classes of society. King George himself wrote on agricultural topics under the pseudonym "Mr. Robinson," while in the northern kingdom the Duke of Buccleugh and "Potato" Wilkie worked shoulder to shoulder for the same purpose.

An equal advance was registered in breeding methods. By 1785 Bakewell had completed his great discoveries in sheep and cattle breeding, and the impetus thus received made itself felt in effectively conducted experiments throughout the remainder of the century.[3]

---

[1] Young, *Annals*, xxiii, 77; xxvi, 116. Sinclair, *Statistical Account of Scotland, 1792-1796*, vi, 439. *Ibid.*, p. 64.

[2] Elkington was the great specialist in work of this kind. A seventeen-page report of his methods is to be found in the *Annals of Agriculture* for the year 1797, xxviii, 77.

[3] Young, *Annals*, xxi, 289; xxii, 19; *ibid.*, p. 337; xxviii, 420; *ibid.*, p. 241. The last-mentioned reference contains a list of sixty-four questions relative to breeding.

Agricultural implements were likewise much bettered,
It is, true that in the more remote sections of the island
crude implements of earlier date were only slowly displaced.   In the Highlands it was still customary, in cul-
tivating, to tie the harrow to the horse's tail.   This was
said to serve the double purpose of saving the harness,,
and breaking in the horse.[1]   Also other localities continued to use a primitive spade, popularly known as a
cascroim.   In Edderaschylis this was simply "a crooked
piece of wood, the lower end somewhat thick, about two
feet and a half in length, pretty straight, and armed at
the end with iron, made thin and square, to cut the
earth."[2]   This implement long survived.   So also did
the Scottish plow, with its clumsy employment of four
horses in place of two.   But little by little methods were
changing.   In advanced districts threshing machines
became common by 1794,[3] while in England contemporaneous records are filled to overflowing with the news
of agricultural inventions.   Threshing and winnowing
machines, improved and reimproved, had already been
introduced.[4]   Machines for all kinds of purposes were
proposed and patented.   There were machines for shoe-
ing oxen,[5] machines for pulling up tree stumps,[6] and
queer cumbrous machines for draining swamps, equipped
with what their inventors termed "inclined float-board
wheels."[7]   Machinery suitable for all sorts and condi-

[1] Sinclair, *Statistical Account*, viii, 48.   [2] *Ibid.,* vi, 288.

[3] *Ibid.,* vi, 504.

[4] Young, *Annals*, xviii, 362.

[5] *Ibid.,* xxvi, 500.

[6] *Ibid.,* xviii, 362.

[7] *Ibid.,* xxvi, 387.   Illustrations of these new machines are to be
found here and there in Young's *Annals*, also in the *Encyclopædia
Britannica*, 3d Edition, 1797.

tions of climate, usage and soil was planned, patented and constructed.

Although new agricultural methods were widely discussed by contemporaneous writers, no one of them caused as much stir as did the proposed utilization of the great areas of waste and unenclosed land. Certain tracts had, in earlier times of scientific ignorance, been considered useless. Other sections, owing to the expense of legal possession, were, wholly or in part, unused, while yet others remained open for public pasture. Arthur Young believed that all of this land, wherever possible, should be enclosed and made productive as the property of private owners. Even the common pasture land, he argued, should be taken, although he recognized that such action would inflict hardships on certain classes of society, for, he said in passing: " The enclosure of the common fields would be beneficial and, to a certain extent, justifiable, for the tenant paid rent for them to the lord of the manor, but it would be effected at great loss to the smaller tenant, and when his common or pasture was enclosed as well, he would be greatly injured, while the agricultural laborer would be permanently disabled."

The process of enclosure, or of converting this public into private land, had made rapid progress throughout the eighteenth century, but not rapid enough to suit the desires of agricultural experts who, like Young, had increased production more closely at heart than equitable distribution. Young was so enthusiastic that he would place all the land of Great Britain, wherever crops might be grown, under the plow. Even forests he regarded with a hostile eye; for he said that there was in England sufficient coal for heat during the winter, and that for other purposes timber could be more profitably imported

from abroad.   Every bit of England's soil, on the contrary, should be used for her food supply.   He even declared that to plant land with timber was retrogressive.[1]

Upper-class England supported Young, and Parliament, ready to assist, ordered investigation.   Committees
of Parliament examined the origin, extent and value of
the waste land of Great Britain, both the benefits that
could be derived from the use of such lands, and the difficulties existent in the way of its immediate absorption by
private capital.[2]

In extent the waste land in Great Britain was astonish-
ingly large.   Out of a total acreage of 73,285,622 acres
there remained unenclosed in 1795, about 23,107,000,
which in pecuniary value was estimated by Watson, the
public-spirited bishop of Llandaff, to equal an income of
some twenty million pounds per annum.   Much of this
land was of good quality.   One million acres only were
incapable of planting.   Of the remainder there were suitable for tillage, 3,000,000 acres; fit for planting, 3,000,-
000 acres; suitable for upland pasture, 1,000,000 acres;
meadow and water mead, 1,000,000 acres.[3]

The committee were convinced that all of this territory
should be utilized.   In the first place, they reported that
the highest and most sterile land should be left to
plantations;[4] for, in the ponderous phraseology of the
eighteenth century, "at first sight it may seem surprising that the spot which will not produce a single blade
of corn will yet support the stately pine, or spreading

---

[1] Young, *Annals,* xxiii, 399.

[2] Parliamentary committees on waste land and bills of enclosure published reports in 1795, 1797 and 1800.   *Vide, Reports from Committees,*
1776-1801, vol. ix.

[3] *Reports of Committee on Waste Land,* ix, 206.

[4] *Ibid.,* p. 210.

oak; these draw their nourishment from sources beyond
the reach of the smaller vegetable productions, and their
leaves are also supposed to derive sustenance from the
air which surrounds them, or the water which they may
imbibe." Land not so barren might with profit be used
for sheep growing.[1] Other soil might be redeemed by
the use of fertilizers and underplowing. Wet and boggy
regions could easily be drained and made usable in the
course of one summer, while dry and arid soil could be
brought to an "astonishing height of produce" by systematic irrigation.

Public land once classified, the feasibility of turning it
into private property was discussed. Here one serious
obstacle blocked the way : the antiquated system of land
tenure which, then as well as now, complicated the title
to all land held in Great Britain. Over most of this
waste or unenclosed territory, there were innumerable
rights of common, confusing well-nigh beyond belief.
A "right of common" the committee defined as "a right
which a person has in another person's property without
any property in the soil." Four different rights of common were recognized : the common of pasture, which
meant a right to graze cattle in the unenclosed territory;
the common of turbary, or the right to cut turf; the
common of estover, or the right to cut wood ; and the
common of piscary, or the right of fishing. These special
privileges were still further involved, for they included
subsidiary qualifications, permissions and sub-rights,
intricate in character and all but infinite in extent, as,
for example, the common of pasture, which included and
was made up of common appendant, common appurtenant, common in gross and common in vicinage.[2]

[1] *Report of Committee on Waste Land,* ix, 207.

[2] Common appendant, is a right belonging to the land and incident

This intermingling of hoary tradition and ancient usage brought forth, as might be expected, a rich harvest for all lawyers, attorneys and counsellors engaged in questions of title. The procedure of enclosure was exceedingly involved. In accordance with English law the following steps were necessary: First, a preliminary meeting must be called for the purpose of advertising the proposed enclosure. Second, after the meeting, a petition to Parliament must be prepared, notices of said petition being affixed to the doors of churches, and in other public places. Third, a special bill must be drawn up and passed by Parliament. To do this, there must be given in evidence the written consent of from three-quarters to four-fifths of the persons interested. No proxies were allowed. Fourth, after the bill had been safeguarded through Parliament, incidentally involving the payment of heavy dues at each step in its progress, commissioners were appointed. These commissioners were generally three in number. Their function corresponded in many ways to that of the modern receiver. They visited the land, inventoried it, surveyed it, heard complaints, if any, and then officially declared it enclosed.[1] This was the technical method of land enclosure in England. In theory, at least, the rights of the laborer, the small leasing farmer and the yeoman were guaranteed by the law; and in theory, at least, the permission of three-quarters of the persons interested had to be obtained before an enclose bill could be passed. Practise did not square

to the tenure. Common appurtenant was a right appertaining to the land, but not incident to any tenure. Common in gross was somewhat similar to common appurtenant, save that it was even further apart from the ownership of the land. Common in vicinage consisted in the customs and privilege of allowing cattle to graze from their own common to an unenclosed adjacent common.

[1] *Report of Committee on Bills for Enclosure,* ix, 231.

with theory. Plans for an enclosure were concocted in secret. The big proprietors, the solicitors and the vicar connived together. Bills were rushed hurriedly through Parliament. Little or no attention was paid to contrary petitions, if, indeed, the protestants had the temerity to present them.[1]

These enclosures were the chief grievance of the poorer agriculturists. The expense was heavy, and, moreover, even if paid, the loss of the fallow and stubble pasture was still serious, and as for the poor cottager: before enclosure "he was a laborer with land; after enclosure he was a laborer without land."[2] Furze and turf no longer were free for all. It was impossible now for the cottager to keep his cow,[3] while the old officialdom of the public common must seek employment elsewhere. The hayward, the pound man, the chimney peepers, viewers and common shepherd were now out of work. There is evidence to show that much more comfort existed among the poorer folk than early in the century. Tea was more generally used. In the poorer districts of Scotland it is said that tablecloths and clocks had become familiar objects,[4] and though here and there customs quite primitive still survived,[5] some authors contend that the lot of the average husbandman toward the close of the century was more comfortable than in the beginning. The evidence, however, is quite disputable, and though to

---

[1] Hammond, *Village Laborer,* pp. 43 *et seq.*   [2] *Ibid.,* p. 100.

[3] Throughout the midland counties it was noticed that the number of cows owned by the laborers became strikingly less. Young, *Annals,* xxvi, 242.

[4] Sinclair, *Statistical Account, passim.*

[5] In Yorkshire the bed was turned, in some instances, into a kind of eighteenth century fireless cooker, keeping warm the oatmeal during the absence of the farmer. Crutwell, *Tour of Great Britain,* p. 118. This custom is said still to survive in Minnesota.

generalize is somewhat dangerous, it is perhaps not unfair to affirm that more comfortable or not, he was
disgruntled and discontented with his life.

Of the farmers who leased their lands, some were
prosperous. This was the case where the land was enclosed and new methods adopted, but in other sections
where this was not done, great discontent prevailed.
As the returns from agricultural labor rose with greater
and greater rapidity, the period of leasing to which the
landlord would consent became shorter and shorter—
and the farmer lost those advantages which came of the
high price of his farm produce. Meanwhile the yeo-
manry, the small proprietors, were also losing ground.
The lamented disappearance of the British yeoman in the
nineteenth century had begun.[1]

As for the land-owning farmers they, like their brethren who leased, were in some instances well-to-do. The
gentlemen farmers,—men of independent wealth and leisure,—were almost invariably prosperous. Indeed, for the
capitalistic farmer,—the farming entrepreneur—whether
gentleman farmer or wideawake yeoman, the end of the
century brought halcyon days. Capital was the *sine qua
non* of enclosure. Ploughs, harrows, fences, and the
other paraphernalia of the new agriculture demanded
capital. They who had capital thrived; others fell by the
wayside.

In Scotland, agricultural conditions were backward.
The new agriculture was there making headway, but at a
slower pace. Complaints were made of the short leases,[2]

[1] The proof that this disappearance took place, for the most part, in
the early nineteenth century, is demonstrated by C. H. Taylor, *The
Decline of Land-owning Farmers in England, passim.*

[2] The short leases which ran from seven to eight years only constantly tempted the farmer to neglect his land. Sinclair's *Statistical
Account*, viii, 107.

and men spoke also of a hard-pressed laboring class.
Nevertheless, in Scotland it was not the new capitalist
agriculture, but the old feudal services that were objected
to.   These services, archaic survivals of an earlier day, not
only were annoying but also, in certain cases, were obstruc-
ting and impeding the advance of agricultural improvement.   Educated Scotchmen thought them disgraceful.
The Rev. James Robertson, of Gargunnock, said in 1794 :
" It would be of great service to the country if all of the
varieties of service usually demanded of the heritors, besides the proper rent, were relinquished.   Great inconvenience arises from the obligations to which the peasants
are subjected ; to pay fowls, to drive coals, peat and dung,
and in the harvest to cut down the proprietor's grain."[1]
The Rev. Adam Forman, of Carmunnock spoke similarly.
" The tenants," he said, " are still subjected to many burdens or services which the proprietors of the land require, such as driving coal, working at hay and other
pieces of labor, which ought to be abolished."[2]   The
truth of these charges was still further substantiated by
the Rev. Adam MacBean, of Delacrossie.   He tells us
that customs were paid by most of the tenants in kind,
such as eggs, fowls, and other articles.[3]   In fact, feudal
service survived in Scotland, of a very pronounced type,
for not only was the working of the heritor's farm compulsory, but we also find here and there the most irksome of
all banalities was still enforced.   This offensive special
privilege consisted in the custom of " thirlage," or the
obligatory grinding of all corn at the heritor's mill.[4]   In-

[1] Sinclair, *Statistical Account,* xvii, 109.

[2] *Ibid.,* xviii, 163.

[3] *Ibid.,* xviii, 117.

[4] *Ibid.,* xviii, 393.

asmuch as every tenant must use this mill, the efficiency
of its operation made little difference to the heritor, consequently we find him unwilling to install new machinery
or to improve the mill in any way. The cost to the
farmer, therefore, was high. In one place, after deduct-
ing for seed and horse corn, it amounted to the value of
one-eighth of the crop.[1]

More fundamental in its effect on British society were
the changes wrought by the parallel revolution in
manufacturing, which, however, scarcely falls within the
scope of this treatise. The inventions of Watt, Crom-
ton, Arkwright and Cartwright, are all, or should be,
narrated in every textbook of English history. These
inventions were made in the eighteenth century, but the
social transformations which follow in their wake are not
experienced, for the major part, until after 1815. Only
the preliminary results of the Industrial Revolution were
realized in the eighteenth century.

The cotton industry was the first to respond to the
stimulus of the Industrial Revolution. By the last
quarter of the century little factories or "twistworks,"
as they were called, began to appear. They bore but
little resemblance to the modern factory. Power was
provided by horses, or more frequently by running
water.[2] Although the superiority of Watt's engine was
conceded by the end of the century, its first use was as
late as 1785, and it was not applied to the spinning of
fine yarn till 1793.[3]

The woolen industry was somewhat belated in its development. Until the time of Edward Cartwright wool

---

[1] Mathieson, *The Awakening of Scotland*, i, 286.

[2] Chapman, *The Lancashire Cotton Industry*, p. 56.

[3] Ure, *Cotton Manufactory*, i, 290.

had been combed by hand. Between 1790 and 1792
Cartwright's second great invention was brought into
use,[1] and from this time on the woolen industry made
rapid strides, at a rate comparable with the manufacture
of cotton.

The improvements in weaving lagged behind those in
spinning. The power loom was applied, it is true, to
commercial use in 1787, but it was not successful until
many years later. By 1813 there were only some 2400
power looms in use, and in 1820 only 14,000. At the
later date upwards of 240,000 hand looms were reported,
and the number even then was said to be increasing.
Indeed, "it appears beyond question," one author tells
us, "that the competition of the power loom was not
very serious prior to 1812, at the earliest, and in many
places not till considerably later."[2] The early power
looms were not very reliable. Cartwright lost most of
his money in trying to make them pay, and, though his
invention was improved, reimproved and finally supplemented by Bell and Miller in 1794 and in 1798, yet in the
later year a Glasgow factory, with all of these improvements, proved to be a failure.[3] Not till the four patents
of Radcliff and the invention of the "dandy" does the
power loom appear to have been firmly established, and
even as late as 1819 its use was regarded as proble-
matical.[4]

Greater progress was made in the metal industries.
A traveler in 1788 states that water and fire engines kept
the tin mines constantly dry and that without Bolton's

[1] Burnley, *History of Wool and Woolcombing*, pp. 105 *et seq.*

[2] For a description of machinery for the manufacture of woolens,
see Young, *Annals*, xxvii, 311.

[3] Baines, *The Cotton Manufacture*, p. 231.

[4] Chapman, *The Lancashire Cotton Industry*, p. 31.

invention they could not be worked in the winter at all.[1]
Nevertheless. the steel industry at this time was clearly
in a transitional stage, for while England's superiority
in that trade was still attributed to her wood supply, and
the charcoal which it made possible, Shropshire coal was
used with success in smelting iron.[2]   The first practical
application of the steam engine to the blasting furnace
had already been made, and new inventions in rolling
and puddling iron were speedily increasing the total steel
production of the nation.[3]   Coal mining had just become
an important industry.   Steam pumps were in use early
in the century, but if any one year be taken to mark the
advance of the British coal trade, it were fairer to take
1794, for in that year Watt's patent for the application
of the crank to the steam engine expired, and coal could
now be hoisted from the mines in an inexpensive manner
by means of the steam engine.[4]   Toward the close of the
century, indeed, the English coal trade began to loom
up as an important factor, and we read of a coal trust
beyond the embryonic stage.[5]   Nevertheless the coal
trade compared to that in the early years of the nineteenth century, was far from remarkable.[6]

England is experiencing at the end of the eighteenth
century a foretaste of the industrial revolution.   Grow-

[1] Shaw, *Tour of the West of England*, p. 380.

[2] *Ibid.*, p. 209.

[3] Scrivenor, *History of the Iron Trade*, pp. 110 *et seq.*

[4] Galloway, *History of the Coal Industry*, p. 115.

[5] Levy, *Monopoly and Competition*, pp. 106 *et seq.*

[6] In London the total amount of coal imported in 1750 was 260,600
tons.   In 1800 it was 410,300, an increase of sixty per cent.   Large
indeed, but compared with an increase of 231 per cent during the next
fifty years, followed by one of 404 per cent during the next fifteen,
its importance is diminished.   Jevons, *The Coal Question,* p. 232.

ing manufactories, expanding trade and a far-reaching
commerce are bringing to England wealth hitherto but
dreamed of. The golden days of the entrepreneur are
beginning. Many indications abound of this new wealth
which is to line the pockets of the chosen few. Car-
riages, silks, muslins, plate glass, the theatre,—a hundred
traces there are of machinery's magic wand.[1] Now has
come the day of the large manufacturing cities, with
their pressing problems of sanitation, water supply,
police protection and the housing of the poor.[2] The
employment of women and children in factory labor to
the great detriment of their health, already has attracted
the attention of the thoughtful observer.[3] The great
shifting of the center of population from the south and
east of England to the north and west is in full headway.[4] And more significant still to the social historian,
the wage-dependent laborer is becoming more permanently a fixture in England than ever before; for his
right to work is now more frequently subjected to the
ups and downs of trade and commerce, interrupted by
the chance invention of a new machine, blocked and
thwarted by circumstances over which he has no control.

This was not always the case. The condition of the
manufacturing population varied greatly. Nowhere was
this divergence greater than among the weavers. In
the case of the muslin or cambric weavers there was no

[1] The posthumous letter of Edmund Burke on "Peace with the Regicide Directory of France," sounds a paean of praise for this material
comfort.

[2] Hutton, *History of Birmingham*, p. 72. Baines, *History of Liverpool, passim.*

[3] For the conclusions of a physician on this subject, as early as
1784, see Cunningham, *Growth of English Trade and Industry*, p.
628.

[4] Dechesne, *L'industrie de la laine en Angleterre*, pp. 107 *et seq.*

machinery to supplant or cheapen their labor, and at the same time a highly stimulated market existed for their wares. Consequently, we find, if one authority is to be trusted, that the trade was considered "the trade of a gentleman. The operatives brought home their work in top boots and ruffled shirts. They had a cane and took a coach, in some instances." "Every house was well furnished with a clock of elegant mahogany or fancy case, and a tea service there was of Staffordshire ware with silver or plated sugar tongs and spoons."[1]

Quite the reverse, however, was the condition of those artizans who wove inferior cloth. They had already, by 1793, begun to feel sharply the competition of the power looms. By that year it was said of the fustian weaver, or he who dealt in coarser cloth, that it was nearly impossible for the weaver to earn the necessaries of life, and a great number of families out of work were said to have been in a most wretched position. The competition of the hand weaver with machinery, which was to work such direful results in the nineteenth century had, indeed, begun. The effect of the revolution in industry of which this invention was but a phase, may be seen in the following letter from a physician :

"To the Rev. Mr. T.[2]

Dear Sir: You desired me to give you my opinion of the present state of want and distress among the weavers in Spitalfields. Being physician to the London Dispensary, where between 2,000 and 3,000 of them annually apply for medical relief, I am called frequently to visit their wretched habita-

---

[1] Chapman quotes Radcliff to this effect in his *Cotton Industry. Op. cit.,* p. 38.

[2] This letter was read from the *Morning Chronicle* at the trial of Maurice Margarot for sedition in Edinburgh, in 1794. *State Trials,* xxiii, 716.

tions, there the first thing that commonly presents itself to view, is an empty loom, and a starving family. Some have had only half their usual work for more than twelve months past; and many no work at all, for the last six months. Sometimes I find one or two children sick, and the wretched parents looking upon them with all the distress which parental affection, and the utmost degree of poverty, can impress on the mind. At other times I find the husband and wife, and not infrequently both, sick in the same bed, and several help-less and half starved children looking up to them for bread. Here anxiety and poverty increase the disease if they did not produce it, which however is often the case. It is impossible for words to give a perfect idea of the distress which prevails amongst this useful class of the people. If any doubt the truth of this representation, all I can say is, come and see. Were they to accompany me in my daily visitations for a short time, they would be fully convinced, that this is a very imperfect outline of the general misery amongst this part of the labouring poor, who would gladly work, if they could be employed; and therefore, the more deserving of help. I am persuaded, sir, that you need only to be acquainted with real distress, to interest yourself in the means of relieving it in the present instance. Both you, sir, and those who second your laudable endeavours and benevolent purposes, will be doing a great work.—I am, dear sir, your sincere friend,

JOHN WHITEHEAD.

Old Bedlam,
Dec. 17, 1793."

The new agriculture and the new industry not only owed their success, but even their origin, to capitalism: a capitalism that populated deserts; ruined ancient cities; turned farmers into mill operatives; and held at its behest and bidding the Parliament of Great Britain. The operations of this capitalism, however, took place in a framework of society which, in itself, demanded reform on every side.

The fundamental laws of Great Britain—those old statutes which organized and governed society—were subjected, in almost every instance, to as keen a criticism as
that meted out to the new capitalism.   Laws for defining
and punishing crime—laws establishing, defining and pro-
tecting the state religion—laws providing for the relief
of the poor—laws relating to the army and navy—laws
determining the powers, composition and the duration of
Parliaments—fiscal laws, game laws and libel laws—the
entire objective and visible structure of society was freely
studied, if not in a conciliatory, at least in a wholesome
fashion.

The glaring inequalities of representation in the House
of Commons attracted the first attention of the reformers.
The constitution of that body obviously was unjustifiable.
One-half of the membership of the House of Commons
was returned by the southern counties of England, which
contained but a fraction of the population.   In 1793 two
hundred and ninety-four members—a majority—were returned by constituencies, the greater part of which had
less than a hundred voters ; none had more than two
hundred and fifty.   At the most, less than fifteen hundred electors returned a majority of the House.   Even
this was merely nominal, for in the words of a recent
authority " it is reasonable to conclude that from 1760
to 1832 nearly one-half of the members of the House of
Commons owed their seats to patrons." [1]

These men were regarded as the delegates of their
patron.   When the nominated member made his mark,
congratulations were offered, not to him, but to his
patron.   On the other hand, if he displayed an undue
independence, it was customary to complain to the

---

[1] Porrit, *The Unreformed House of Commons,* i, 311.

patron direct.   In Parliament, and in society, statesmen
were spoken of freely as Lord so-and-so's members.
The nine representatives of the people in Parliament
controlled by Sir James Lowther were popularly known
as Lowther's ninepins.[1]

The state of the Scotch representation was even worse
than that of England.   Electors in Scotland were so few
in number that members of Parliament were frequently
on calling terms with all their constituents.   They varied
in number from twelve, in Bute, to two hundred and five
in Ayreshire.   In seven, the average was only eighty.
The entire number to all practical purpose responded to
the beck and call of that prince of politicians, Henry
Dundas.   These men were controlled by means of patronage, and it was said: "There was scarcely a gentle
family in Scotland . . . which had not at some time in
some of its members received some Indian appointment
or other act of kindness from Henry Dundas."[2]

The conflicts of party politics in the seventies and
eighties of the eighteenth century, emphasized with an
ever-increasing lucidity the fact that a majority of the
House of Commons were, in no true sense, representative of the nation as a whole, but were, on the other
hand, none other than the delegates of influential families.
In the scathing words of Fox, "there is one class of
constituents whose instructions it is considered the duty
of members to obey.   With those who represent popular
towns and cities, it is a disputed point whether they
ought to follow their instructions, or obey the dictates
of their own consciences; but if they represent a noble
lord, or noble duke, then it becomes no longer a ques-

[1] Porrit, *op. cit.*, i, 313.
[2] Stanhope, *Life of Pitt*, i, 311.

tion of doubt, and he is considered no longer a man of honor who does not implicitly obey the order of the single constituent. He is to have no conscience, no liberty of his own. He is sent here by the lord of this, or the duke of that, and if he does not obey the instructions which he receives, he is held to be a dishonest man. Such is the mode of reasoning in this House. If he dares to disagree with the mode of reasoning of the duke, or lord, or baronet whose representative he is, then he must be considered as unfit for the society of decent men." [1]

Toward the end of the century some effort at reform had been made. Pitt, in 1785, vainly endeavored to bring about a moderate reform. The country at the time was apathetic—or at least unwilling to force the situation, as it might have done, by powerful and insistent pressure.[2] With the coming of the French revolution, the upholders of class privilege, sustained by a frightened conservatism, more than ever were determined to maintain the *status quo.* The friends of Parliamentary reform were few in number and well-nigh powerless. In 1793 a motion of Grey's, asking leave to submit a petition for Parliamentary reform by the "Friends of the People," was defeated. And this, despite the fact that the "Friends of the People" was by far the most conservative of the radical societies. No new effort was made till 1797. At that time Grey brought in a new measure. It proposed to abolish many of the more crying abuses of the old system, while at the same time extending the suffrage in a very limited degree. The proposal was buried beneath the government's majority, and the debate

[1] Woodfall, *Parliamentary Debates,* iii, 329.

[2] J. Holland Rose, *William Pitt, and the National Revival,* pp. 203-206.

on the subject is scarce worth recording, save that in it
Fox gave notice of the proposed secession of the Whigs
from Parliament.   The Tory preponderance of 1791 had
become, in 1797, a Tory mastery.

The ecclesiastical laws of England in the restrictions which they imposed were quite medieval.   Laws
dating back to the time of Elizabeth and Charles II were
still on the statute books.   The more severe of these, it
is true, were suspended by the Act of Toleration in 1689,
in behalf of all persons who foreswore popery, or who
acknowledged their belief in the Trinity—that is, all who
were not Roman Catholic or Unitarian might hold religious services without molestation.   No dissenter, however, of any creed was exempt from the Test and Corporation Acts.   These two laws forbade anyone holding
any office under the crown, or, indeed, even in the local
corporations of the country (i. e., the town governments) who had not taken the sacrament according to
the rites of the Anglican church.

In 1790 the friends of toleration in the House of Commons endeavored to repeal the Test and Corporation
Acts.   They pointed out the peaceful character of the
dissenters, and their loyalty to the house of Hanover.
They made much of the irreligious character of the Test
Act, by which the Lord's Supper was made an essential
preliminary to all offices, from exciseman to admiral.
"It is a stain on the fair memory of the nation," claimed
a prominent member of the House of Commons, "that
the legislature of a country should deliberately, and by
express enactment, . . . strip the altar of its purity, and
make it the qualification desk for the tax gatherer and
public executioner." [1]   Not a few members of the House

───────

[1] *Parliamentary Debates,* xxvii, 173.   Mr. Powys, in reply to

of Commons thought likewise, and fought with him for a repeal. The "Church and King" men were of a different opinion, and Fox's motion for a repeal was negatived by a majority of one hundred and eighty-nine.

The Roman Catholics and Unitarians, exempted, as we have seen, from the benefits of the Act of Toleration, were subjected to special disqualifications. By the law of England, as late as 1791, a priest by the fact of his presence in the country committed the crime of high treason. Anyone who heard mass, or who attended or kept a Catholic school, committed a crime punishable by fine or imprisonment. Unitarian services were illegal as well, and to preach Unitarianism involved the crime of blasphemy, for the denial of the Trinity was so considered. These laws, which marked out the Catholic and the Unitarian as offenders beyond the pale of the ordinary dissenter, were not enforced, but they remained on the statute books, to the discomfiture of both Catholic and Unitarian, and for their repeal energetic measures were set on foot.

The Roman Catholics largely succeeded in their endeavors. Whigs, Tories, and even dissenters themselves, were not averse to some measure of Catholic emancipation. The government was distinctly favorable. It had for some time given small salaries to those Catholic priests in Scotland whose income had been impaired by the confiscation of estates in France.[1] Catholicism was a conservative bulwark, as prominent conservatives acknowledged. With the advance of the French Revolution the status of the Roman Catholic Church steadily

Fox, argued that the way would be open for "the Jew, the Mohammedan, the disciples of Brahma, Confucius, and every other head of a sectary" (Mr. Fox cried, "hear! hear!").

[1] Amherst, *Catholic Emancipation*, i, 279-280.

improved in the minds of England's governing class.
The church, at any rate, was opposed to radicalism, and
radicalism was a more dangerous spectre by far than the
return of the Stuarts to the throne.

A law for the relief of Roman Catholics was enacted
by Parliament; in 1791 the mass was made legal in
England. No other concessions were granted. The
doors of Catholic churches could not legally be locked.
Catholic churches could not have steeples, and they
must be licensed, nor could Catholic vestments be worn
in any private house, where the number of persons con-
gregated exceeded five. Furthermore, Catholic peers
could not take their place in the House of Lords, nor
could Catholics become members of the House of Commons, or vote for members. No crown office could be
held by a Catholic, nor could a Catholic be legally married, save in an Anglican church, or be buried in a
cemetery where the service was not read by an Anglican
clergyman.[1]

Still, partial as this relief was, it placed the Catholic
in a position far more pleasant than that held by the
Unitarian. Catholic services could, at any rate, be
legally conducted. Unitarian services, as such, were a
direct violation of the law of the land. In 1793 an attempt was made to relieve the Unitarians. Fox, who
at this time championed their cause, pointed out the
inconsistency of Parliament in ameliorating the condition of the Catholics, while retaining in full force the
statutes against Unitarianism. "The Unitarians," he
said, "took the same rule of conscience for their guide
that the Trinitarians did, the Scriptures of the Old and
New Testament: they believed in the immortality of the

[1] Bernard Ward, *The Dawn of the Catholic Revival in England,
1781-1813*, i, 314.

soul; a state of rewards and punishments; their rules of morality were the same; their demeanor as citizens was sober and exemplary. As to differences of opinion between them and the established church, these were matters of discussion rather for theologians than any other body of men."[1] Fox's relief measure did not propose to repeal the test in corporation laws; it simply placed Unitarians on the same basis with other dissenters. The proposal, nevertheless, met with violent opposition. Burke venomously led the attack. The Unitarians "he condemed as base cowards, who had hitherto passed their lives in holes, corners and lurking places, not daring at any time to show themselves as a class of men, till they saw impending storms—till the political world was threatened with convulsions."[2] They were also concocting a plot to destroy the constitution of their country. They believed in French ideas, than which nothing could be more vile, and as for his part "he wished to leave his child those blessings that had been handed down to him by his ancestors; to leave them laws, religion, morality, discipline, and subordination in an army, manliness in their men and chastity in their women."[3] Pitt also objected to the repeal of the penal statutes which affected Unitarianism. He thought that, as the laws did no actual harm, it was best to let sleeping dogs lie. To repeal the acts might look like an attack on the established religion of the country, etc. In these opinions a majority of the House evidently concurred, and Fox's motion was lost by a vote of 142 to 63.

In practice, the greater part of the English ecclesias-

[1] *The Senator,* 1792, p. 790.
[2] *Ibid.,* p. 796.   [3] *Ibid.,* p. 801.

tical legislation was a dead letter. The dissenters quietly went their own way, not nearly as zealous on their own behalf as their friends were for them. Some of them felt that the government was "a shield held over their head." And at any rate their major interest was in the world to come. But nevertheless, the religious restrictions established by law, archaic and absurd as they were, were an indisputable source of annoyance.

Many have written of the severity of the English criminal law, generally with much exaggeration. The second edition of Blackstone's Commentary, published in 1769, declared that 160 offences were punishable by death. That statement has been freely drawn upon as evidence of the great harshness of the English law. It is, in itself, of insufficient proof. According to the English custom of the eighteenth century, many laws were passed, defining in each case numerous specific crimes. For instance, no general law of forgery existed. Forgery, as such, was not a felony, but forgery in the instance of South Sea bonds, exchequer bills, etc., was a capital crime.[1] In this case a general enactment, which punished forgery with death, would have been far more severe than five or six different statutes, punishing forgery in certain circumstances. Again, a great number of specific laws defined stealing as a felony. Special laws there were for theft from a ship in distress, for taking linen from a bleaching ground, and for cutting down trees in an orchard.[2] A single statute, inflicting the death penalty for all kinds of stealing, would undoubtedly have been more drastic than fifty laws applying to as many different kinds of theft.

[1] Stephens, *History of the Criminal Law of England*, i, 470.
[2] Colquhoun, *Police of the Metropolis*, 5th edition, 1797, pp. 284-286.

Furthermore, the severity of the law had been, toward the end of the eighteenth century, tempered by the growth of conditional pardon-granting. It was quite generally the custom to commute the death-penalty of prisoners by sending them to Australia, and, in fact, so frequent had these commutations become, that in 1768 a statute was passed to facilitate the pardoning process still further.[1] The administration of justice. however, if not as barbaric and inhuman as we have been led to believe, was bad enough. Too many offences, undoubtedly, were punishable by death. The severity of the law, also, increased rather than diminished crime. Tender-hearted jurymen oftentimes preferred to acquit petty offenders rather than to convict them of a capital offense, and this miscarriage of justice set many prisoners free. On the other hand, the uncertainties of the law were justly criticised. Too much depended on the whim of the judge. No one could tell whether the criminal would be punished or set at liberty.

Though the laws which so jealously defined the religious status of the Englishman were archaic, though the laws which defined and punished offences against persons and property were excessively severe, in both instances the plea could be made that in practice the theory was greatly modified. No such exception can be urged for the poor laws. Ominous, indeed, in outline, it is not easy to exaggerate the frightful results of their operation. In accordance with the English law of 1782 (Gilbert's Act), none but the impotent were allowed in the workhouse. All able-bodied men were to have work found for them near their homes. The intent

[1] Stephens, *History of the Criminal Law of England,* i, 471.

of this act was a kindly one ; the result was unfortunate, for a huge increase in the poor rates took place, without any corresponding relief of suffering.

This policy of state pauperization begun in 1782 was carried to greater lengths by the Speenhamland Act of 1795. In compliance with its rulings wages were to be supplemented from the poor rates in accordance with the fluctuation of the price of wheat and the number of children in a family.[1]

The Act proved to be very discouraging to the independent laborer. Frequently he found that his wages were lowered as a result of the law, for the responsibility of paying him rested no longer with the employer, but with the parish. The individual employer could not improve the condition of his men, nor could the men improve their own lot, for the former was obliged to pay in the form of poor rates a proportion of the wages of those men whom his neighbor employed, while the latter was constantly discouraged by the knowledge that his less-provident fellow received state relief which equaled the reward of his own labor.

The workman, pauperized by the poor law, was forbidden, both by the common law and by special statutes, from all combinations which might force a higher rate of wage. The common law doctrine said to have been invoked as a legal subterfuge for this purpose was that known as Illegality of Proceedings in Restraint of Trade. This doctrine had been constantly supplemented by Parliamentary enactments, which forbade combinations in particular trades. Finally, in 1799, a blanket statute was placed on the

---

[1] Nicholls, *History of the English Poor Law,* ii, 131. For a good account of the so-called " Pig-stye " era of the English poor law, see Hammond, *op. cit.,* p. 161 *et seq.*

books, which forbade all combinations of workingmen.[1]
This act was passed apparently without debate, and it is
not even referred to in the Annual Register for 1799.

[1] Sidney and Beatrice Webb, *History of Trade Unions,* p. 63.   A
legal controversy of great length has arisen over the question of the
common law involved in this statute.   Stephen, *Criminal Law, op. cit.,*
iii, 211, holds that the common law doctrine mentioned above was
not the basis for the act of 1799.   Sir William Earle, *Trade Unionism,*
p. 57, holds that it was.   For a summary of the argument see Chal-
mers-Hunt, *The Law Relating to Trade Unions,* p. 119.

CHAPTER I.

DEFINING THE ISSUE.

REPRESENTATIVE CHAMPIONS OF CONSERVATISM: BURKE, HANNAH MORE, AND JOHN REEVES.

IN so far as the time of its nativity may be established, revolutionary radicalism was born in October, 1790. Then was published Burke's "Reflections" on the French Revolution. This book was the conservative call to arms; it was more. Hammer and anvil it proved for the vague and undefined radicalism of its day—a hammer and anvil which beat with incredible rapidity inchoate, nebulous sentimentality into firm, hard dogma. By its publication the slow sifting of English public opinion was rapidly quickened. The older radicalism of 1790 became suddenly a side issue. Coincidentally "His Majesty's Opposition" became, though less evidently, distinctly a third party. Its place, in number of adherents, in vitality, and perhaps even in influence, had been largely usurped by the fast-forming, rapidly coalescing group of younger radicals.

All these demarcations may be said to date from the appearance of the "Reflections." From that point the schism within the Whig ranks may be intellectually traced; so likewise may the swing toward Toryism of many old reformers. Undoubtedly, great impetus and head was given to the radical cause by the publication of this book. It afforded a common object of attack. It was,

indeed, the conservative platform; the reasoned accepted
defence of things as they were, which the conservative
element in the nation was as glad to defend as was the
radical to attack.

Edmund Burke, as a politician, statesman and philosopher, has been exhaustively studied. Every action of
his life, every whim of his fancy, has been expanded,
analyzed, cherished. Such scrutiny is quite remote from
our purpose. Burke, in the study of radical thought and
action, stands simply as conservatism incarnate. Why
he was conservative : by what motives real or imagined,
open or ulterior, he was influenced, we need not consider.[1] Burke. indeed, as an individual, might even fade
from our memory provided his prominence in generating
the discussions of his day be appreciated, and the real
purport of his position as the conservative champion be
clearly understood.

It would be an easy matter to select from this book
of Burke's many passages intemperate or virulent. Likewise one could cull from the same source absurd conclusions and historical misstatements aplenty. Friend and
foe alike recognize the vulnerability of Burke in this
particular, and criticism of such faults we may readily
pass over. Also Burke discusses many details of French
history upon which we may not linger. Indeed, wholly
eliminating questions of taste, rhetoric and minute fact,
to what general principles does Burke nail his flag ?

Government, Burke defines as " a contrivance of human

---

[1] Some critics openly defend Burke's attitude; others think he
sought a peerage for himself or his son; still others that he was in-
sane. As an illustration of intensive Burkian study, the ingenious explanation that the " Reflections " were a logical outcome of Burke's
attitude toward the Regency Bill of the year previous is sufficient.
Laprade, *England and the French Revolution,* p. 17.

wisdom to provide for human wants."[1] "The science of the construction of the Commonwealth is like every other science, not to be taught *a priori*."[2]

The British construction, Burke was persuaded, had been thus fashioned. He saw no reason for change. The preponderant voice of property in the councils of the nation was justified. " Nothing is a due and adequate representation of a state that does not represent its ability as well as its property, but as ability is a vigorous and active principle, and as property is sluggish, inert and timid, it never can be safe from the invasions of ability unless it be out of all proportion predominant in the representation."[3] To make this superiority doubly secure, he adds that property should be held only by a few. The maintenance of the Law of Entail secured this, and Burke believed that it was good. A religious establishment he pronounced only secondary to a property-controlled government. "This consecration of the state by a state religious establishment," he affirms, "is necessary also to operate with a wholesome awe upon free citizens."[4] A perfect democracy he thought " both shameless and fearless," because the citizens fall into such a state that their own will is the ultimate standard of right and wrong. The church prevents this evil and the people know the value of the church, for " in England . . . there is no rust of superstition which the accumulated absurdity of the human mind might have crusted over in the course of ages that the people of England would not prefer to impiety."[5] Hardly too much emphasis can be laid, according to Burke, on external authority which an established church imposes. Even British education, he exults, conforms to this idea, for, by

[1] Burke, *Reflections*, p. 70.   [2] *Ibid.*, p. 71.   [3] *Ibid.*, p. 59.
[4] *Ibid.*, p. 109.   [5] *Ibid.*, p. 106.

sending the younger sons of the nobility on their tours in care of clerical gentlemen, the ascendency of religion is lastingly stamped on the plastic intelligence of those who will eventually guide the destinies of the nation.

Burke approves of the above-mentioned checks for preventing destructive change. He is not opposed to reform, he tells us, "when the useful parts of an old establishment are kept, and what is superadded is to be fitted to what is retained." If reform comes in this way, then, and then only, may we change and innovate, or, in Burke's words "in what I did I should follow the example of our ancestors."

Burke does not, in his "Reflections," suggest that any innovation is desirable. He is convinced not only that the British nation is in a very satisfactory condition, but also that his countrymen are of the same mind. In a celebrated passage he dismisses all radical agitation as follows: "Because half a dozen grasshoppers under a fern make the field ring with their importunate chink, whilst thousands of great cattle repose 'neath the British oak, chew the cud and are silent, pray do not imagine that those who make the most noise are the only inhabitants of the field, nor of course that they are many in number, nor, after all, other than the little, shriveled, meager, hopping, loud and troublesome insects of the hour." [1]

Thus spoke Burke. In justice to him it is fair to recall the intensified horror with which he viewed the trend of French affairs. The depth of that feeling we of the twentieth century may not accurately gauge, but we do acknowledge its existence. Furthermore, throughout his turbid, and often unjust, denunciation of events in France, Burke is in reality defending a principle, pro-

---

[1] Burke, *Reflections*, p. 100.

fessed by the radicals themselves: the test of a medicine lies in the cure. Very well, Burke tells us; the experimental cure has been tried and found wanting.

Burke's book interprets the spirit of conservatism, but its interpretation is one-sided. His masterpiece reflects conservatism as presented in its best aspect. A little pamphlet, "Village Politics," best reflects it as presented to an ignorant agricultural and industrial class. "Village Politics, addressed to all the Mechanics, Journeymen and Laborers in Great Britain," was a phenomenally popular book. Presumably written by Will Chip, a country carpenter, the actual author was that estimable lady, Hannah More, and her purpose was the inculcation of true principles among the lower classes.

Hannah More said of the book herself: "It is as vulgar as heart can wish, but it is only designed for the most vulgar class of readers."[1] The English "squirearchy" was unanimous in upholding it as an admirable sedative for the lower orders, and largely on that account "Village Politics" had a tremendous sale. The bishop of London wrote to "Mrs." More: "'Village Politics' is universally extolled. It has been read and greatly admired at Windsor, and its fame is spreading rapidly over all parts of the kingdom. I gave one to the attorney-general, who has recommended it to the association at the Crown and Anchor, which will disperse it throughout the country. Mr. Cambridge says that Swift could not have done it better. I am perfectly of that opinion. It is a masterpiece of its kind."[2] There were many who agreed with the Bishop, and wide approval was expressed by the gentry, who bought copies wholesale.[3] Clergy-

[1] Hannah More to Mrs. Boscowan, 1793. Roberts, *Life and Correspondence of Mrs. Hannah More,* ii, 345.

[2] *Ibid.,* p. 343.　　　　　[3] *Ibid.,* p. 348.

men aided in its distribution. In the newly founded Mendip schools, "Village Politics" was said to have been greeted with delight, and indeed many copies were sent to Hannah More, with the intimation that she should emulate the methods of the unknown author.

The little tract which excited this interest was a dialogue between Jack Anvil, the blacksmith, and Tom Hod, the mason. Tom is filled with novel ideas. He reads books. He is discontented and desires a new state of affairs in England. Jack Anvil rallies him on his belief. "I tell thee, Tom," he says, "we have a fine constitution already, and our fathers thought so."

Tom: "They were a pack of fools and had never read the 'Rights of Man.'"

Jack: "I'll tell thee a story. When Sir John married, my lady, who is a little fantastical, and likes to do everything like the French, begged him to pull down yonder fine old castle. . . . 'No,' says Sir John, '. . . this noble building raised by the wisdom of my ancestors . . . shall I pull it all down . . . only because there may be a dark closet, or an awkward passage or inconvenient room or two in it. Our ancestors took time for what they did; they understood foundation work; no running up your little slight lath and plaster buildings, which are up in a day and down in a night.' . . ."

Tom: "But the times, but the taxes, Jack."

Jack: "Things are dear, to be sure, but riot and murder is not the way to make them cheap. . . . Beside, things are mending. . . and I dare say if the honest gentleman who has the management of things is not disturbed by you levellers things will mend every day. But bear one thing in mind, the more we riot the more we shall have to pay. The more mischief is done, the more will repairs cost. The more time we waste in meeting to redress public wrongs, the more we shall increase our private wants. . , "

Tom: " But the subject is not below the king. All kings are crowned ruffians and all goverments are wicked. For my part I am resolved to pay no more taxes to any of them."

Jack: "Tom, Tom, if thou did'st go oftener to church . . . The book tells you that we need obey no government but that of the people, . . . but mine tells me that every one be subject to the higher powers, for all power is of God. Whosoever resisteth the power resisteth the ordinance of God. . . . Tom? I have got the use of my limbs, of my liberty, of the laws, and of my Bible. The two first I take to be my *natural* rights; the two last my *civil* and *religious* rights: these, I take it, are the *true Rights of Man*, and all the rest is nothing but nonsense, and madness and wickedness. My cottage is my castle ; I sit down in it at night in peace and thankfulness, and 'no man maketh me afraid.' Instead of indulging discontent, because another is richer than I in this world (for envy is at the bottom of your equality works) I read my Bible, go to church, and look forward to a treasure in Heaven."[1]

The picty and wisdom of Will Chip made so great an impression that other dialogues were planned. Three a year were to be published under the title of " Cheap Repository Tracts." The bishop of London, a royal duke, and William Wilberforce were patrons of this series. Under their auspices the Repository Tracts were widely circulated throughout the country.[2]

---

[1] Hannah More, *Works*, i, 225-240 *passim*.

[2] Among them were: *Betty Brown, the St. Giles Orange Girl; Black Giles, the Poacher; Sorrowful Sam, the Blacksmith; Patient Joe, or the Newcastle Collier; The Gin-shop, or a Peep into Prison; A Riot,*

No statement of the conservative platform, however simple, can with justice fail to mention "The association for preserving liberty and property against republicans and levellers." This organization was formed on November twentieth, 1792, "at a meeting of gentlemen at the Crown and Anchor Tavern."[1]

The chairman of this meeting was a certain John Reeves, formerly one of his Majesty's judges. Radicalism had no more bitter enemy than John Reeves. His association was active in the prosecution of real and supposed libels against the crown; in publishing and distributing cheap tracts on behalf of the Tory party; and in founding other societies throughout the country.[2]

---

or Half a Loaf is Better than no Bread. This latter pamphlet was written in 1795. It was said to have prevented the destruction of property during a coal strike. The wise Jack Anvil soothes once more the troubled waters in a speech, of which this is an extract:

> "And though I've no money, and though I've no lands,
> I've head on my shoulders, and a pair of good hands;
> So I'll work the whole day, and on Sundays I'll seek
> At church how to bear all the wants of the week.
> The gentlefolks, too, will afford us supplies.
> They'll subscribe—and they'll give up their puddings and pies.
>   DERRY DOWN."

[1] *Annual Register,* 1792, p. 92.

[2] The original resolutions of the society were:

"First, that the persons present at this meeting do become a society for discouraging and suppressing seditious publications tending to disturb the peace of this kingdom, and for supporting a due execution of the laws made for the protection of persons and property.

"Second, that the society do use its best endeavors occasionally to explain these topics of public discussion, which have been so perverted by evil designing men, and to show by irrefragable proof that they are not applicable to the state of this country; that they can produce no good, and certainly must produce great evil.

"Third, that this society will receive with great thanks all communications that shall be made to it for the above purposes.

"Fourth, that it be recommended to all those who are friends to the

Reeves himself was more zealous than wise. Particularly
was this true of his authorship of "Thoughts on English
Government." This pamphlet was so ultra-partisan in character that it was accused of libelling the House of Commons, and, in a debate against the coercive measures of
Pitt, a Mr. Sturt for the opposition quoted effectively
from the "Thoughts" to the effect that "the government
of England is a monarchy; the monarchy is the ancient
stock from which have sprung those goodly branches of
legislature, the Lords and Commons. . . . But these still
are only branches, and derive their origin and nutriment
from the common parent; they may be lopped off, and
the tree is a tree still—shorn, indeed, of its honors, but

established law and to peaceable society, to form themselves in their
different neighborhoods into similar societies for promoting the same
laudable purposes.

"Fifth, that this society do meet at this place or elsewhere every
Tuesday, Thursday and Saturday.

"Sixth, that these considerations and resolutions be printed in all
the public papers, and otherwise circulated into all parts of the kingdom."

Among the publications of the society were: "Dialogues on the
Rights of Britons, between a farmer, sailor and manufacturer;" A
Dialogue between a laborer and a gentleman;" "A Dialogue between
Mr. T——, a tradesman in the city, and his porter, John W——." These
dialogues, which the Society published, and others which it approved
of, were written on the model of Hannah More's "Village Politics." For instance in "Plain English for All Parties," Will Blunt
exclaims: "We can none of us be independent one of another. The
rich stand in need of the poor, and the poor in need of the rich; the
money of the one is as necessary to buy the materials, such as wool,
iron, timber and cattle, as the labor of the poor is to increase the rich
man's property. To what purpose would it be to sow corn, breed cattle,
and weave woolen or cotton, if there were not people enough to buy it."

A similar pamphlet was entitled "Free Communings; or a Last
Attempt to Cure the Lunatics now Laboring under that Dreadful Mal-
ady Commonly Called the French Disease." The characters in this
pamphlet were, Mr. Timothy Crab, a reformer, and Mr. Charles
Hearty, a Royalist.

not like them cast into the fire." If the radical publications are to be prosecuted, how about this Tory pamphlet, cries Mr. Sturt, which says that the House of Commons may be lopped off.[1] This lead was eagerly followed by several of the Whig leaders. A select committee discovered the authorship of the "Thoughts," which were published anonymously, and Reeves was indicted and tried for seditious libel. He was acquitted, but the jury said they were of "the opinion that the pamphlet which has been written by J. Reeves, Esq., is a very improper publication."[2] The "Thoughts" is not as representative of Tory opinion as the "Reflections" or "Village Politics." Nevertheless the Bourbonism which it expresses is frequently to be encountered.

Our treatise, as an analysis of radical opinion, does not pretend to do more than to state the conservative position in as fair a light as possible. The fact that important supplements were made by Burke to the Reflections,[3] that Arthur Young rushed to his assistance,[4] that learned judges and other dignitaries defended the conservative intrenchments, does not invalidate the claim that the three writers we have quoted represent with fair com-

[1] *Parliamentary Register*, xliii, 287.

[2] *State Trials*, xxvi, 594.

[3] *Appeal from the New to the Old Whigs*, 1791. *Letter to the Duke of Portland*, 1793. *Throughts on the Prospects of a Peace with the Regicide Directory*, 1796.

[4] Young, *The Example of France a Warning to England*, 1794. For this book Young received a great many letters of congratulation from private friends and numerous votes of thanks from Loyalist associations. "Correspondence of Arthur Young," British Museum, *Additional MSS.*, vol. ii, pp. 250, 253, 267 *et seq.* Young was accused of being in the government's employ. He denied this in a letter dated December 25th, 1795.

prehensiveness the Tory ideal.   At any rate there can be no question concerning the "Reflections" and "Village Politics."   No upholder of the old order caviled at these books; they stood side by side; both were read widely; both bore the *imprimatur* of a united Tory party.

CHAPTER II.

PAMPHLET SKIRMISHING.

THE OLDER RADICALS BRIEFLY SURVEYED : PRICE, PRIEST-
LEY, HORNE TOOKE AND MAJOR CARTWRIGHT.   CUR-
SORY TREATMENT OF SCURRILOUS, ANONYMOUS
AND INCIDENTAL LITERATURE.

BURKE'S pronunciamento called forth thirty-eight replies.   Many Tories flew to arms in his defence; cudgels
were freely handled by both sides.   Following hard upon
the publication of the "Reflections" were issued numberless "Counter-reflections," "Tracts," "Strictures,"
"Inquiries," "Refutations," "Remarks," "Animadver-
sions," "Letters" and "Addresses."   This great out-
pouring virtually began with Burke.   It increased in volume and intensity throughout the years 1794 and 1795,
amid the hard times and the excitement of the treason
trials.   Lessening to a considerable degree with the
naval victories of the next two years, accompanied as
they were by an ever-growing British patriotism, hostile
in the same breath to France and to imported French
ideals, a brisk pamphlet skirmish between the friends of
Burke and those of his chief enemy, Paine, was maintained, even until the end of the century.   This controversy may in part be treated with scant respect, for only
by the elimination of a large portion of it may we form a
just estimate of radical opinion.

The writings of the Whig minority we shall omit
altogether.   They were not radical at all.   Furthermore,

their ranks, since the defection of Burke, had become much thinned. Able men were enrolled among them; able men defended their principles outside of Parliament; but they were few in number, and their voice was as one crying in the wilderness,—a futile cross-current in the midst of a storm.[1]

Then, too, for the purpose of demarking as clearly as possible the radical opinion of the day, one other body of writers must be dismissed with an equally curt notice. That body comprised what might be termed the group of older Radicals. Among them were very distinguished men. Their names are as well, if not better, known as those of the younger and more influential radicals of the decade. Still it is fair to dismiss them with but brief mention. They belong to an earlier school of thought, and their work was well over by 1791. Some of them lingered on, it is true, until the nineteenth century. But their ideals were those of an earlier day, the aspiration of which do not fall within the province of this discussion.

As illustrative of the work and aims of these elder statesmen in the radical camp, brief mention may be made of Richard Price, Joseph Priestley, John Horne Tooke and Major Cartwright.

Price, from several points of view, represents fairly the temper of the earlier reformers. A stanch believer in theoretical freedom, he boldly and forcefully defended

[1] Cappell Lofft, *Remarks on the Letters of Edmund Burke*, 1790. Lofft has been generally classified as a Whig, because of his friendship with Fox and other Whig leaders. His career, however, was remarkably independent of party. So also was Dr. Samuel Parr's. Parr hoped for the " cramming of such ministers as Pitt, such bishops as Horsley, and such reformers as Horne Tooke into a basket, [said basket] to be tossed into the ocean." Parr, *Works,* vii, 650.

the American Revolution.   A Unitarian minister of distinction, he consistently fought for the repeal of the test
laws.   Disgusted with the corruption rampant among
Whigs and Tories alike, he championed the cause of a
thorough reform of the House of Commons, and finally,
as a warm-hearted, sympathetic man, he enthusiastically
approved of the earlier stages of the French revolution.
But beyond these ideas Price did not go far, nor did his
fellow old-time reformers.   Born in 1723, Price, though
not ranking high in pulpit oratory,[1] became soon after
the middle of the century widely recognized as a writer
upon religious and metaphysical subjects.   Shortly after
this, in 1772, in publishing a book on the subject of the
national debt, he evinced a profound knowledge of
finance[2] and speedily attained an international reputation
as an economist.   We find him in continuous communication with Turgot, while the American Continental Congress sought his assistance in the regulation of its
finances.[3]   As a man of affairs Price now stood high.
His writings were received with favor.   His work, both
educational and religious, was highly appreciated.   Aside
from all this a single act, and that the last public effort
of his life, has assured Richard Price historical prominence.

On the fourth of November, 1789, in his meeting-house
in old Jewry, Price preached one of the best-known sermons in history.   That sermon fully summarized the
ideals of the early reformers.   Price is looking backward, not forward.   He is praising liberty, it is true, but
it is the liberty achieved in theory by the revolution of
1688.   His chief thesis is to affirm and demonstrate a

---

[1] William Morgan, *Memoirs of the Life of Rev. Richard Price,* p. 30.

[2] Price, *An Appeal to the Public on the National Debt.*

[3] Morgan, *op. cit.,* p. 76.

three-fold right obtained by that revolution, to wit, that
the people have the right to choose their kings; the right
to cashier them for misconduct; and the right to form a
government for themselves. These ideals more nearly
resembled ancient traditions than dangerous innovations,
and yet, forsooth, because Burke singled out this sermon
for attack, we must, according to certain writers, think
of Price as the chosen champion of the French revolution
in England.[1] But Price was already an old man: his
work was done. He died destined not even to behold
the struggles of the revolutionary party in England.

The career of Joseph Priestley was not unlike that of
Price. Also an eminent Unitarian clergyman, Priestley
had two major interests: theology and experimental
chemistry. In the history of both Unitarianism and
chemistry he ranks with the highest, but as an exponent
of theoretical radicalism, he occupies no considerable position, for not only was his radicalism, if we may call it
such, of the somewhat antiquated type represented by
Price, but likewise its expression and influence were, by
1791, already a thing of the past.

As indicative of Priestley's early ideas, he tells us, in
1771, that " the English government is a mixture of regal,
aristocratic and democratical power, and if the public education should be more favorable to any one of these than
to another . . . the balance of the whole would neces-
sarily be lost.'[2] This old theory of the separation of
powers and of the three-fold division of the state preserving liberty by a balance of authority, Priestley held early in

---

[1] Laprade, *England and the French Revolution*, devotes three pages
to Price, while dismissing Paine with a curt mention.

[2] Joseph Prisetley, *An essay on the first principles of Government*,
p. 106. A copy of this book, given by the author to John Wilkes, is in
the possession of Columbia University.

his career. He believed in it also throughout a long life. In a volume appearing in 1788, and reissued in 1793, in speaking of the benefits enjoyed by limited monarchical governments, he says: " These governments, consisting of so many parts, each of which has a negative on all resolutions of consequence, are a check and balance on one another." [1]

This was Priestley's idea of politics. His chief interest, however, did not lie in social and political affairs. It was said that he never preached a sermon devoted to politics; he cared little for society and never attended a public meeting if he could help it.[2] One might even hold that his name would hardly have been associated with the history of radicalism had not his house been wrecked by a mob.

The riot in which this occurred created vast excitement. Its cause was a celebration held in honor of the second anniversary of the fall of the Bastille. A public dinner was given, eminently respectable in tone; a churchman presided, and the toasts save in one instance were mild. During the course of the dinner, however, a rabble gathered outside the tavern. Encouraged by the tacit approval of some magistrates present, and proceeding in accord with true mob psychology, it took the short step from overflow of invective to destruction of property. Priestley's house, with the costly scientific apparatus which it contained, was destroyed. The Non-conformist chapels were attacked, and to quell the riot troops were quartered in Birmingham. The disturbance was to some extent a preliminary gust of the revolutionary storm. More largely was it due to Priestley's personal enemies, negligence on the part of the government, and hatred of the Dissenters.[3] One result was

[1] Priestley, *Lectures on history and general policy*, p. 355.

[2] Thorpe, *Joseph Priestley*, p. 153.

[3] Yates, *Memorials of Dr. Priestley, passim;* Laprade, *England and the French Revolution*, pp. 43-52.

to drive the poor preacher into an unprofitable controversy with Burke, and to shed upon him an unwelcome
limelight. Another was that Priestley, disgusted with conditions in England, emigrated to America.[1]

A more humorous and delightful representative of old-
time radicalism was John Horne Tooke. Tooke, like
Priestley, had been swept into the radical current by ad-
ventitious circumstances and against his will. In 1794
Tooke was tried for high treason—why, it is difficult to
say. There was no evidence against him; still the government selected him as an object of attack. An example
evidently was to be made of a rash gentleman, and Tooke
was tried for high treason. He was triumphantly vindi-
cated. Nevertheless, a hue and cry had been raised, and
Tooke, willing or otherwise, from this time on was eyed
askance as an evil radical.

Tooke's major activities, like those of Price and Priestley,
belonged to earlier days. His life and training were those
of a gentleman of the old school. His parentage, to be
sure, was humble,—a circumstance Tooke skilfully concealed.[2] He was a scholar, a clergyman of the Church of
England,—facts he never allowed himself to forget.

His exciting early career concerns us but little. A party
to the confused entanglements of the Junius controversy
and the Wilkes affair,[3] Tooke soon abandoned the lure of
theology for the excitement of public life. Resigning his
living he became a lawyer. For parliamentary reform he
fought courageously; in the crusade against rotten boroughs he was a leader; not for the purpose, be it noted, of

---

[1] Thorpe, *Priestley,* p. 155.

[2] Stevens, *Memoirs of John Horne Tooke,* i, 21.

[3] For an ingenious proof that Tooke was none other than the
mysterious Junius, see Graham, *Memoirs of John Horne Tooke.*

introducing innovations, but rather for the maintenance of
the old rights and privileges of Englishmen.   The substance of his political philosophy may readily be deduced
from his speeches in the Westminster election of 1796.
He then declared: " The voters are tied to a tree of corruption, and in this country its height and weight and bulk
are enormous."   The tree is shaken, and a united effort
will pull it over.   And again he assures them " that all
constitutional and necessary check is taken away from the
courts of justice."   " The voters might perceive it by sen-
tences passed contrary to legal precedent, fit only for the
devils in hell to pronounce."[1]   This check on the courts
should be restored.   For to Tooke, as to Priestley and Price,
checks and balances were the desiderata of politics.

The ex-clergyman, however, incurred the especial dis-
pleasure of the government.   Because Tooke hated both
Toryism and Whiggism[2] they could not conceive of him
otherwise than as a dangerous man.   An action was
brought against him, and the result was the famous
Tooke trial, the verbatim report of which affords amus-
ing reading.   Horne Tooke conducted the greater part of
his own defence.   Angered as he was by the attitude of the
judge and prosecuting attorney, and sure of his evidence,
he took a huge delight in bantering his opponents.   Even
toward the judge he exhibited a marked playfulness of
manner.   Indeed, with an untroubled heart he must have
answered both thrust and parry, for the evidence of his
own innate conservatism, his dislike of Paine, and his contempt for universal suffrage was overwhelming.[3]

[1] *Speeches of John Horne Tooke during the Westminster Election*, p. 7.

[2] Stephens, *Memorial of Tooke*, i, 438.

[3] Tooke's dislike of Paine: Evidence in the *State Trials*, xxv,
112.   Tooke throws a letter to Paine unopened into the fire, *ibid.*,
p. 248.   Tooke opposes the sending of delegates to Edinburgh for the

After his release from prison Tooke made an unsuccess-- ful canvass for Parliament. He tried once more and was elected but as an ex-clergyman, he was declared ineligible. Abandoning public life he became more and more interested in literary subjects, in his garden, and in giving dinner parties at Wimbledon, his country estate. At the end of the century we discover him a carefully-dressed old person, with silk stockings, long wrist ruffles and powdered hair.[1] And his opinions befitted his appearance. In his last address to his friends at Westminster in 1804, he assures them that so long as he lives he will maintain a steadfast adherence to the ancient freedom of his country, as it has been prac- tically enjoyed under those honest old gentlemen, George I and George II.[2]

John Cartwright, or, as he was generally known, Major Cartwright, can hardly with propriety be omitted from our discussion of the British reformers. In a way Cartwright represented both the older and the younger school of radi- cal thought, for his eighty odd tracts are scattered through- out the period covered by both. Cartwright believed stead- fastly in universal suffrage, which was in no great favor with the older men, yet at the same time socially he be- longed to their group. Throughout his career he was the country gentleman in politics. He carried his Majesty's commission in the militia[3] and had been a naval officer.

Radical Convention, *ibid.*, p. 87. Tooke opposes Universal Suffrage, *ibid.*, p. 93. Tooke accused by the Radicals of making an aristocratic speech, *ibid.*, p. 253. Sheridan, Philip Francis and Bishop of Glou- cester all testify at this trial in favor of the prisoner. Stephens, *Memorial,* ii, 346.

[1] Stephens, *op. cit.,* ii, 234.

[2] *Ibid.*, p. 263.

[3] The attendance upon radical meetings kept Cartwright from pro- motion in the militia. "A Letter to the Duke of Newcastle," by John Cartwright, p. 51.

Furthermore, his reforming ideas were more theoretical than practical. They all looked backward to a so-called day of English freedom. " I ought to have a vote because I am a man," and because my ancestors had it, argued Cartwright, and upon that philosophical foundation the greater part of his public life was laid. He regarded suffrage as a fetich which would cure all evils, and this belief he stated in season and out of season for fifty years.

So stupidly and awkwardly written were these appeals of the Major that no one regarded him very seriously.[1] He was said to be free from any Machiavellian touch. One may well believe it, for even the best-known of his eighty odd tracts are intolerably dull and prosy. But everybody liked Major Cartwright. He was not altogether an extremist. He disapproved of Paine,[2] as his friends were always glad to repeat, and in the meantime the goodness of heart and sincerity of spirit of Major Cartwright atoned for many aberrations.

Certain pamphleteers deserve less consideration than that afforded to the older radicals. Briefly may we dismiss those partisans of the pen whose writings are in character low and scurrilous, exulting in rhodomontade to the exclusion of thought and reason. Pamphlets of this nature, all too many, unfortunately, poured forth in equal volume from both Tory and radical camps. Let one author suffice for a Tory warrior of this sort—William Cobbett, writing under the pseudonym of Peter Porcupine.[3]

[1] Kent, *A Historical Sketch of Radicalism,* p. 70.

[2] *Life and Correspondence of Major John Cartwright,* edited by his niece, F. D. Cartwright, p. 192.

[3] Cobbett, the famous English radical, imbued with patriotic fervor in his early days, wrote during the period of the French revolution as the most irreconcilable of Tories. E. D. Smith, *Life of Cobbett,* p. 107.

The pamphlets of Peter Porcupine, it so happened, were
written and printed in Philadelphia, but their chief influence was in England.   Indeed, so popular were they there,
that the Philadelphia imprint was generally believed to
have been adopted for purposes of concealment.   His
first pamphlet, " A Bone to Gnaw for the Democrats,"
was immediately reviewed and answered by the deli-
cately worded reply, " A Kick for a Bite."   " The Kick,"
as might be expected, brought back retaliation from Porcupine, and a flood of abuse followed after.   " Hireling,"
" Pork Patriot," " Mr. Hedgehog " and other edifying
epithets were freely bandied about,[1] and Porcupine forthwith became well known as a defender of church and king.[2]

    " The Bone to Gnaw " is, indeed, too indecent for ex-
tended quotation.   France, described as a low woman of
the town, is represented as making love to John Bull.
" No," says John, " you heathenish cannibal; you reek
with blood.   Get from my sight, you stabbing strumpet.
. . . She is a cruel spouse, John, something like the brazen
image formerly made use of in Hungary for cracking the
bones and squeezing out the blood and guts of those condemned to its embrace." [3]   Of such stuff was composed the
" Bone to Gnaw "; nevertheless we find it highly praised in
England.   J. R. Greene, a Tory magistrate and editor of the
Anti-Jacobin, wrote a preface for the work and, in his
first issue of the *Anti-Jacobin Review,* gave a criticism of
Cobbett's pamphlet the place of honor.   Herriott, edi-

---

[1] Smith, *Cobbett, op. cit.,* p. 135.

[2] Cobbett tells us that when he opened his shop " I put in my windows, which were very large, all the portraits that I had in my possession of Kings, Queens, Princes and Nobles.   I had the English
Ministry, several of the Bishops and Judges, the most famous Ad-
mirals, and in fact every picture that I thought likely to excite
rage in the enemies of Great Britain." *Ibid.,* p. 162.

[3] *Bone to Gnaw,* p. 60.

tor of *The True Briton,* Pitt's subsidized paper,[1] recommended Peter Porcupine, whose coarseness even the clergy condoned.[2]   In fact, Peter Porcupine was approved by the highest authorities in England, for we learn that when Cobbett returned to England in 1798, he was dined by Windham and presented to Pitt and many other notables.[3]

Indecent fulminations were not the exclusive property of the conservatives; several periodical publications of the radical party showed a similar tendency.   One of them, taking title from Burke's phrase " the swinish multitude," was styled " Pig's Meat."[4]   Another, which received the appellation " Hog's Wash," was edited by a certain Daniel Isaac Eaton.   This Eaton was tried by the government for seditious libel in attacking the king by open innuendoes, and although he was acquitted,[5] no more copies of " Hog's Wash " were printed; and, indeed, it may fairly be assumed that the coarser qualities of the publication did not meet altogether with popular approval, for in the thirteen numbers issued before the trial an evident purification of tone was in progress.[6]

---

[1] Laprade, *England and the French Revolution,* p. 77.

[2] The Rev. William Beloe is quoted as saying: "That the writer is occasionally a little coarse in his style and expression cannot be denied, but perhaps he could not attain more refinement except at the expense of some strength." Smith, *Cobbett,* p. 238. The *British Critic* also eulogizes Cobbett repeatedly.   It calls him " our good ally " (*British Critic* for 1797, page xii, Introduction), and recommends highly *The Bloody Buoy, ibid.,* p. 201.   A special diatribe by Cobbett against Priestley. *A twig birch for butting calf,* also meets with approval.

[3] Smith, *Cobbett,* p. 251.

[4] The editor of " Pig's Meat " was Spence, the land nationalizer. *Cf. infra,* pp. 108 *et seq.*

[5] *State Trials,* xxiii, 1013.

[6] The first five numbers are entitled simple *Hog's Wash.*   The sixth

Nevertheless, this weekly, even in its semi-cleansed condition, is quite comparable with the work of Peter Porcupine. By verse and by fable Eaton sought to supply popular matter for his magazine. In " The Land of Apes," the conditions of England are foully depicted.[1] Other little stories have matched crudity only by obscenity. " The Story of the Honest Cobbler," [2] is an illustration in point, as is also a bit of humor dubbed " Aristocratic Insolence and Democratic Bluntness." [3] In an article on the origin of nobility we are told that princes and potentates are descended from " cruel butchers of men: oppressors, tyrants, perfidious truce-breakers, robbers and parasites," [4] and so on, in an endless flood of vituperation. Of such language one speedily sickens, and turns with relief to other types of discussion.

A large proportion of the decent literature may be eliminated with as little attention as is warranted by the scurrilous publications. Thus the bulk of the religious writings may be dismissed, for most ecclesiastics held the anti-slavery cause to be of far more consequence than domestic reform. By the Rev. John Akin we are told that Britains are " personally free, politically free and commercially free;" [5] therefore they should devote their energies toward conferring these benefits on the poor slaves and benighted heathen. Other clergymen, the majority of

number is called *Hog's Wash, or Politics for the People.* The seventh and eighth numbers, *Politics for the people, or Hog's Wash,* whereas the last numbers are known simply as *Politics for the People.*

[1] *Hog's Wash, or Politics of the People,* no. 6.

[2] *Hog's Wash,* no. 2.

[3] *Politics for the People, or Hog's Wash,* no. 7.

[4] *Hog's Wash,* no. 3.

[5] John Akin, *Food for National Penitence, a discourse intended for the approaching fast day.*

the Anglican and perhaps also of the Non-conformist, were frankly Tory.   No uncertainty marks the utter-
ances of these divines.   Their exhortations ring out loud
and clear.   But we will not linger over them.   When we
are told that the radical writers are " quacks, who, under
the specious appearance of philosophy and reason, would
administer their empiric remedies, and purge away the
health of the country;" when we are assured that " we
will not deprive the British lion of his teeth and fangs and
leave him the laughing-stock of every puny beast of the
forest;" and, after we are informed finally that there is no
persuasion more favorable to the British constitution than
the Established Church,[1] there is little more for us to know.
Samuel Horsley, Bishop of St. Asaph, delighted to use
similar language,[2] while many of the Scottish clergy in
equally felicitous terms made clear the conservatism of
their attitude.   Celebrations of the martrydom of Charles I
became more and more frequent.   Upon that sacred day
the evils of the French revolution were a common topic for
sermons.   Texts of all kinds were put into requisition, one
divine selecting " By that time he stinketh." [3]

The leading dissenting clergymen after 1791 deserted
the radical cause, if they can be said ever to have belonged

[1] *An important defense of the Established Church.*   The writer tells
us that he believes in keeping peace with all men, " but when we perceive the ray darting from the deadly scales of the hidden serpent,
it is our duty to drag the monster to the light, and to display him in
his naked deformity."

[2] Before the House of Lords in an anniversary sermon, *Morning
Chronicle,* Feb. 16, 1793.   His speeches, however, were generally more
temperate, as, for instance on the third reading of the Treason Bill.
Horsley, *Speeches,* p. 167.

[3] Laprade, *England and the French Revolution,* p. 154.   Andrew
Bunaby, William Gilbank, John Scott and others are enumerated by
Laprade, pp. 154-155, while in Edinburgh the printed sermons of
George Hill and Thomas Somerville are quite similar in kind.

to it.[1]   Their activities were more engrossed with the
founding of missionary societies than in seeking the repeal
of the Test Act.   The suspicious government was soon to
learn that their designs were remote from concerns terres-
trial.[2] A few dissenting clergymen continued to hold radical opinions; [3] others boldly insisted that they were faithful
defenders of the existing order; while a majority preached
apologetic sermons.   "The crystallized thought of God" is.
to be sure, demonstrated quite clearly by many of the clergy,
and the ways of His providence are pointed out to us with
naïve freedom,[4] and so also is the path along which society
shall travel.   All of these ideas found a considerable circulation, and from an antiquarian point of view are of interest; [5] but their tangled phraseology and cloudy mysticism
render them for our purposes quite unpractical.   In brief,
then, it is not unfair to conclude that from the dissenting
clergy the cause of radicalism received but trifling support,
and from the Established Church less.

Little attention, either, need be paid to a large number
of anonymous tracts.   These are generally humorous or

[1] This, of course, does not apply to Priestley or Price whose work
was over by 1792.

[2] Bogue and Bennett, *A History of the Dissenters,* iv, 206; Stoughton,
Religion in England under Queen Anne and the Georges, pp. 293,
336, 348.

[3] Mark Wilkes, *The Origin and Stability of the French Revolution,*
sermon preached in St. Paul's chapel, Norwich.

[4] James Hinton, *Vindication of the Dissenters.*

[5] John Bicheno in *The Signs of the Times* demonstrates from Daniel
and the Book of Revelations, that 1789 was the turning point in
Christian history.   From that date he tells us it will take thirty years
to root out Popery and to prepare mankind for civil and religious
liberty.   Forty-five additional years would find the Jews converted and
Christianity extended to the uttermost confines of the earth.   Everything then being in readiness for the second coming of Christ, the
world would end in 1862.

satirical and at times their meaning is veiled in allegory. Frequently it is explained by fictitious dialogue. Rarely interesting, frequently stupid, as indicative of public opinion, they have but little value. The story of the visit of Brissot's ghost to a radical meeting is typical.[1] The ghost tells the members of the society that they already have " equitable laws [and] an amiable king under whose mild government every class of subjects enjoy liberty and equality in the highest degree." The ghost then, by the well-worn analogy of the human family, points out that, inasmuch as children have no voice in family government, so indeed the lower classes should not expect to share in the government of the nation. A few words about France follow in warning. He then vanishes, and the radicals depart, no longer believing in their foolish whims.

Dialogues and letters are numerous. Here we are introduced to a dialogue where the fears of a conservative are allayed; there we find a series of letters purporting to be written by Brother Bull to Brother Jonathan. These may be classed in the same category.[2] Several tracts written by Old Hubert are equally representative. Old Hubert describes the strange country of Bull Land, where the king may be an idiot, the priests lazy and inefficient, the laws complicated and unjust, and all social conditions in-

---

[1] *Brissot's Ghost, or Intelligence from the Other World.* A large catalogue of this type of pamphlet might be made. *Thoughts on a late Riot in Birmingham; The Flower of the Jacobins; The Patriot; An Address from a Poor Man to his Equals* will serve as illustrations. The last mentioned tract contains a spirited dialogue between a workman and Mr. MacSerpent. " The Reeves Manuscripts " in the British Museum contain an enormous number of Tory manuscripts of this kind.

[2] *One pennyworth's of truth for a penny,* also *One pennyworth's more of truth for a penny.* Like pamphlets are *The present state of the British constitution deduced from the facts,* and *Comments on proposed war with France.*

iquitous. One Tory writer cuts to the heart of the question when he insists that at bottom the point at issue is one of property. So likewise does an unknown radical who asserts that " a poor man, whose enthusiasm is a good deal subdued by hard labor, by cold domicile, by scanty wages, by a press of taxation, and by the necessary care of a family," is not aroused by the idea of a patriotic war.[1] Such, however, are exceptions. In the main but little reasoning power is exhibited by these effusions of the anonymous pen.

Finally we shall put to one side writings of yet another kind. There were men whose influence, for one reason or another, was no true measure of their ability. There were also many who, because they endeavored in the narrow compass of a pamphlet to compress too many complaints and too many remedies, deserve but transitory notice in a résumé of radical theory. William Hodgson and George Dyer were men of this stamp. The former, a well-known botanist and physician, became a warm adherent of the more radical tenets of the French *doctrinnaires.* These opinions made trouble for Hodgson. In a tavern brawl, he called the king a German hog butcher.[2] Placed in jail for this offence, Hodgson planned his book, " The Commonwealth." This production, an eighteenth century Utopia, is somewhat crassly and feebly executed. The artillery of Hodgson is mainly directed against religion. Men never agree upon religion, he says, and inasmuch as there are some two-hundred-odd different creeds, which he enumerates, it is folly to believe that one is more pleasing to God than another. Furthermore, popes, muftis, druids, dominies and other divines exercise an authority which is bad. Hodgson would do away with it. " The Commonwealth " also advocates civil marriages, easy divorces, national work-

[1] *The Crisis stated,* 1793.
[2] *The World,* Dec. 10, 1793.

shops, old-age pensions, improved public schools, and the abolition of capital punishment. There is to be but one tax —a tax on land of four pence per acre. That tax will more than provide for the expenses of clerk hire sufficient to run the government. There will be a favorable balance which will make possible the remission of taxes altogether every fourth year. On such a year, he says, " I will provide that they celebrate a feast of economy." [1]

The ideas of George Dyer were less chimerical. Dyer was a Christ Hospital boy, and a graduate of Cambridge. Unitarian opinions prevented his advancement in the Church and Dyer became a literary free lance of a somewhat eccentric type, and, although well known and much liked by many literary celebrities,[2] he remained always on the borderland of real literary attainment. In 1793 Dyer published " The Complaints of the Poor People of England." The humanitarian sympathies of the man may be seen in his treatment of this subject. " But God never said," wrote Dyer apropos of the game laws, that " the squire may shoot the partridge or the pheasant, though the laborer shall not; or that Sir Robert may draw a fish out of the river, and that his poor tenants be imprisoned for the same offense." The army and navy, he thought, were overtaxed with officers. The army was too aristocratic, and aped the Prussian system. He mentioned an offender who was lashed four and twenty-five times, and quoted the reply of a non-commissioned officer who, invited to serve as an officer of the Prussian

[1] Hodgson, *Commonwealth*, p. 103. Aside from the "Commonwealth," Hodgson wrote *The System of Nature*, and *Proposals for Publishing by Subscription*, a treatise called *The Female Citizen, or a historical inquiry into the rights of women*, various scientific works, a Life of Napoleon; and other miscellanies emanated from his pen.

[2] Charles Lamb said of Dyer that " for integrity and single heartedness he might be ranked among the best patterns of his species."

army, said, " I would rather be in hell eight years than in the service of Prussia." There is red tape to be found everywhere. Special privilege controls the hospitals. The public schools are far from democratic, and the existence of flogging in them is most brutal. So also is capital punishment; and as for the criminal and civil code, it is quite impossible.[1] Not very logical or closely reasoned is this outburst of Dyer's.[2] But, filled as it is with the spirit of aroused democracy, it is worthy of remembrance.

[1] Dyer, *The Complaints of the Poor People of England, passim.*

[2] The worst that the Tory *Critical Review* could say of this book was " The complaints of the poor is a plausible, and in some degree, popular term, but it is a great pity that there should be individuals so officiously acute in finding out the inconvenience and suffering of those who are not immediately susceptible of their oppression, or even of its existence." The *Critical Review*, 1793, p. 333.

CHAPTER III

The Radical Creed

THE RIGHTS OF MAN AND THE RIGHTS OF WOMAN
WOLLSTONECRAFT AND PAINE
MACKINTOSH AND BENTHAM

FIRST in the field to reply to Burke was a woman. Burke's " Reflections " were published in November, 1790. Ere the year closed his book was refuted. Before the smooth-flowing *Vindiciae Gallicae* of Mackintosh and the pretence-stripping pamphlets of the " vulgar " Paine had gone to press, there came with swiftness and penetration a woman's defence of all mankind. Mary Wollstonecraft's " Vindication of the Rights of Man," opened the radical campaign—a campaign which sooner or later drew into the *melée* the keenest intellects of England. To the " Reflec tions " of Edmund Burke no fewer than thirty-eight re- plies were forthcoming. Mary Wollstonecraft's, first in priority of time, has, in thought if not in diction, no su- perior.

There is little hesitancy in her attack on Burke. " I per- ceive," she writes, " from the whole tenor of your ' Reflec- tions,' that you have a mortal antipathy to reason, but if there is anything like argument or first principles in your wild declamation, behold the result—that we are to rever- ence the rust of antiquity, and those unnatural customs which ignorance and self-interest have consolidated into the sage fruit of experience." Progress is retarded by the worship of the mouldy past. The eighteenth century ought to admit " that our canonized forefathers were unable or afraid to revert to reason without resting on the crutch of authority." Wollstonecraft would throw away that crutch. " Let us reason together," she argues, and look upon the world around us as it is. It is true that the world is far from lovely or ideal, but candor and sincerity demand that we know it honestly as it is. Purity of morals is destroyed " by smearing sentimental varnish over vice to hide its natural deformity."

The school mistress had no respect for the immaculate constitution of England. It guarantees property, no doubt, but at the same time " the liberty of an honest mechanic is often sacrificed to secure the property of the rich." Why should the life of a deer be more prized than the life of a man? Why, under our excellent constitution, should men be kidnapped for service in the navy? " Why cannot large estates be divided into small farms? Why does the brown waste meet the traveller's view when men want work? "

And as for the much-praised House of Commons, what could be more farcical than British elections? The members of the House are but puppets. " After the effervescence of spirit raised by the opposition and all the little tyrannical acts of canvassing are over—quiet souls!—they only intend to march rank and file to say yes or no." " You were (she says to Burke) behind the curtain. You must have seen the clogged wheels of corruption continually oiled, and the sweat of the laboring poor squeezed out of them by increasing taxation. You must have discovered that the majority of the House of Commons were openly purchased by the crown, and that the people were oppressed by the influence of their own money. . . . You must have known that a man of talent cannot rise in the church, the army or navy, unless he has some interest in a borough."

Yet you talk of virtue and of liberty, and deride the French
national assembly. What right have you to do that? If
" unlettered clowns " may bring about " a crisis that may
involve the fate of Europe, and more than Europe," you
must allow us to respect unsophisticated common-sense,
but at any rate why praise the British House of Commons,
that " dead weight of benumbing opulence where the sheep
obsequiously pursue their steps with all the undeviating
sagacity of instinct." [1]

Objection is made also to Burke's fulsome laudation of
the Church of England. " It is a well-known fact," affirms Wollstonecraft, " that when we the people of England have a son whom we scarcely know what to do with—
we make a clergyman of him." [2] The intelligence of the
clergy is in consequence low, and so also is their regard
for the sacredness of their calling. Of course there are
individual exceptions, but a majority of them " perform
the duty of their professions as a kind of fee simple," and
as for Burke's claim that the education of the ruling class
is ennobled and idealized by its connection with the cloth;
it calls forth a hearty laugh from everyone who is aware
of the position held by the clerical tutor. He is snubbed
and scorned by his employer and is, in fact, " the modern
substitute for the jesters of Gothic memory." The clergy
dare not resent the patronage which means their livelihood,
" an airy mitre dances before them " and they wrap themselves in " their sheep's clothing and submit."

Property, that other great pillar of the state, should not
be exalted to the seventh heaven. " When you call yourself the friend of liberty, ask your heart whether it would
not be more consistent to style yourself a champion of

---

[1] Wollstonecraft, *Vindication of the Rights of Man,* London, 1790,
passim.

[2] *Ibid.,* p. 77.

property, and the adorer of the golden image which power
has set up." What are the facts? Property is too rigid
in England. Reason and humanity are sacrificed at the
altar of the family estate. The eldest son is made a little
god; the other sons have often small choice between poverty and fawning servility, while the girls are bartered for
the convenience of the family. " Property," she maintains, " should be fluctuating or it is an everlasting ram-
part; a barbarous feudal institution, which enables the rich
to overpower talents and depress virtue." [1] Burke's attitude toward the poor is without palliation. His curt
declaration that they must respect the property in which
they have no share, and his advice that they seek their
consolation in eternal justice, Wollstonecraft denounces.
It is " a contemptible, hard-hearted sophistry in the specious form of humility and submission to the will of
heaven, for it is, sir, possible to render the poor happier
in this world without depriving them of this consolation which you so gratuitously grant them in the next."
" Your respect for rank has swallowed up the common
feeling for humanity. You seem to consider the poor
as only the live stock of an estate; the feathers of hereditary nobility." [2] Wollstonecraft admits that poverty is un-
esthetic and disgusting, but even so, decency demands that
a little intelligence, a little reason be exercised on the problem—break up the large estates into small farms—forbid
the private ownership of huge forests—care for the town
mechanic, whose livelihood is at the whim of the flux of
trade or fashion. Let us have food and shelter here before
we talk of heaven above or of hell beneath. " Hell stalks
abroad—the lash resounds on the slave's naked sides; and
the sick wretch who can no longer earn the sour bread of

[1] *Vindication of the Rights of Man, op. cit.,* p. 47.
[2] *Ibid.,* p. 31.

unrelenting labors, steals to the ditch to bid the world a
long good-night." [1]   And in the meanwhile Burke regrets
" the empty pageant of a name," sighs for " the idle tap-
estry which decorates the Gothic pile," and mourns " the
droning bell which summons the fat priest to prayer."

Burke's triangular fortress of private property, the established church and the British constitution, falls to the
ground on every side.   The school mistress, however, has
a final blow.   She not only undermines the philosopher's
conclusions, but dynamites as well his mental processes.
She is rather reluctant to do it.   She fears that " by the
mere mention of metaphysical inquiry " his nervous system would be deranged, for Burke's mentality does not
seem overstrong to Mary Wollstonecraft.   Putting aside
all subtleties of speech and tongue-fencing, what do you
mean, she demands of Burke, by speaking of " the moral
constitution of the heart?"   The " inborn sentiments "
which you praise so highly—how do you recognize them;
where do they come from?   What are they?   " The appe-
tites are the only perfect inbred powers that I can discern."
Children are born ignorant.   They are neither moral nor
immoral.   It is not nature that fashions their lives, but
nurture.   As the environment is, so is the child.   There
are no natural instincts towards goodness or badness.   If
there were any, she inquires, " what moral purposes can
be answered by extolling the good disposition, as it is
called, when these good dispositions are described as instincts; for an instinct moves in a direct line to its ultimate end, and asks for no guidance or support.   But if
virtue is to be acquired by experience or taught by example, reason perfected by reflection must be the director
of the whole host of passions. . . .   Reason must hold the

[1] *Vindication of the Rights of Man, op. cit.,* p. 45.

rudder or let the wind blow where it listeth. The vessel will never advance smoothly to its destined port, for the time lost in tacking about would dreadfully impede its progress." [1]

" Sentimental jargon " about " the moral constitution of the heart," says Wollstonecraft, has " long been current in conversation and even in the books of morals, though it has never received the regal stamp of reason." It is all very well, she continues, to talk about " a mysterious kind of instinct which resides in the soul," but the trouble is " this subtle, magnetic fluid, which runs around the whole of society is not subject to any human rule." It befogs our intelligence and obscures the issue. Why should we not rely on our own intelligence, and consign to the rubbish heap once and for all this old talk about " the moral constitution of the heart." Let us decide for ourselves; " if we don't stop submitting to authority " we might as well admit that " capacity of improvement is a cheat, an *ignis fatuus* that leads us from inviting meadows into bogs and dunghills." [2]

The modern anthropologist and psychologist slowly and painfully have come to the conclusion " that a great part of what has been mistaken for nature is really nurture, direct or indirect, conscious or more commonly wholly unconscious." [3] This truth which we of the twentieth century are but beginning to appreciate, a book with the imprint 1790, the hurried output of a few weeks' labor, asserts in clear and emphatic language, and the book was the work of a woman.

The author of the " Rights of Man " was soon still further to sustain and amplify her thesis. In 1791, Mary

[1] *Vindication of the Rights of Man, op. cit.,* p. 68.

[2] *Ibid.,* p. 27.

[3] Robinson, *The New History,* p. 253.

Wollstonecraft's corollary to her defense of humanity made its appearance. The " Vindication of the Rights of Woman," the product of six weeks' labor, was greeted with astonishment, consternation and praise. Both book and author were freely discussed. Said the *Analytical Review,* " the lesser wits will probably affect to make themselves merry at the title and apparent object of this publication. . . . But we have no hesitation in declaring that if the bulk of the great truths which this book contains were put in practice the nation would be better, wiser and hap-pier." [1] On the other hand, the *Critical Review* broke forth in this reactionary wail: " We call on men, there-fore, to speak, if they wish the women to be puppets of this new scheme. We call on' women to declare whether they will sacrifice their pleasing qualities for the severity of reason. . . . We may anticipate their answer and leave Mary Wollstonecraft to oblivion." [2] Many felt that the *Critical Review* had spoken well. Some, indeed, for con-science' sake refused to read the book. Hannah More, who doubted at one time the expediency of Sunday-schools because children might learn to read Thomas Paine as well as the Bible, was one of these. " I have been much pes-tered," she wrote to Walpole, " to read ' The Rights of Woman,' but I am invincibly determined not to do it. . . . There is something fantastic and absurd about the very title." [3]

The book analyzes the position of woman. Wollstone-

[1] *Analytical Review,* March, 1792.

[2] *Critical Review,* June, 1792. These extracts are taken from Rausch-enbusch-Clough, *A Study of Mary Wollstonecraft,* p. 45.

[3] Walpole replied, " I would not look at it, though assured that it con-tained neither metaphysics nor politics; but as she entered the list of the latter, and borrowed the title from the demon's book which aimed at spreading the wrongs of man, she is excommunicated from the pale of my library." *Ibid.,* p. 44. Lordly Walpole also speaks of Wollstonecraft as " that hyena in politics."

craft admits the inferiority real or assumed of her sex. It
has been brought about by three causes. First,—the
physical inferiority of woman is not a serious drawback
for the superiority of reason over brute force receives
more recognition as the years go by. Secondly, woman
has in the past always been held subject to the will of man,
and custom has made it the norm. Thirdly, woman's
ridiculous training has brought her sex to this sorry condition. " The storehouse of knowledge is closed to them."
Their education is absurd, fatuous; an anachronism.

Wollstonecraft, convinced that nurture alone makes for
progress, takes for her main theme the education of
woman. Conventional education she denounces as horrible:
" Women are told from infancy, and taught by the example of their mothers, that the little knowledge of human
weakness justly termed cunning, softness of temper, outward obedience and a scrupulous attention to a certain kind
of piety," would accomplish all that was necessary, and as
for wealthy women, " confined in cages like the feathered
race, they have nothing to do but plume themselves and
move with mock majesty from perch to perch." [1] There is
some seriousness in the education of man. He is prepared
for business, for the professions, for public life. His mind
has a chance to expand, develop, and to reason. Poor
woman is not expected to reason. Her thinking is to be
done for her. The modesty of her sex demands that she
be guarded, protected and cherished.

" And will moralists pretend to assert that this is the
condition in which one-half of the human race should be
encouraged to remain, with listless inactivity and stupid
acquiescence? Kind instructors! What are we created
for? To remain, it may be said, innocent; they mean in a

---

[1] Wollstonecraft, *Vindication of the Rights of Woman*, p. 118.

state of childhood. We might as well never have been born, unless it were necessary that we should be created to enable man to acquire the noble privilege of reason, the power for discerning good from evil, whilst we lie down in the dust from whence we were taken, never to rise again." [1] The defenceless woman, the white muslin heroine, Wollstonecraft excoriates. " In the most trifling dangers they cling to their support; with parasitical tenacity, piteously demanding succor; and their natural protector extends his arm, or lifts up his voice, to guard the lovely trembler—from what? Perhaps the frown of an old cow, or the jump of a mouse; a rat would be a serious danger." The entire system of female education must be revolutionized. " We should hear of none of these infantile airs," she said, " if girls were allowed to take sufficient exercise, instead of being confined to a close room till their muscles are relaxed, and their power of digestion destroyed." The remedy is simple. Boys and girls in the primary schools should be kept together. Women should know something about anatomy. They might study the art of healing and become physicians—in fact, declares Mary Wollstonecraft, " I may excite laughter by dropping a hint," and the hint intimates the possibility of women entering politics. [2] No emphasis, however, is given to this point. Her insistence is upon the feminist movement in its larger aspect: " The laws respecting women make an absurd unit of man and his wife, and then by the easy transition of considering him the only responsible being, she is reduced to nearly a cipher." Society should provide for honest, independent women, and encourage them to earn an independent livelihood.

[1] *Vindication of the Rights of Woman, op. cit.,* p. 131.

[2] This idea was to be developed in a second volume which was never written,—Rauschenbusch-Clough, *op. cit.,* p. 36.

History is beginning to pay a tardy tribute to Mary Wollstonecraft. As the wife of Godwin, and as the mother of Mrs. Shelley, she has been long a familiar figure—but a figure only. Mary Wollstonecraft, the woman of passion and the woman of intellect, has been too long in the shadow. Her whole life was far from easy.[1] Struggling against the poverty engendered by the failing fortunes of a middle class family, she endeavored to establish a school. The project failed, and nothing remained for her but the position of a governess. Shortly after this time, however, Johnson, the publisher, issued a contribution from the governess on education. " The Vindication of the Rights of Man " soon followed and Wollstonecraft, as an influential member of that little group of advanced radicals which foregathered around Paine, Holcroft, Godwin and others interested in social reform and revolutionary ideas, was now in her element. Wollstonecraft moved to Paris, where she lived with an American, Captain Gilbert Imlay. Though a child was born to them, Imlay soon left the mother, never to return; and for Mary Wollstonecraft many bitter experiences were in store. William Godwin, the philosopher, at last won her heart. She and Godwin lived happily together, and shortly before the birth of their daughter they were married. Their happiness was short-lived, for Mary died when her daughter was born. This daughter, Harriet Godwin, afterwards became the wife of Percy Bysshe Shelley.[2]

Mary Wollstonecraft was well-nigh forgotten amid the bleatings of timidity, exclamations of hatred, and shouts

[1] G. Stanley Taylor, *Mary Wollstonecraft, a Study in Economics and Romance, passim.*

[2] Free use has been made of Rauschenbusch-Clough, *Mary Wollstonecraft, a study,* and G. S. Taylor, *Mary Wollstonecraft, a Study in Economics and Romance.*

of approval which greeted the writings of Thomas Paine. Paine, centre and life of the radical movement, as genuinely embodied the spirit of radicalism as did Burke the heart and soul of conservatism.[1] By everybody of the period this was recognized. Paine's " Rights of Man " had a wider circulation and a more profound influence than any book issued in the radical cause. Evidence of this, varied in character and overwhelming in quantity, greets us on every hand. Turn to the State Trials for Treason of the years 1794-1795, and the enormous vogue of the " Rights of Man " stands out in bold relief.[2] The same story is echoed by the press.[3] It is demonstrated by the frequent and reiterated discussion of Paine in contemporaneous pamphlets, and in numerous replies which his writings

[1] Those writers who regard Price as the great opponent of Burke fail to catch the real spirit of the times. Laprade, *England and the French Revolution,* pp. 11-24, develops this theory, and contrasts the semi-conservative Price with the ultra-conservative Burke, to the entire exclusion of real radicalism.

[2] Trial of John Horne Tooke, *State Trials,* xxv, 107. Here we are informed that the Radical Society of Sheffield resolved: " That they considered the ' Rights of Man ' the most important book written on reform." For praise of Paine by the Manchester Constitutional Society, *ibid.,* p. 134. Similar praise from the Radical Associations in Norwich, *ibid.,* p. 146. The Corresponding Society urges a cheap edition of Paine, *ibid.,* p. 156.

[3] *The Public Advertiser* estimates on February 21, 1792, that fifty thousand copies of the " Rights of Man " had been sold.
Conway, the biographer of Paine, says that a careful contemporaneous estimate of the number of copies sold by 1793 was upwards of two hundred thousand. (Conway, *Life of Paine,* i, 346.) The second part was issued on March 13, 1792. On the second of July of the same year Paine wrote to Washington that 11,000 out of 16,000 issued had been sold. (*Dictionary of National Biography,* xliii, 73.) A twopenny edition, translated into Gaelic, had a wide circulation in the Highlands. (Mathieson, *Awakening of Scotland,* p. 124.)

called forth.[1] It is indicated by venomous hatred of Paine assumed in certain aristocratic quarters. We are told that it was fashionable to wear " Tom Paine " shoe nails, that he might be trampled under foot. " Tom Paine " pitchers were manufactured bearing painted serpents with Paine's head and this accompanying inscription:

"Observe the wicked and malicious man,
  Projecting all the mischief that he can."

The burning of Paine in effigy was a common sight,[2]

[1] Among them were—*A rod in brine for a tickler for Tom Paine* by an Oxford graduate; *Various Opinions of the Philosophical Reformers Considered, particularly Paine's Rights of Man,* by Charles Hawry, Vicar of Bampton, (" Monthly Review," vii, 1792, p. 354, says that Hawry has generally classified all reformers as fools, madmen, heretics, or learned Thebans); *Notes upon Paine's Rights of Man,* 1791; *Reform, a farce, modernized by Aristophanes, and published with annotations by S. Foote, Jr.; An Examination of Mr. Paine's Writings by William Fox.*

Many others might be cited. On the continent the " Rights of Man " was widely known. In the *British Critic* for 1797 (vol. ix, p. 682), a book is reviewed which indicates the general international interest created by Paine's publication. It is entitled *Adam Smith, Auteur sur la richesse des nations et Thomas Paine; essai de critique publie dans toutes les langues,* by S. A. Joersson. This book went through many editions.

In America the " Rights of Man " received favorable comment from Jefferson and other prominent men.

Sir Samuel Romilly said, " It is written in his own wild but forcible style; inaccurate in point of grammar; flat where he attempts wit, and often ridiculous when he indulges in metaphors; but for all that full of spirit, and energy, and likely to produce a great effect. It has done that a good deal already, and in the course of a fortnight has gone through three editions, and what I own has a good deal surprised me, has made converts of many persons who were before enemies to the revolution. (Romilly, *Autobiography,* p. 318.)

[2] For the burning of Paine in effigy see Conway, *Writings of Paine,* ii, 226. Paine was hung also in Jersey in effigy, with the red cap of liberty and the " Rights of Man." *Sun,* Jan. 18, 1793. The writer of the day assures us in 1792 that "this month Thomas Paine, author of the 'Rights of Man,' etc., was burned at most of the towns

while, on the other hand, celebrations were held in his honor.[1]

This book of Paine's, which created such a furore, was, in many ways, not ultra-radical. Many people at present would consider it conservative; yet after its appearance certain good folk refused to open it. That champion of liberty, Charles James Fox, boasted that he had not read the second part, and no fewer than fifteen members of his Whig club, out of respect for his opinion, destroyed their copies.[2] Why this intense bitterness of spirit? The question is easily answered when Paine's marvelous style is taken into account. Matchless for the purpose in hand, terse and epigrammatic, his homely phrases were seized on with avidity by the people for whom he wrote. They became catchwords; household proverbs; verbal banners to flaunt before the astonished vision of a comfortable aristocracy and a contented conservatism.

Hardly indeed can we account for Paine's ascendency on any other ground. He is not more extreme than the great bulk of his school, neither does he excel the abler of

and considerable villages in Northumberland and Durham." For a good account of the anti-Paine propaganda in country towns, see *Thomas Poole and his Friends*, by his daughter, Mrs. Henry Sanford, i, 34-37.

[1] Paine was not fond of banquets or personal display. He disliked public speaking, and refused to attend one big banquet held in his honor in London. In 1791, however, as the guest of a banquet of the Revolution Society, much to-do was made over him, as extracts from the following song will indicate:

"He comes, the great reformer comes!
Cease, cease your trumpets, cease, cease your drums!
Those warlike sounds offend the ear,
Peace and friendship now appear.
Welcome, welcome, welcome, welcome!
Welcome, thou reformer, here!"

Conway, *Life of Paine*, i, 324.

[2] *Oracle and Public Advertiser*, May 9, 1797.

his contemporaries in the cogency and logic of his reasoning. It is true that he treated with scant respect many cherished institutions of his day;[1] it is true that he was republican at heart and a believer in representative democracy. But so likewise were most of his fellow-radicals. In his view of history, Paine was in some ways more conservative than Burke, while his theory of governmental activity and function would at the present time be considered quite old-fashioned. Governmental control of industrial affairs is not even intimated. The less money spent by the government, the better, Paine argued, and in his celebrated letter to Secretary Dundas[2] he declared that Pitt was but " a school boy " in his pride at raising taxes. A real political genius would only take pride, he intimates, in lessening the supply and necessity of taxation. Certain suggestions, certain hints appear in the " Rights of Man " which might imply an extensive system of governmental education, labor bureaus, and old-age pensions, but, save in the proposal of pensions, the plan outlined is fragmentary and tentative; even in the matter of old-age pensions Paine expects to accomplish his scheme with a decreased tax rate.

What does an analysis of the " Rights of Man " show? Paine is as expert as Burke in vituperation. The sins of the one, if they do not cancel, at least balance the sins of the other. In outlining his theories, then, we will afford him the same courtesy given to his illustrious rival. Bursts of temper and abuse we may well rule out, as also all ideas, hypotheses and theories which are not pertinent to the main thread of his argument.

[1] "After all," cries Paine, "what is this metaphor called a crown; or rather what is a monarchy? Is it a thing? Is it a name—or is it a fraud? Is it a contrivance of human wisdom, or of human craft to obtain money from a nation under pretence of fraud?" Paine, *Works*, II, p. 366.

[2] *To Mr. Secretary Dundas,* Paine, *Works,* iii, 18.

The " Rights of Man " was written in two parts. The first part, published in February, 1791, is a direct indictment of Burke's thesis; scathing and bitter. Freedom from the heavy weight of antiquity we must possess, maintains the author. " Vanity and presumption of governing beyond the grave is the most ridiculous and insolent of all tyranny. Man has no property in man, neither has any generation property in the generations which are to follow." The French nation has been animated by this principle. "The Augean stable of parasites and plunderers" across the channel needed a revolution and in cleaning their house the French have done well. Violence and bloodshed accompanied this change, but who was responsible for it? The aristocracy, Paine says, plotted against the revolution, and took the offensive, and as for heads on pikes and other unpleasant spectacles, have not all the conservative governments of Europe long made such sights familiar? " Lay then the axe to the root," he demands, " and teach governments humanity. It is their sanguinary punishments which corrupt mankind." Do not blame the people for copying their example.[1] This running defence of the French revolution need not detain us long, nor need part one of the " Rights of Man." The second part, published in March, 1792, combining theory and practice, tells us what we care to know most about, namely, Paine's diagnosis of contemporary discontent and his proposed remedy.

" When in countries that we call civilized we see age going to the workhouse and youth to the gallows, something must be wrong in the system of government." Why is it, Paine continues, " that scarcely any are executed but the poor. The fact is a proof among other things of the wretchedness of their position. Bred up without morals, and cast upon the world without prospects, they are the

[1] Paine, *Rights of man*, Part 1, *passim*.

exposed sacrifice of vice and legal barbarity." [1]   The basic
evil is bad environment accompanied by poverty, "lack
of education for the young and a decent livelihood for the
old," as he puts it.

Where does the responsibility for this state of affairs
rest?   It rests with the government, and in England the
government is thoroughly bad. Its keynote is special privilege.   The existence of chartered corporations which control the membership of the House of Commons is the seat
of the disorder.   These charters give no indication of liberty—quite the contrary.   "If charters were constructed
so as to express in direct terms that every inhabitant who
is not a member of the corporation shall not exercise the
right of voting, such charters would on the face be charters not of right, but of exclusion." [2]   Paine saw clearly
that the House of Commons was made up in bulk of representatives of these special privileges.   Not otherwise was
it with the House of Lords, for "it amounts to a combination of persons of special interests.   No better reason
can be given," he said, "why the house of legislature should
be composed entirely of men whose occupation is in letting
landed property than why it should be composed of those
who hire, or brewers, or bakers, or of any other separate
class of men." [3]

Nor is this a matter of pure theory.   In practice the system works poorly, and Paine believes that British finance
affords the proof.   The taxes are raised in an unjust manner, and he tells us why. [4]   Once raised the money is foolishly spent, and Paine again tells us why, presenting at the
same time an ideal budget which demonstrates concisely
his theory of the functions of government.   He estimates

[1] Paine, *Works,* ii, 462.

[2] *Ibid.,* ii, 465.   [3] *Ibid.,* ii, 468.

[4] For a discussion of the incidents of taxation see *ibid.,* ii, 471, 472.

that there remained of the national income, after deduct-
ing the interest on the national debt, the net sum of eight
million pounds. Of this sum he claims that " five hundred
thousand pounds is more than sufficient to defray all the
expense of government, exclusive of armies and navies." [1]
That is, from this sum all necessary salaries and expenses
of administration might be met. Five hundred thousand
more pounds would provide for a skeleton navy; an equal
sum would suffice the army. Of the six and one-half million pounds which remained to be disposed of, four million,
or one-half the total revenue of the country he assigns to
the relief of the poor and to education. This he would
do roughly as follows: (1) provision to be made for two
hundred and fifty thousand poor families; (2) education
to be provided for one hundred and thirty thousand children; (3) comfortable pensions granted to one hundred
and forty thousand aged people; (4) donations, or premiums, to be given for births and marriages, together with
an allowance for funeral expenses of people dying out of
work and away from their friends. State employment and
lodging-houses ought also to be provided for workmen in
the cities of London and Westminster.

This is Paine's plan. He is not very felicitous in the details. He apportions the money unscientifically; that given
for direct poor relief is altogether too large. A diminutive
sum is given to the state labor bureau. This bureau is evidently entirely experimental, and yet that Paine thought
of it at all is commendable. Of the remaining two and one-
half million pounds, Paine would spend one quarter in
pensioning the disbanded officers and men of the diminished army and navy.[2] Enough would be left to warrant

---

[1] Paine, *Works*, ii, 482.

[2] *Ibid.*, ii, 482. Paine calculates that as this money grew less and less
with the diminished number of pensioners certain special taxes might
be removed, such as those on soap, candles, etc.

the removal of the tax on houses and upon windows which bears heaviest of all on the middle class of people. Remove it entirely, and we are left with a balance of one million pounds. Any number of ways, he tells us, may be found in which to divide this money. Some of it might go to underpaid revenue officers; the inferior clergy also ought to be considered. Incidental expenditures would probably consume what remained.

Having spent the revenue, Paine now explains to us his ideal basis of taxation. He aptly remarks, that " when taxes are proposed the country is aroused by the plausible language of taxing luxuries. One thing is called a luxury at one time, and another at another. But the real luxury does not consist in articles, but in the means of procuring them, and this is always kept out of sight." [1] The only fair way to do, he argues, is to levy an income tax. It should be a progressive income tax, for not only would the greater income be produced that way but also in so doing we should deal a blow at primogeniture. Primogeniture, which Paine terms " an attaint upon character," should be done away with, " not only because it is unnatural and unjust, but because the country suffers by its operation. By cutting off the younger children from their proper portion of inheritance, the public is loaded with the expense of maintaining them, and the freedom of election violated by the overbearing influence which this unjust monopoly of family property produces." Nor is this all. It occasions a waste of national wealth. Many acres of rural England are rendered unproductive by the great extent of parks and chases which this law serves to keep up, and this at a time when the annual production of grain is not equal to the national consumption.[2]

[1] Paine, *Works*, ii, 496. [2] *Ibid.*, ii, 500.

The "Rights of Man" contains in addition valuable suggestions for the furtherance of international comity.[1] A treaty is advocated between England, France, the United States and Holland. In accordance with this treaty no new ships may be built by any of the signatory powers, while their existing naval establishments are to be reduced to one-half of their existing strength. "If men will permit themselves," he says, "to think as rational beings ought to think, nothing can appear more ridiculous and absurd . . . than to be at the expense of building navies, filling them with men, and then hauling them out into the ocean to see which can sink each other the fastest." [2]

Commerce does not depend upon ships of war. The prosperity of one country is the prosperity of another. Paine knew his Adam Smith. Break down all artificial barriers is his plea. Boundaries, custom houses, national regulations, all impede prosperity. Peace abroad, economy and generous provision for the poor at home, comprise, in short, the principal articles of Paine's political philosophy.[3]

The "Rights of Man" brought much money to Paine with which he was very generous. Despite the fact that he was living in comparative poverty at the time,[4] he turned

---

[1] Paine's method of reducing the national debt is omitted, as it includes some technical discussions. *Works*, ii, 504-507.

[1] Paine, *Works*, ii, 511. The four nations mentioned are to see to it that others cease from building warships.

[3] In this book Paine says nothing about religion which could be offensive to anybody—in fact, he significantly states that he has avoided the subject "because I am inclined to believe that what is called the present ministry wish to see contention about religion kept up to prevent the nation turning its attention to subjects of government." (*Works, ii,* 515.) That Paine's republicanism was somewhat incidental is his scheme of things, is indicated by his defence of a limited monarchy in the French Constitution.

[4] Conway, *Life of Paine,* i, 288.

over to the London Constitutional Society the thousand pounds which he obtained from royalties,[1] enabling it to scatter copies broadcast. All radicals were interested in its circulation. Suggestions were made for abstracts and abbreviated editions.[2] Copies were said to have been circulated in all shapes and sizes, and even to have been used for the wrapping of candy.

Part Two was in particular demand. Paine refused an offer of a thousand pounds from his publisher, Chapman, for he feared that its extensive use might be checked.[3] He need have had no fear on that score. No book of its generation had, in Great Britain, the vogue of the " Rights of Man."

Other political writings of Paine add but little to the radical synthesis, nor did they vie in circulation or influence with the " Rights of Man." ·" Address to Addressors " and " A Letter to Secretary Dundas " we have quoted elsewhere. " Agrarian Justice " does, it is true, lean far more towards socialism than the earlier books. It was, however, not published until 1797, well to the end of our period. Nor have we made mention of " The Age of Reason," the authorized edition of which was not published until 1796. It was promptly suppressed by the government,[4] and its influence in England was of no great

---

[1] *State Trials,* xxiv, 491.

[2] *Ibid.,* xxv, 156.

[3] The evidence that Chapman desired the copyright, either to change, or to suppress the book entirely, is given in Conway, *Life of Paine,* i, 30. An account also is here given of a libellous account of Paine's life.

[4] A poor dealer named Williams was apprehended for selling a copy of " The Age of Reason." As the man had two children ill with the smallpox, and was otherwise distressed, Erskine was said to have pleaded in vain with Wilberforce, the philanthropist, and Porteus, Bishop of London, for leniency.

moment until the very end of the century.[1] Much maligned
as that book was, and interesting as an analysis of it might
be, its study is omitted, so far afield is the work from the
general tenor of the radicalism of our period.

Thomas Paine was, from many points of view, the best
known international figure of his day. Such a claim seems
at first sight somewhat exaggerated, but who else represented as he did three nations? Friend of Washington
and Jefferson, champion of the revolting colonies, his
place in American history is assured. France also knew
well this Americanized Englishman. He bore, as her representative, the key of the Bastille to Washington. He was
also a member of the French convention, and an influential
member, if we may judge from his speech on behalf of the
French king. In England, too, Paine had long ceased to be
the poor exciseman, without influence and without friends.
Between the American and the French revolutions we find
him visiting, on terms of familiarity, Burke, Portland,
Fox, and other Whig leaders.[2] Certainly no American at
this time received a warmer welcome in England.

Nor did Paine's English prestige disappear with the
publication of the " Rights of Man." It changed its
character, it is true, but Paine to many thousands in
Great Britain now became a popular hero, where before
known to a few only as a successful bridge builder and
pamphleteer. And, although he lived in London very
quietly at the house of his friend, the bookseller Rickman,[3] that house was the centre of attraction for God-

[1] The nickname " devil's disciple " was apparently not in general
usage until toward the end of the century. A group of his adherents in
Glasgow were known as the " Hell Fire Club." *Glasgow, Past and
Present,* i, 249 (Glasgow, 1884).

[2] Conway, *Life of Paine,* i, 244.

[3] Rickman's children were named Paine, Washington, Franklin,
Rousseau, Petrarch, Volney. *Ibid.,* i, 25.

win, Horne Tooke, Romney, Holcroft and others of like mind. Quite content Paine must have been, for he was no demagogue who longed for popular applause. Indeed, if we are to accept the testimony of Rickman, Paine was more fond of a quiet conversation and a game of dominoes than of general society.[1]

Paine was not to stay in England long. In 1792, acting on the advice of his friends, he fled to France. His flight came none too soon. Twenty minutes after he sailed from Dover, orders arrived from the Home Office to detain him.[2] The English government, baffled of their prey, proceeded in somewhat silly fashion to try the fugitive for a seditious libel. The trial was a farce. Erskine made a noble effort on Paine's behalf, but it was useless. If there had been any question of the verdict, its result would have been guaranteed by a letter which Paine wrote to the attorney-general. The letter was read at the trial. Paine said in it: " The time, sir, is becoming too serious to play with Court prosecutions, and sport with national rights. . . . That the Government of England is as great, if not the greatest perfection of fraud and corruption that ever took place since governments began, is what you cannot be a stranger to; unless the constant habit of seeing it has blinded your sense. But though you may not chuse to see it, the people are seeing it very fast, and the progress is beyond what you may chuse to believe. Is it possible that you or I can believe, or that reason can make any other man believe, that the capacity of such a man as Mr. Guelph, or any of his profligate sons, is necessary to the government of a nation? I speak to you as one man ought to speak to another; and I know also that I speak what other people

[1] Conway, *Life of Paine,* i, 321.
[2] Gilchrist, *Life of William Blake,* i, 95.

are beginning to think." [1]　Do anything you desire,
Paine continues: I have weightier matters on hand,—and
he had.　The king of France was soon on trial for his life.
Among those who pleaded for him was the much-execrated
radical, Thomas Paine.

Wollstonecraft and Paine have formulated the creed of
radicalism; still further to define its tenets, we should
speak briefly of Sir James Mackintosh and Jeremy Bentham.　To dismiss the work of Mackintosh and Bentham
as an appendix to that of Wollstonecraft may seem ques-
tionable; yet Mackintosh was but half a radical, and his
answer to Burke, though brilliant, is largely a refutation of
erroneous statement of fact.　As for Bentham, while none
can question his radicalism all must admit that his work
and influence belong to the nineteenth century.

The fiat has gone forth that the *Vindiciae Gallicae* of
Sir James Mackintosh is the ablest reply to Burke which
history records.　Let us admit that the vindication is most
beautifully written.　Let us also admit that it contains the
most lucid, comprehensive and emphatic expression of the
radical spirit in English literature; and it is that expression so fitly supplementing the thought and argument of
our two previous authors, that we would emphasize.

Mackintosh insisted that we should pay more attention
to reason and justice and less to tradition and custom.　He
regarded with impatience precedents deduced from the
good old days.　"A pleader," he said, at Old Bailey,
"who would attempt to aggravate the guilt of a robber or
murderer by proving that King John or King Alfred punished robbery and murder, would only provoke derision.
A man who should pretend that the reason why we have
the right to property is because our ancestors enjoyed that
right four hundred years ago would be justly condemned.

[1] *State Trials,* xxii, 405.

Yet so little is plain sense heard in the mysterious nonsense
which is the cloak of political fraud that the Cokes, Black-
stones and Burkes speak as if our right to freedom depended on our ancestors.

" In common cases of humanity we would blush at such
an absurdity. No man would justify murder by its antiquity, or stigmatize benevolence for being novel. The
genealogist who should emblazon the one as coeval with
Cain, or stigmatize the other as upstart with Howard,
would be disclaimed even by the most frantic partisan of
aristocracy. This Gothic transfer of genealogy to truth
and justice is peculiar to politics. . . . Justice and liberty
have neither birth, youth, race or age. It would be the
same absurdity to assert that we have the right to freedom
because the Englishmen of Alfred's reign were free, as
three and three are six because they were so in the reign
of Ghengis Khan." [1]

Mackintosh perceived with very clear vision that radicalism must face the future rather than the past. In this
matter he even out-radicaled Thomas Paine, for Paine,
though rarely rivaled in independence of spirit, thought
it wise to justify freedom, not indeed from Alfred's reign,
but from an even earlier period,[2] while the pages of other
radical writers bristle with inferences and arguments
drawn from the reigns of King Alfred and Henry VII,
to say nothing of the glorious revolution of 1688, to the
befuddling of their thought and the weakening of their
argument.

Mackintosh, then, wasting no time in appeals to an-

[1] *Vindiciae Gallicae*, p. 304.

[2] Paine, *Works,* ii, 304. Paine said that the only trouble with those
who argued from history about the freedom of man was that they
did not go far enough back in history. He himself began with Adam.

tiquity, outlines the radical position. It is not a matter of
theory at all, he argues; certain abuses exist in Great
Britain; they should be done away with. Our complaints
are not chimerical. The point at issue is simply a question
of fact. We are boldly challenged, he says, " to produce
our proofs. . . . Most unfortunately for us, most unfortunately for the country, these proofs are too ready and
too numerous. . . . We find them in that monumental
debt the relique of waste and unprofitable wars. We
find them in the black and bloody list of persecuting statutes that are still suffered to stain our code. We find
them in the ignominious exclusion of great bodies of our
citizens from public trusts." [1] And to complete the list of
abuses which Mackintosh enumerates, he mentions the
criminal code; the lack of representative government; the
efforts to suppress and stifle public opinion; The Test Act,
and all anti-Catholic laws; the remnant of feudalism still
extant in Scotland; and finally the excise laws, which he
claimed greatly hindered the manufacturing interests.

The "Vindications" were published in April, 1791. Mackintosh was at that time twenty-six years old. No special
success had hitherto attended his life. His father, too
poor to educate the boy for the Bar, assisted him in obtaining a medical degree, but at Edinburgh, Mackintosh was
more interested in philosophy and politics than in medicine.
He drifted to London, attended political meetings, and
wrote this reply to Burke. It proved to be the making of
Mackintosh. The " Vindications " went through three editions within the year, and a generous publisher willingly
paid the author several times over the thirty pounds bar-
gained for. Employment came immediately in the newspaper world. The admiration of Mackintosh for the French
Revolution, however, soon waned. He became a lawyer and

----

[1] *Vindiciae Gallicae, passim.*

a prominent government official, and we find him on good terms with Burke. In fact, in 1797, he publicly denounced the principles of the revolution, but nevertheless, throughout a long public life, he remained in practice steadfastly on the radical side.[1]

If Mackintosh gives, with charming literary appreciation, an epitome of the radical spirit, the definite practical application of radicalism to social reform appears more prominently in the writings of another author.

Part and parcel of the radical attack came a scathing denouncement of England's legal system. Upon no point were the radicals more united. The delays of the civil procedure; the barbarities of the criminal code; the harsh and inhuman treatment of prisoners attracted alike the attention of all reformers. Against the stupid brutalities of the English prison, humanitarianism arose in special revolt, and upon that subject was focussed the life-long efforts of John Howard and the analytical brilliance of Jeremy Bentham. John Howard's epoch-making book, "The State of the English Prisons," had been published in 1777, and in 1790 the philosopher died. To do more than to mention his work would exceed the limit of this treatise.

The views of Bentham are explained in his "Panopticon."[2] This book has borne the brunt of much ridicule. In reading the first sentence, "Morals reformed—health preserved—instruction diffused—public burdens lightened —economy seated as it were upon a rock—the gordian knot of the poor laws not cut, but untied—all by a simple idea

[1] After serving in an official position in India, Mackintosh became a member of the House of Commons, and sturdily resisted the reactionary policy of the government in the first quarter of the nineteenth century.

[2] Bentham, *The Panopticon, or the Inspection House,* 1791.

in architecture," we can scarcely doubt that the author
has a somewhat sanguine temperament.   We might even
suspect that his plan was in many respects chimerical, and
so, to some extent, it was.   Bentham is over-sanguine about
his ideal prison-house which, by its construction, would
make light and air possible in every cell, while providing
at the same time for the inspection of the entire building
by one keeper, stationed in the centre.   In this architectural
device as such we have no direct interest.   Indeed, for the
Panopticon as a building we care nothing.   But it was
more than a building.   It was a building governed by certain principles.   Those principles were at once so just,
so practical, so humane, that they cannot but command
our admiration.

Four different theories of Bentham's regarding the
treatment of the prisoners, particularly merit attention.
First, he believed that the prisoner should be rationally
employed.   The compulsory labor required should be always, if possible, of two different kinds, for variety would
make the work less irksome.   " Occupation," he said, " is
in itself sweet in comparison to enforced idleness." [1]   Although believing that work should be compulsory, Bentham
would not have it oppressively hard.   He considered it bad
for all concerned, both financially for the government, and
physically for the prisoner.   Financially, to employ prisoners in beating hemp, rasping logwood and chopping rags
is very uneconomical, for the work can be done more
cheaply by machines; [2] and the prisoner himself will simply
be more brutalized than before by a monotonous routine.

In the second place Bentham demanded a decent food

---

[1] Bentham, *Works,* iv, 144.

[2] Aside from machinery, animals could provide this power better
than men, he tells us, and in a long footnote he discusses the use of
elephants in a treadmill. *Ibid.,* iv, 145.

supply for his Panopticon. He believed that not enough
food was ordinarily given for the support of the body,
and he quoted Howard to the effect that, in a certain
prison in 1788, " everybody is sick; they always will be,
for they are slowly starving." To prove the laxness of the
law in this regard, Bentham quoted from the National
Penitentiary Code as follows: " Every offender is to be
sustained with bread, and any coarse meat or inferior food.
and water or small beer." " For humanity, for health and
for comfort, what does this do? " cried Bentham. " Nothing. In what respects can the prisoners be the better for
this article? None. What says it? That the food shall
be sufficient? No! That it shall be wholesome? No!
Not even as much as that. What then? That bread shall
form a part of it. They are to have what? Bread and
something besides. What is that something to be? Is it
to be meat at all events? No! But either meat, so that it
be coarse, or anything else whatever, so that it be of an
inferior kind! Inferior to what? That the statute has not
told us, and it would have been rather difficult for it to
have told us." [1] Great care should be taken, says Bentham, that the law provide wholesome and sufficient food.

Health also is essential. To insure health we must have
cleanliness. Bathing is to be insisted upon. Shirts,
breeches, blankets and sheets must be frequently laundered.
Between physical and moral delicacy he assures us a connection has been observed which, though fathered by the
imagination, is far from being imaginary. Washing is a
holy rite, and those who dispute the spiritual efficacy will
not deny its physical use.[2] Furthermore, we must have
not only cleanliness but also exercise. To secure this he
advocated walking in a wheel or treadmill. This wheel
would be erected on the outside of the Panopticon with

[1] Bentham, *Works,* iv, 155.   [2] *Ibid.,* iv, 158.

covered flaps of canvass to pull down in inclement weather. Bentham, indeed, instructed his architects to provide for big windows in all the cells. Glass costs no more than stone walls, he wrote, and is far more satisfactory. There must be also an abundant water supply in each individual cell; and by a very complicated heating plant an even temperature is to be maintained throughout the year.

Finally, Bentham devised by his plan a solution of the ex-convict problem. He believed that convicts should have four options after serving a term in the Panopticon: (1) they might enter the land service; (2) they might enter the sea service for life; (3) have security given for their good behavior by relatives, friends or bondsmen, to whom they should be under certain obligations; (4) enter a kind of subsidiary Panopticon. This establishment would be run on the Panopticon principle. It would, however, insure greater liberty to the occupant, though not entire freedom. For instance, he might marry, if he wished, and carry on a trade for which the government would provide.[1] It was a cardinal tenet of Bentham's faith that the future of the criminal is an obligation which society must recognize. The criminal should, if possible, be reformed, and never is he to be treated like a brute.

The fact that Bentham's imagination ran riot in the planning of details in no way detracts from his humane and rational apprehension of the essential postulates of penology. Very dear to him was this scheme of the Panopticon. Although he was writing several of his most important books[2] at this time, or shortly after, he kept the Panopticon always in view, and even after it had been partially adopted without success, Bentham insisted that the hatred of King George was alone responsible for the failure.

[1] Bentham, *Works*, iv, 166.

[2] *The Truth Against Ashurst*, written in 1792, but not published until 1822. *A Protest against the Law of Taxes*, published in 1795.

CHAPTER IV

THE DEVELOPMENT OF THE RADICAL PLATFORM

GODWIN ON PROPERTY; SPENCE ON LAND NATIONALIZATION;
GERRALD ON WAR; FREND ON THE CHURCH; BAR-
LOW ON THE ADMINISTRATION OF THE LAW;
THELWAL ON INJUSTICE

THE most radical book of the decade was written by a slender dissenting minister of gentle manners and quiet habits. The author was William Godwin, and his book he called " Political Justice." On its preparation was lavished all the erudition and enthusiasm which profound reading and scholarly instincts could afford.

Godwin had some years previously given up the ministry for uninterrupted literary work. While at his labors it was his custom to arise at five in the morning and to work with constant assiduity until midnight. He had no time, inclination or money for pleasure, for only with the strictest economy was he able to follow out his plan, and, save for the attendance of an old woman to cook his chop, he altogether dispensed with service. Finally, in 1792, the child of his brain, " Political Justice," made its appearance. It was a large volume divided into two books, containing a total of somewhat over five hundred pages. The plan and scope were surprisingly extensive, and surprisingly revolutionary as well. In it Godwin, the ex-clergyman, argues, and argues emphatically, in favor of a complete state of anarchy, with the usual concomitant conditions that civil institutions, laws, penalties, private property and government should cease to be.

Though forcefully and logically written, the book had comparatively little popular interest. This was due to two causes. In the first place, Godwin's style, more or less desiccated—or, in its most favorable light, extremely dispassionate—is not such as would attract the public imagination. He is quite philosophical throughout; never angry; never abrupt; anxious and insistent upon qualifying and defining with scholastic zeal his statements and ideals. Secondly, his book sold for three guineas. Three thousand copies were shortly disposed of, it is true, and for them Godwin received in royalties a thousand guineas. Nevertheless, this sale was confined very largely to the wealthier classes. Poorer folk scarcely knew of its existence, and this the government recognized for they never brought an action against Godwin or suppressed his book.[1] Compared with Godwin, Paine was a conservative, but Godwin, the philosopher, was harmless; Paine, the voicer of discontent, a dangerous enemy.

Uninfluential though this book was with the great body of the nation, no survey of the radicalism of its day would be complete without it. Godwin had many friends among the younger radicals; indeed, he was one of their number,[2] and with his friends his influence and prestige were not negligible.[3] Furthermore, Godwin's arguments concerning

[1] *The British Critic* for July, 1793, said: "A much heavier fate than persecution awaits him, and one for which perhaps his mind is not equally prepared; the worst that can attend ambitious authorship of system-making, neglect. Two bulky quartos contain too much reading to be popular; and one pound sixteen is too serious a sum for any man to give."

[2] Godwin, *Political Justice*, ii, 218.

[3] And his influence was lasting, for Shelley acknowledged in his later years that practically all of his radicalism had been inspired by his father-in-law.

private property, closely knit and cogently stated, may well be reproduced as embracing everything which, from the radical viewpoint, may be urged against that institution.

The subject of private property, he said, " is the keystone that completes the fabric of political justice." And Godwin believed that the institution of private property was absolutely wrong. In his own words, " with grief must it be confessed that however great are the evils that are produced by monarchies and courts, by the imposture of priests, and the inequalities of the criminal law, all these are imbecile and impotent compared with the evils which arise out of the established administration of property." [1]

Private property, claimed Godwin, brought about five great evils. The first of these was the lack of an independent spirit. " Accumulation brings home," he said, " a servile and a truckling spirit." And for illustration he selected the fawning pauper, the submissive servant and the obsequious shopkeeper. " Observe the tradesman, how he studies the passions of his customers, not to correct but to pamper them. The vileness of his flattery and systematic constancy with which he exaggerates the merits of his commodities." The age of chivalry is not gone. The feudal spirit still survives, that reduces the great mass of mankind to the rank of slaves and cattle for the service of a few.[1] In the second place, the constant projection of property before the vision of mankind as the most desirable of all objects led man astray and perverted his judgment. Godwin was pursuaded that " the ostentation of the rich perpetually goaded the spectator to the desire of opulence." [2] Of what use was it, he argued, to instruct the child in integrity and unselfishness when, as soon as he enters the

---

[1] *Political Justice,* ii, 218. The reference to the age of chivalry is obviously an ironical reference to Burke's use of the term.

[2] *Ibid.,* p. 219.

world and inquires " 'Why is this man honored?' the ready
answer is, ' Because he is rich.' If he inquire further why
he is rich, the answer is, in most cases, from the accident of
birth, or from a minute and sordid attention to the cares of
gain." [1] This glorification of property Godwin pronounced
much more serious than the swollen pension roll of the government, for " hereditary wealth " he believed to be " a
premium paid to idleness, an immense annuity expended
to maintain mankind in brutality and ignorance." Con-
tinuing his argument, Godwin held that private property
retarded not only the development of genius but the growth
of intelligence as well, for property either surfeited those
who held it, or by its unequal distribution compelled others
to spend their days in sordid cares.[2] The fifth charge in
the indictment was that property created the chief causes
of crime; for " the true crime," he declared, " in every instance is in the selfish and partial propensities of men thinking only of themselves, and despising only the emoluments
of others; and of these the rich have their share.[3]

Since private property, then, is wrong in theory, Godwin proposes its abolition. This, he urges, would come
about by a changed attitude of public opinion. He does
not desire or expect that any compulsion will be necessary.[4]
As an exceptional means the law might be invoked for this
happy consummation. Presumably, however, a revolution
of opinion, and a just estimate of wealth, will do it more
effectually. Godwin does not think that much difficulty
will be met with. He reviews, in his ultra-logical fashion

[1] *Political Justice,* ii, 220.   [2] *Ibid.,* ii, 221.

[3] *Ibid.,* ii, 223. It is characteristic of Godwin that in this matter of
the bearing of property on crime, the whole question is discussed on
very philosophical grounds, quite apart from the interest of the ordinary citizen.

[4] *Political Justice,* ii, 210.

the principal obstructions. " The frailty of the human mind," he affirms, is more an apparent than a real objection. " To sell all that thou hast and give to the poor," he insists is rather practical.[1] For as soon as the ideal changes its character and is transformed, no man will care for possessions.

The question of permanence gives him no trouble. A purer theory of happiness is going to supplant the existing attitude of society. If the equality sought for were introduced by a magistrate or by authority, doubtless it would not endure. But equality coming from general consent has a far more permanent value.[2] Neither will the allurements of sloth be a destructive influence. Mankind will not care for as many luxuries, and furthermore, inasmuch as everybody will do his share of labor, but very little time will be demanded of the individual.[3] The further criticism of his ideas embodied in the theory that the benefits of luxury had increased the value of our civilization, he meets with the parry that luxury, while conferring benefits, does so only temporarily, and that the transition stage where that is done is now past. Finally, when told that the destruction of property rights renders society rigid and inflexible, Godwin replies that he has no notion at all of men eating in a common hall; quite the reverse, for he hoped that more, not less, liberty would result from a rational understanding of its nature.

Perhaps no more attractive or quaint figure is to be met with among the radical reformers than Thomas Spence. Spence was a one-idea man, and that idea was land nation-

---

[1] *Political Justice,* ii, 225.   [2] *Ibid.,* ii, 229.

[3] *Ibid.,* ii, 233. Godwin calculated that one-half hour a day employed in manual labor by every member of society would sufficiently supply the whole with necessaries.

alization. To Spence land nationalization and the millennium were synonymous. Through the storm and stress of
a long, hard life, he clung with determination to this ideal;
and so absorbed was he in this theory that his friends
thought him more or less childish,[1] and paid far less attention to his utopias than they deserved. The government,
on the contrary, believed him to be a dangerous man,
dogged his footsteps with spies, and, from time to time,
put him in prison, a persecution which confirmed Spence's
faith in the eternal justice of his cause.

Spence early in life was a teacher, and a member of the
Philosophical Society of Newcastle. Before this Society
he presented his famous plan for social amelioration as
early as 1775. Spence was promptly expelled from the
Society.[2] He left Newcastle, and settled in London where
he set up a shop. It was a peculiar shop; in it the proprietor earned his living by selling salops, but his heart
lay in a side line which he carried, namely, books. The
book chiefly recommended in the time of the French
Revolution by this curious merchant was familiarly known
as " Spence's Plan." [3] In reality it was nothing more or
less than a reprint of his famous lecture. To circulate this
lecture, or plan, extensively, Spence was prepared to make
any sacrifice. The " Plan " was sold at the ridiculous price
of a half-penny per copy. For purposes of advertisement
this unique scheme was adopted : copper medals were struck

[1] Wallas, *Life of Francis Place,* p. 62.

[2] According to the Dictionary of National Biography, liii, 38, Thomas
Spence was expelled, not for writing his lecture, but for hawking it
around the streets. Spence however claimed that he was expelled for
writing it, and his position is substantiated by Davidson in his *Land
for the Landless,* p. 6, and by Adler in his *Introduction to Spence.*

[3] The official title was " On the Mode of Administering the Landed
Property of the Nation as a Joint Stock Property in Parochial
partnership by Dividing the Rent."

by the order of Spence, bearing on one side the words, " Spence's Glorious Plan is Parochial Partnership without Private Landlordism," while on the other side was engraved, " This Plan will Produce Everlasting Peace and Happiness, or, in fact, the Millennium." These medals, the same size as copper pennies, would, from time to time, be thrown from his windows by the handful. They served indeed to advertise his " Plan," and also his eccentricities.

According to Spence's scheme there was to be no more private property in land. All of Great Britain, he held should be owned by the people in common instead of by individuals. The title to the soil was not to rest with the state, but with the different parishes of the United Kingdom. He proposed that a national law should be passed, by which, on a day appointed, it might be legal for the inhabitants of each parish to meet and to take possession of " their long-lost right to the soil." " The land, with all that appertains to it, is in every parish made the property of the corporation or parish, with as ample power to let, repair, or alter any part thereof as a lord of the manor enjoys, over his lands, houses, etc.; but the power of alienating the least morsel in any manner from the parish either at this or at any other time is denied." [1]

Rent, however, is not to be abolished. It is to be paid to the parish instead of to the landlord. Part then is to be given to the national government in lieu of general taxation, the rest is to be used by the parish " in maintaining and relieving its own poor and people out of work; in paying the necessary officers their salaries; in building, repairing and adorning its houses, bridges and other structures; in making and maintaining convenient and delightful streets, highways and passages, both for foot and car-

---

[1] Spence, *The Meridian Sun of Liberty*, p. 8. For the parish to give land awly, Spence maintains, is as horrible as selling children.

riages; in making and maintaining canals and other con-
veniences for trade and navigation; in planting and taking
in waste grounds; in providing and keeping up a magazine
of ammunition, and all sorts of arms sufficient for all the
inhabitants in case of danger from enemies; in premiums
for the encouragement of agriculture, or anything else
thought worthy of encouragement." Once this was accomplished, all taxation apart from rent could be done
away with. Freedom of trade and commerce would be
assured, and the bane of special privilege would be lifted
forever.

There were various other features of the scheme. The
possibilities of his idea, indeed, Spence elaborated with
considerable fulness and *naïveté*. But the story of the reformed parish of Bees, with its old landlords, Lord and
Lady Drone, and all the little Drones, working busily away
in their reformed life, is apart from our purpose. Suffice it to say, that Spence's theory is considered by many
as the father of the Henry George system of the Single
Tax.

As the years went by Spence sold fewer salops, and more
books. By 1793, his shop, apparently, was a bookshop pure
and simple. He named it the "Hive of Liberty." On
every publication going out from his door was inscribed
the motto, "The Hive of Liberty, 8 Turnstile Street,
Holborn." From the "Hive" was published throughout
1793, 1794, and 1795 the periodical "Pig's Meat, or
Lessons for the Swinish Multitude." Also the famous
lecture, refurbished, was published again in 1793, and still
once more in 1796, as "The Meridian Son of Liberty." [1]
For this Spence went to jail. Nevertheless, there appeared
in 1805, a "Constitution, or Spensonian Declaration of

[1] George Adler, *Der altere Englische Sozialismus und Thomas
Spence*, p. 21.

Rights." With these ideas Spence busied himself to the last day of his life.[1] He died in 1814.

The spirit of militarism, to their credit be it said, was condemned by all British radicals. None denounced it with more force and eloquence than Joseph Gerrald. Gerrald, born of British parentage in the West Indies in 1763, educated at the famous school of Dr. Parr in England, returned to the West Indies, and drifted thence to Pennsylvania, where he studied and practiced law. In 1788 he went to England on a legal mission, and there decided to remain.[2] His winning personality making friends for him everywhere, it was not long before he leaped into prominence. In 1793 was held the famous Edinburgh Convention of the British radical societies. Gerrald was a London delegate. He proved to be an eloquent speaker and it was said that " his morning *levee* at the Black Bull Tavern was crowded with worshippers." At this convention Gerrald and the other leaders were arrested. An inadequate and most unfair trial was given them,[3] and Gerrald himself was transported to Australia. A victim of consumption, he died five months after his arrival, barely thirty years of age.[4]

[1] A Spensonian song book was published, which contains a Jubilee Hymn. One stanza is as follows:

> " Sing to the Lord of Hosts,
> And pass around a toast,
>   To Tommy Spence.
> Who through great peril ran,
> Having devised this plan,
> The perfect Rights of Man.
>   True Common Sense."

[2] *Dictionary of National Biography,* xxi, 237.

[3] Cockburn, *An Examination of the Trials for Sedition in Scotland, passim.*

[4] Gerrald's name may be found engraved on the Calton monument erected in Edinburgh to perpetuate the memory of political martyrs.

Before the convention met, however, which brought about the untimely end of the young radical, Gerrald had been busily engaged in promoting its existence. To this end he wrote a pamphlet [1] in the form of an open letter to the people of Great Britain on the proposed convention, which had a wide circulation. It was published by order of the London Correspondence Society, and easily ranks as one of their best propagandist publications. In this tract Gerrald paid his respects to war, and to the history of war. " If we look back," he writes, " to the wars which have desolated Europe for these last three hundred years, then these melancholy truths must strike the most careless observer: that they might have been decided by negotiations instead of being decided by arms; that they arose, not from the jarring interests of the people, but from the ambition and avarice of courts, and at the end of each war, the situation of the people was much worse than at the beginning of it." [2] Gerrald next proceeds to illustrate this statement by a brief summary of the wars of England since the revolution of 1688. The war of the Spanish Succession, he said, sacrificed 150,000 lives, and left England with a thirty million-pound debt. The pretext of the war was to give " a king to another people " who did not want him.[3] In the Spanish war of 1739 " the blood of British subjects was again poured out to maintain a Pragmatic Sanction; to preserve the balance of power, and to enable us to talk that cabalistic jargon which, while it assails the ears, neither informs the understanding or improves the condition of men. The balance of power, fellow citizens, means nothing more than

[1] Joseph Gerrald, *A Convention the Only Means of Saving us from Ruin.*

[2] *Ibid.*, p. 7.

[3] *Ibid.*, p. 12.

to extend the dominions and to increase the revenues of kings, for when did war meliorate the situation of the people?"[1] In 1756 came the next war. This caused horrible suffering "from the Great Lakes to the Ganges." In Germany, before Havana, and in other places, thousands died for a boundary dispute that might have been settled by jury.[2]

Indeed, Gerrald claims, no war is justifiable, save on grounds of self-defense. Under the old Scottish law, he continued, a king could not make war without the consent of his people. In America, a dangerous dispute between Pennsylvania and New Jersey was settled in 1784 by arbitration. Why not take advantage of these old-new precedents?

England is now engaged, he maintained, in a war of aggression. "The opening of the budget, like the opening of the box of Pandora, will pour forth innumerable evils and enormous taxes upon the good people of England. . . . A tax on Irish linen; a tax on shoes, and upon a number of articles which constitute the necessaries of life, are to be proposed and carried."[3] And for what? Simply that the merry old round may begin again.

There is one, and only one, reason why this state of affairs should be. "The great source of evil is that the people of Europe have in general as little connection with their respective governments, except, indeed, as they are the objects of their plunder, as they have with the governments of China and Japan. Does a gazette extraordinary, which announces the taking of a Condé or Valenciennes enable you to procure one pint of beer or a morsel of bread for your helpless, famishing children? Does the firing of cannon, the illumination of shops, lighten your labor, feed

---

[1] Gerrald, *A Convention,* p. 15.

[2] *Ibid.,* p. 19.   [3] *Ibid.,* p. 62.

your hunger, or clothe your nakedness? . . . I am free to confess that glory acquired by His Royal Highness of York on the plains of France has no charms for me, nor am I delighted to hear that the German eagle, that emblem of tyranny and massacre, now flies over the walls of a town where lately waved the banner of freedom. By war, kings extend their dominions and increase their revenues, while the inferior animals which have been hunting with the lion are amply rewarded. . . . by the honor of having sweated and bled in such company." [1]

War must be abolished, insists Gerrald. We must bring about this reform, and a good many others which he enumerates. If we do these things, he contends, " the poor, who are now worked too hard and taught too little, will have their persons better protected, their labor better rewarded, and their minds better instructed, and that class of men— the extremely indigent—will soon cease to exist." [2]

In religious reform, few of the younger radical school were interested. While not particularly hostile, their general attitude toward religion was one of indifferentism. In their ranks, however, was one notable exception. William Frend, Fellow of Cambridge University, knew no superior as a sane and broad-minded critic of contemporaneous ecclesiastical abuses. The son of a successful tradesman, he was sent early in life to France, and from there to Quebec, for a practical business education. Indifferent to commercialism, his heart set on scholarship, he entered Cambridge, graduated with high rank,[3] and became a clergyman of the Established Church.

[1] Gerrald, *A Convention*, p. 75.   [2] *Ibid.*, p. 117.

[3] So good was his reputation as a scholar that he was offered the post of tutor to Archduke Alexander of Russia, at a salary of two thousand pounds a year.

Doctrinal differences very soon ·disturbed him. Persuaded at length of the truth of Unitarianism, he shortly found himself engaged in a conflict on behalf of greater intellectual freedom. This conflict was waged over the University regulation which compelled all candidates for the degree of Bachelor of Arts to subscribe to the thirty-nine articles of the Church of England. To make clear his position in the controversy Frend published a pamphlet,[1] in which he tells us that, as far as the doctrines of the church are concerned "a young man of twenty cannot know whether they are right or wrong, and therefore the University, contrary to her principles in other studies, obliges the student to subscribe to things he does not understand."

All university tests concerning religious faith, he averred, were wrong in principle. To remove them altogether would harm neither the Church nor the State. "I deny," he wrote, "that the church is attacked, and were an attack made on the church I deny that it would be detrimental to the State. Would the State be ruined if all kinds of subscriptions were removed, whether the subscribers be parsons, or doctors of physic; would our soldiers be less courageous; would our sailors be less dangerous; would the clergy be less pious; would stocks rise and fall . . . , would the taxes be increased?"[2] He saw no reason why any dissenter should be debarred from the university. No distinction should be made at all between Englishmen in the matter of University privileges. Indeed he saw no reason why religious qualifications should shut out a man from any civil office. That Howard the philanthropist could not legally be made a Justice of the Peace was to Frend

[1] William Frend, *Thoughts on Subscriptions to Religious Tests Particularly that Required by the University of Cambridge for the Degree of Master of Arts.*

[2] *Ibid.*, p. 15.

ridiculous.[1] No good reason existed for desiring religious
uniformity, anyhow, for what could be more foolish than
to quarrel over original sin; or to object to putting oil on
the head of a sick man.[2]

Frend soon found himself an object of suspicion to the
University authorities, who particularly disliked [3] his great
influence with the undergraduates.[4] Meanwhile his radical opinions grew apace. In 1793 he published perhaps his
most important book. Its title, " Peace and Union," indicated, to some extent, the idea of the author. He believed,
evidently, that by a conciliatory discussion of existing evil
and necessary reform, it might be possible to bring together
in some kind of harmonious co-operation the warring fac-
tions in England's social and political life, and to that end
" Peace and Union " was written.

In this book Frend discusses many abuses which he perceived then rife, but upon none of them was he more level-
headed than on the abuses of the existing ecclesiastical establishment.[5] Three reforms were advocated: the abolition of the tithing system; the reform of the liturgy; and
the repeal of the Test Act. Under the tithing system the
general relation of the Church to the State is discussed.
The Church of England, he states, is a political institution,
" for the design of it is to celebrate at certain times re-

[1] Frend, *Thoughts on Subscriptions*, p. 20.

[2] *Ibid.*, p. 29.

[3] S. T. Coleridge, at that time an undergraduate, was among his
warmest friends.

[4] Frend, *Peace and Union recommended to the Associated Bodies of
Republicans and Anti-Republicans.*

[5] Very little attention was paid to religious reform by the average
radical of the younger school. As a body, indeed, it might fairly
be said that they were either Deists who thought but little of organized religion, or moreover agnostics who thought any religion hardly
worth thinking about. Kent, *Sketch of Radicalism*, p. 130.

ligious worship, and to instruct the people in certain doctrines laid down by Parliament."[1]

This political conection Frend distrusted. He feared that
as long as it continued, too much authority would be exercised by the politically influenced clergymen. " Ten thousand men in black," he explains, " under the direction of
an individual, are a far more formidable body than ten
times that number in arms, and more likely to produce the
greater injury to civil society."[2]   The granting of tithes,
says Frend, appears to be both " injurious to religion and
detrimental to the State." It tends to make the pastor
independent of his flock. It is unfair to the Non-conformists. It retards the systematic development of agriculture,
and even from the point of view of the beneficed clergymen, it is far from a satisfactory system of support.[3]

Secondly, the liturgy of the English Church, in Frend's
eyes, was antiquated. " It is far, indeed, from the standards of purity in its arrangement, language or doctrine,
which is required from such compositions."[4]

Finally, he demanded the repeal of the Test Act. The
attitude of the English Church and of the English government towards Non-conformists was disgraceful.[5] If
the disqualifications under which they lived were removed the great Non-conformist body of the nation
would become more devoted to the institutions of their
country, not less so. No danger menaced the Church
of England from this measure of justice. The greatest source of the Non-conformist strength, Frend believed, lay in the oppression to which they were subjected.
Take this away, and the number of dissenters would not

---

[1] Frend, *Peace and Union*, p. 37.   [2] *Ibid.*, p. 39.
[3] Frend, *Thoughts on Subscriptions to Religious Tests*, p. 16.
[4] Frend, *Peace and Union*, p. 41.   [5] *Ibid.*, p. 47.

materially increase. A few more might hold office, that
was all. Something should be done, and that soon, thought
Frend, for Christianity, in his opinion, had made but little
progress in fourteen hundred years, and largely because of
ecclesiasticism. Ecclesiastical courts, ranks, titles and caste,
were all repugnant to the spirit of Christianity. He would
render them all extinct.[1]

These opinions were not suffered to go unpunished.
Frend, tried by a University court, was banished from
Cambridge. From the action of the University authorities
he appealed to the Court of King's Bench, but no satisfaction was granted him.[2] His University career was now
virtually ended. He kept up a lively interest until the end
of his life, however, not only in social reform, but also in
all intellectual agitation in England. Called " the last of
the anti-Newtonians and a noted oppugner of all that dis-
tinguishes algebra from arithmetic," he found time nevertheless to write exhaustively on such diverse topics as
" Christian Theology," " The National Debt," " The Slave
Trade," " Astronomy," and "Ways and Means of Freeing
London from Smoke." Frend died in 1841, a stanch
radical to the end.

" Once teach a man that some are born to command, and
others to be commanded, and after that there is no camel
too big for him to swallow." [3] These words are taken

[1] Frend, *Peace and Union*, p. 54.

[2] Frend believed himself to be the victim of a petty intrigue, an account of which he gives us in "A Sequel to the Account of the Proceedings in the University of Cambridge against the Author of a
pamphlet entitled ' Peace and Union,' etc." London, 1795.

[3] Joel Barlow, *Advice to the Privileged Orders, in the Several States
of Europe, Resulting from the Necessity and Propriety of a General
Revolution in the Principle of Government*, London, 1792. Other editions and reprints: Paris, 1792; New York, 1792; London, 1793; Paris,
1793; London, 1795; New York, 1796.

from "Advice to the Privileged Orders," by Joel Barlow. They well express the spirit of the pamphlet from which they come; for it traces back almost all social and political discontent to what the author calls " aristocratic tyrannies." Here is the fountain source of injustice; here is the origin of such meaningless expressions as right of conquest, compact between king and people, and other sophistries.

Aristocratic tyrannies are cherished and maintained in many ways, " hence for that reason, the arming of one class of our fellow creatures with the weapons of bodily destruction, and others with the mysterious artillery of heaven." Authority and tradition are also evoked in their behalf. Barlow has as little respect as Mackintosh for authority. " Aristotle," he explains, " was certainly a great politician, and Claudius Ptolemy was a great geographer; but the latter has said not a word of America, the foremost quarter of the world, nor the former of representative republics, the resource of afflicted humanity." And, he continues, " since I have brought these two great luminaries of science so near together I will keep them in company a moment longer, to show the strange partiality that we may retain for one superstition, after having laid aside another, though they are built on similar foundations. Ptolemy wrote a system of astronomy; in which he taught, among other things, that the earth was the centre of the universe, and that the heavenly bodies moved around it. This system is now taught (to the exclusion by anathema of all others) in Turkey, Arabia, Persia, Palestine, Egypt, and wherever the doctrines of Mohammed are taught; while at the same time and with the same reverence the politics of Aristotle are taught at the University of Oxford. The ground which supports the one is that the sun stopped its course at the command of Joshua, which it could not have done had it not have been in motion; and the other, that the powers that be are ordained of God. Mention to a Mussulman the Copernican system, and you might as well speak to Mr. Burke about the rights of man; they both call you an atheist." [1]

Aristocratic tyrannies, indeed, are perpetrated by every wile which craft may invent, or tradition excuse. And the survival in Europe of the feudal system, the church, standing armies, customary administration of justice, and the revenue and expenditure of European states are given in evidence by Barlow as proof of his assertions. The administration of justice in aristocratically ridden states is especially atrocious. " If I were able," he writes, " to give an energetic sketch of the office and dignity of a rational system of jurisprudence, describe the full extent of its effects on the happiness of men, and then exhibit the perversions and corruptions attendant upon this business in most of the governments of Europe, they would furnish one of the most powerful arguments in favor of a general revolution, and afford no small consolation to those persons who look forward with certainty to such an event." [2]

Justice, Barlow argues, is not concerned solely in restraining vice. To prevent vice is a duty equally important, and even more sacred in character. Society should give every man a fair chance, for, he tells us, " none can deny that the obligation is much stronger on me to support my life than to support the claim my neighbor has upon his property. Nature commands the first; society the second." Justice should take into consideration this primitive will to live. " Vindictive justice " or punishment is but a small part of justice, for it is subordinate to two other principles. In the first place justice should take it upon

---

[1] Barlow, *op. cit.,* p. 29.   [2] *Ibid.,* p. 81.

herself to instruct everyone, " not only in the artificial
laws by which property is secured, but also the artificial
industries by which it is obtained." Secondly, if the individual is a weakling, mentally deficient, or in other ways
unable to look out for himself, justice rests under an obligation to protect him. Only in the last extremity is punishment to be inflicted.

The administration of justice should be based upon these
principles. The actual practice is quite different. " In
England the people at large are as perfectly ignorant of
the acts of Parliament after they are made as they possibly
can be before. They are printed by one man only, who is
called the king's printer—in the old German characters
which few men can read—and sold at a price that few can
afford to pay. But lest some scraps of comments upon
them should come to the people through the medium of
the public newspapers, every such paper is stamped with
a heavy duty; and an act of Parliament is made to prevent
men from lending their papers to each other; so that not
one person in a hundred sees a newspaper once in a year.
If a man at the bottom of Yorkshire discovers by instinct
that a law is made which is interesting for him to know,
he has only to make a journey to London, find out the
king's printer, pay a penny a page for the law, and learn
the German alphabet. He is then prepared to spell out his
duty." [1]

The laws are complicated. They are expensive. Furthermore, the very form and method employed in presenting a case for trial is unsystematic and archaic, " more difficult to learn than the construction of the most complicated machines, or even the motions of the heavenly
bodies." To illustrate this, Barlow traces the history of a

---

[1] Barlow, *op. cit.,* p. 95.

case in the court of chancery. " The suitor," he says, " begins his incomprehensible operation by stating his claim in what is called a bill, which he leaves at a certain office belonging to the court, and obtains an order for the subpoena for summoning the defendant. This being done, the court requires the defendant to send an attorney to write his name at another office of the court. This writing of the name is called an appearance; it answers no possible purpose but that of increasing expenses and fees of office, for which it is a powerful engine. For if the defendant does not comply, an expense of thousands of pounds is involved. A *capias,* a process for outlawry, a commission of rebellion, and an order and commission for sequestration are pursued in their proper routine till he consents to write his name." [1]

The first step is over. The defendant has at last written his name. Once that is done, he is entitled to a delay. During this delay he makes a demur or answer; at the expiration of the days of grace four more weeks are given him. " But though he is entitled to this further delay, and neither the plaintiff nor the court can refuse it, still he must employ a solicitor to make a brief for counsel, and this solicitor must attend the counsel, and give him and his clerk their fees for moving the court for this delay, which cannot be refused. The counsel must attend the court and make the motion; the solicitor must attend the court, and pay for the order, entry and copy, and then must cause it to be served." [2]

After the four weeks have passed the defendant may have another delay of three weeks, and after that another one of two. Both of these respites must be applied for in the way we have outlined. Furthermore, this method as

---

[1] Barlow, *op. cit.,* p. 104.　　　　[2] *Ibid.,* p. 105.

described may be much further involved by " motions, petitions, decrees, orders, etc., for amending the bill, for referring to masters the insufficiency of answers, reports
upon those answers, and further answers, and exceptions
to masters' reports and orders and decisions relative to
them." [1]

Barlow then rapidly summarizes the fortunes of a bill
in chancery by stating that " to proceed through all the
forms to the end of a suit in chancery would be to write a
commentary on many volumes of practice, and would be
calling the patience of the reader to a trial from which it
certainly would shrink. But there are parts as much worse
than what we have described as this is worse than common
sense. Strip from the administration of justice the forms
that are perfectly useless and oppressive, and counsellors
will have much less to do; while the whole order of attorneys and solicitors will fall to the ground."

The author of this tract was an American. Graduated
with distinction from Yale in 1778, he served as chaplain
in Washington's army. After the war he wrote poetry of
some little merit,[2] and became an editor of the *American
Mercury*. In 1788 Barlow was appointed European agent
of the Scioto Land Company. Going to France he received
a hearty welcome. There were many buyers for his land,
and Barlow himself was lionized in Paris.

In London, too, he was a familiar figure. Member of
the London Constitutional Society, he took an active
part in the propaganda which the Society carried on.[3]
In London he wrote, " The Address to the Privileged
Orders." The author was proscribed by the government.
His private letters were intercepted, and he himself fled to

---

[1] Barlow, *op. cit.*, p. 107.

[2] Tyler, *The Literary Strivings of Joel Barlow, passim.*

[3] *State Trials,* xxiv, 526, 527.

France.   Mrs. Barlow wrote him there from England in
1793 that " Mr. Burke makes honorable mention of you in
Parliament.   Sometimes he calls you the Prophet Joel." [1]
Both in England and in America, indeed, Barlow and his
book were widely known.   In London, also, Barlow wrote
" The Conspiracy of Kings," a poem.   It was a brief, and
to the eighteenth century imagination, a stirring produc-
tion, suitable for insertion in newspapers and broadsides.
It was said to have been more popular in England than the
" Advice to the Privileged Orders." [2]

The versatile American now turned to other occupations.
In 1796 he undertook a mission to the Barbary States for
the United States Government.   Returning to Paris, he
continued his business career, made a fortune, and took
a deep interest in the invention of the steamboat, conduct-
ing experiments with Fulton on the Seine.   He then went
back to America, bought a country seat near Washington,
and continued his experiments in steam navigation, while
entertaining Jefferson and many other prominent politicians.   In 1811 Barlow once more crossed the ocean to
negotiate a treaty of commerce.   In search of Napoleon,
he traveled to Poland, and died there in 1813.

Friend of Coleridge, Thomas Paine and Wordsworth;
poet, philosopher, economist and patriot, John Thelwal
stands pre-eminent among his fellow-radicals as a de-
nouncer of abuses in the industrial and economic life of the
nation.

Struggling like so many of his contemporaries with

---

[1] Todd, *Life and Letters of Joel Barlow,* p. 89.   Jefferson wrote to
Barlow: " Be assured that your endeavors to bring the trans-Atlantic
world into the world of reason are not without their effect here."
John Adams mentions Barlow's book in his third letter on Government
to John Taylor, 1814.

[2] *Ibid.,* p. 90.

early adversity, he, too, ultimately found himself in literature.   Poet of a somewhat conventionalized type in 1787, Thelwal, by the early nineties, was swept headlong into the radical current.   No half-hearted convert was he.   From 1792 till the end of his career, his life was given over with singular zeal and perseverance to the cause of radicalism. As a lecturer and as a pamphleteer, as a .campaigner and as an editor, his work was invaluable.

The government feared him mightily.   No other radical writer was watched more closely.   He seemed equally dangerous to the authorities either as a fiery orator of the London Corresponding Society, or as editor of the vitriolic *Tribune.*   Driven from pillar to post; tried for high treason; permanently deprived of his manuscripts and books; beaten and assaulted by hired thugs; he yet persisted undauntedly on his chosen path.

For this continual persecution Thelwal himself was in part responsible.   Possessed of a store of invective comparable to that of Burke or Paine, he was, as Paine never was, an orator of considerable power.   Furthermore, he was without fear.   Legally debarred from discussing politics, Thelwal immediately lectured on the psychology of the laws of freedom and the love of the fair sex.   In this lecture,[1] for purposes of illustration, the position of the king rooster in the farmyard was freely and pointedly explained.   No one doubted, or could doubt, the innuendo implied by the King Chanticleer, who lost his life by strutting about a little too proudly, with " his ermine spotted breast."   Largely as a result of this lecture came his trial for high treason.[2]

---

[1] *The Story of the Farmyard* was published by Eaton in his *Politics for the People;* Cestre, *Life of Thelwal,* p. 78.

[2] The indictment for high treason read in one place, "A very fine, majestic animal, the game cock, meaning our lord the King," etc.

Thelwal soon devised a better way to accomplish his purpose than by lectures on psychology. He would lecture on ancient history and to that end published the prospectus [1] of a series of Lenten lectures. In this prospectus the way in which the law is to be circumvented is clearly indicated. First the law is quoted, then, writes Thelwal, "all . . . . that the lecturer or debater is enjoined from doing by this act of Parliament is to avoid all mention of this country, its grievances, its laws, its constitution, government and policy, and provided he does this—which most certainly I shall do—he may discuss the principles of liberty and justice, and expose all the vices and horrors of tyranny and usurpation." [1] A sentence from Rapin, an eighteenth century historian, might condemn the orator to a penalty of a hundred pounds, says Thelwal, but if the story of Greece or Rome is substituted for modern England, the facts recorded by Thucydides, Sallust and Tacitus may be expatiated upon with impunity. [3]

These lectures created great excitement. They must have been widely popular. [3] Thelwal was soon able to charge one shilling a night, instead of sixpence, his early price. He said that the great expense of buying books, hiring halls, etc., made that step necessary. Great difficulty was indeed experienced. At times his bills of advertisement were torn down as quickly as posted, while hired rioters frequently made the delivery of his lecture impossible. [4]

At times he barely escaped personal injury. While lecturing at Yarmouth on Classical History, according to

[1] *A Prospectus of a Course of Lectures to be given every Monday, Wednesday and Friday, during the ensuing Lent, in strict conformity with the restrictions of Mr. Pitt's Convention Act."*

[2] *Ibid.,* p. 18.

[3] The first lecture of a series planned on "The Moral Tendencies of a System of Spies and Informers" went through four editions by 1794.

[4] Cestre, *op. cit.,* p. 81.

Thelwal, certain clergymen and militia officers on the first
two evenings attempted to create a distrubance, with the
assistance of noisy boys, who were paid by a naval officer.[1]
He weathered this storm, but on the following evening a
band of about ninety armed sailors rushed in and attacked
the two-hundred-odd people in the audience. The sailors
assaulted the women and wounded many people with their
cutlasses. Someone kicked over the lights. Cries of
" where is the parson " were heard. Thelwal escaped, but
was caught by his enemies, only in turn to be rescued by his
friends. The evidence in this fracas was very clear.
Charges were preferred against various individuals, and
an acrimonious wrangle ensued over the refusal of the
municipal government to take action in the matter.

The spirit of Thelwal's writings may best be indicated
by his reply to Burke: " The Rights of Nature." [2] In the
first part of this answer Thelwal says: " We have heard
much of the rights of property and of the rights of nations,
and of the rights of man we have heard some things well
worth serious consideration. Much also have we heard of
the rights of the peerage, the rights of Parliament, and of
the rights of the crown. But let us for once inquire into
the rights of the laborer." [3]

Thelwal wrote that progress came not from the intellectual stimulus of philosophers and philanthropists, no
matter how clear-thinking they might be, but rather from

---

[1] Thelwal, *An Appeal to Popular Opinion on Kidnapping and Murder, including a narrative of the late atrocious proceedings at Yarmouth,* p. 21.

Another meeting of Thelwal's was broken up by soldiers in 1797.
This was at Norwich. *A Topographical and Historical Account of
the City and County of Norwich,* p. 252.

[2] Thelwal, *The Rights of Nature against the Usurpation of Establishments,* a series of letters in reply to Edmund Burke.

[3] *Ibid.,* p. 77.

the inarticulate body of the nation which, maddened to the point of fury by wrongs endured, demanded a new life. " Hume's commentaries," he observed, " slept for thirty years, and the Utopia for whole centuries on the shelves of the learned, and even the popular language of Thomas Paine would not have provoked any alarming discussion had not the general condition of mankind predisposed them to exclaim ' we are wretched; let us inquire the cause.' "

The basic cause of social distress, Thelwal asserted roundly, was the unequal distribution of property in Great Britain. Conditions in the workhouses, he exclaims, are altogether similar to those existent in the slave-ridden British colonies,[2] and he compares, with telling effect, these conditions with the luxury found among the nobility of England.[3]

This inequality was brought about by several causes. In the first place there was taxation. This was really much more than it was popularly supposed to be, for most taxes were concealed. " You think not of taxes," he affirmed, " save when the collector comes to your door. You forget that your stomachs have been gauged and your backs measured by rates, by customs and by excises, and that, eat, drink and wear what you will, fifteen shillings out of every twenty must go for tithes, or for taxes." [4]

[1] Thelwal, *Rights of Nature*, Part I, p. 82.

[2] *Ibid.*, p. 34. Thelwal took far more interest in the anti-slavery movement than did the average radical.

[3] *Ibid.*, p. 35. Thelwal tells us of a canine palace at Godwood, erected by the Duke of Richmond, which contained " a commodious kitchen, parlours, diningrooms, bedrooms, lying-in rooms, and pleasure grounds for morning fun, pleasure grounds for evening fun, baths, etc."

[4] *Ibid.*, Part II, p. 94. Thelwal indicates the taxes indirectly paid by the reader of his pamphlet by tracing the taxation of that pamphlet from the tax paid on the rough timber to that paid on the warehouse of the publisher.

Many other complaints were made against the economic
organization of society. A very unfair custom of fining
the workmen existed in the textile trade. There were employers " who took the liberty, when the work was brought
to them, to scotch the spinners (as it is called), at their
own will or pleasure." This arbitrary power, Thelwal believed, was the result of monopolies. They must be
checked, for increased production, unaccompanied by just
distribution is a mockery.[1] This just distribution Thelwal
thought would come in time, through the very accumulation
of property, which was thus not an unmixed evil. He distinctly forecast the coming of the trade union as the result
of men working together in large groups.[2]

No man perceived more clearly the significance of economic fact. That his portrayal should be perfervidly
rhetorical is unfortunate, but not surprising. If he chooses
to speak of " oppression heaped upon oppression, till it
overtops Olympus," [3] or of " the proud vaults and splendid
charnal houses of illustrious ancestry," [4] he merely followed the literary usage of his day, and the precedent of
that master mind, the champion of conservatism, who is
held even now as a great master of English diction. These
faults we may forgive in John Thelwal, because he fought
bravely for the right as he saw it.

---

[1] *The Tribune,* ii, 34. These scotchings, or deductions, made on
various pretexts, amounted sometimes to one-quarter of the full value
of the work. Quoted from Cestre, *op. cit.,* p. 163.

[2] Thelwal, *Rights of Nature,* Part I, p. 19.

[3] *Ibid.,* Part I, p. 61.

[4] *Ibid.,* Part II, p. 98.

CHAPTER V

Radicalism and Political Reform

Annual Parliaments and Universal Suffrage the Ultimatum. Doctrinnaire Theories of the Radical Reformers

All radical writers advocated political reform; it was perhaps the first article of their creed. They were both vociferous and repetitious in urging its necessity. Nor was their arraignment of existing political conditions lacking in vigor. Said Paine, apropos of the monarchy: "When extraordinary power and extraordinary pay are allotted to any individual in a government, he becomes the centre around which every kind of corruption generates and forms. Give to any man a million a year, and add thereto the power of creating and dispersing places at the expense of a country, and the liberties of that country are no longer secure." [1] Said Gerrald, on the subject of representation: "There are not, there cannot be, more than two kinds of representation: persons and property. But the present system represents neither. Persons are not represented because 5,723 persons who are influenced as we have seen by a much smaller number return a majority of the House of Commons, though the adult males throughout Great Britain amount to one hundred twenty-five thousand. Property is not represented, for the County of Cornwall, one of the poorest in the sixty-two, sends forty-five members to Par-

---

[1] Paine, *Rights of Man*, Part II, p. 408.

liament, while the County of Middlesex, which contains
the greater part of the wealth of the kingdom, sends only
eight.   In some boroughs the man who boils a pot has the
privilege of voting for a member of Parliament, though
he who possesses a hundred thousand pounds in the funds
has not." [1]   A tempting opening in the Tory armor was
this state of political Britain, and the reformers with one
accord laid bare whatever scandals they could find therein.

As to the precise direction which political reform should
take there was not the same unanimity.   The more cautious
among them contended for a reform on the basis of Pitt's
proposals of the year 1785.   The fact that Pitt then recognized the need of reform was loudly proclaimed by all
radicals alike, as substantiating their claim that the House
of Commons was not truly representative of the people.
Few, however, were content with Pitt's moderation.   The
Rev. Charles Wyvill maintained that Pitt's plan " was a
wise proposal and well adapted to the state of public opinion in 1785. . . . But since that time the denial of redress and a long protracted discussion had produced their
usual effects.   Upon the subject of constitutional rights
the ideas of the public had been expanded, and a more
extensive redress is sought for in many parts of England
and through Scotland than Mr. Pitt's original plan proposed." [2]

Wyvill was willing that the great factory towns should
be adequately represented.   He approved of extending the
franchise to the middle class, but for him no universal
suffrage.   Listen to his argument: " For, should the right
of universal suffrage be now granted, who could for a
moment doubt that in quiet times our profligate population

[1] Gerrald, *A Convention*, p. 102.

[2] Christopher Wyvill, *A State of the Representation of the People of
England*, p. 27.

would be submissive and venial; that their submission and
veniality would increase the preponderance of the great
and destroy the salutary influence of those disinterested
and independent men who are chiefly to be found in the
middle class of mankind.   And, in times of national distress and discontent, it can admit of as little doubt that
artful demagogues might soon inflame the passion of the
populace to a wild and ferocious rage for liberty; and thus
raise a hurricane by which society would too probably be
overturned to its deep foundations."   By and by, continues the author, perhaps we might approach with reason
and religion working in harness " the simplicity and purity
of our forefathers," and if we ever thus won back the innocence and integrity of primitive times then, and then only,
might we have universal suffrage.

A majority of the radicals did not draw their inspira-
tion from Pitt; they found it rather in a certain letter
written in 1783 by the Duke of Richmond.   The reformers
were thoroughly conversant with this letter.   Its principles
were quoted and incorporated in their various pamphlets
and appeals.   It was cited by their leaders as important testimony in the criminal trials in which they were defend-
ants, while even the duke himself was summoned to Old
Bailey that he might testify to his authorship.[1]   In this
letter Richmond declared, " I have no hesitation in saying
that, from every consideration which I have been able to
give to this great subject. . . . I am more and more convinced that the restoring of the right of voting universally
to every man not incapacitated by nature for want of
reason, or by law for the commission of crimes, together
with annual Parliaments, is the only reform that can be
effectual and permanent.   I am convinced that it is the only

[1] *State Trials,* **xxiv,** 1048.

reform which is practical."[1]   Half-way measures, he maintained, would do no good.   The weight of corruption was
too heavy; the people at large must cleanse their own house,
and, continues the duke, "I am convinced that the only
way to make them feel that they are concerned in the business is to contend for their full, clear and indisputable
rights of universal representation."   To facilitate his reform he presented a bill in the House of Lords, providing for annual elections and for a census of Great
Britain, in order to redistribute the seats in the House of
Commons, on the basis of one representative for approxi-
mately every two thousand six hundred voters.

If anybody remained in ignorance of the declaration of
Richmond it was not the fault of the radicals.   Richmond,
in a measure the patron of the London Corresponding
Society, the leading radical organization, was quoted in
the publications of the Society.   Also, in various pamphlets,
his letter appeared in full,[2] while the radical tracts in general made many references to it,[3] one of them summarizing
the attitude of the radicals towards the duke's statement
as follows: "The plan offered by the Duke of Richmond
seems the only one that has met with public approbation;
and it is clear that either that or one of a similar nature
upon the same principles is the only one that can restore
to the people their original and inherent rights, and a strict
and equal justice to every individual in the nation.   This
plan is universal suffrage; mental insanity and incapacity

[1] *State Trials,* xxiv, 1049.

[2] *Authentic Copies of a Declaration of the Rights of Englishmen, a
Bill for a Reform in Parliament, and a Letter to Lieut-Colonel
Sharman, by his Grace, the Duke of Richmond.*

Daniel Holt, *A Vindication of the Conduct and Principles of the
Printer of the Newark Herald.*   Newark, 1794.

[3] Daniel Stuart, *Peace and Reform against War and Corruption, in
Answer to a Pamphlet written by Arthur Young, entitled, "The Example of France a Warning to Britain,"* p. 95.

arising from public crime being the only bar against that privilege." [1]

The proof that this letter was in large measure the keystone of the radical attitude on the question of suffrage neither rests entirely on the importance given to it in the radical tracts, nor does it depend upon the emphasis given to it by the radical clubs and associations; for further indications of the important rôle it played among the radicals, we have but to look at the defence of Muir, Daniel Isaac Eaton and Thomas Hardy when placed on trial by the government. [2]

Radicalism, then, sought universal suffrage and annual parliaments. It cleverly buttressed its demand by incorporating in it the expressed opinions of Pitt and the Duke of Richmond. Its endeavor to demonstrate that universal suffrage and annual parliaments were ancient rights of Englishmen was not quite so strategic. Forgetful of Mackintosh and his calm statement that political justice does not depend upon precedent, the reformers sought unanimously to find in the records of antiquity the proof of man's pristine independence. A few instances of this reasoning will suffice. Gerrald's defence in Edinburgh recalls to us the recent controversies of Fustel de Coulanges, Vinagradoff and Maitland. No exegesis of the Magna Carta will suffice for Gerrald, nor indeed is the Witanagemot of our Saxon forbears satisfactory. He needs must go back to Tacitus and there discover the early seeds of the English constitution,—*"De Germania: De Minoribus rebus principes consultant, de majoribus omnes—ita tamen ut ea, quoque, quorum penes plebenarbitrium est, apud principes protractentur."* [3] Searching inquiries were made by

---

[1] *The Gulf of Ruin, or a Quick Reform: which will you Chuse?* p. 6.

[2] *State Trials,* xxiii, 194, 1044; xxiv, 915.

[3] *State Trials,* xxiii, 958. " I have adopted the reading of Colerus and Aedalius in preference to the common reading which is *pertractentur,"* he tells the jury.

other writers into the purpose and intent of the Magna
Carta and the Parliament of 1265. A lively controversy
over the interpretation of the latter event arose between
Arthur Young and Daniel Stuart. After triumphantly
tearing to shreds the argument of his opponent, Stuart
announces: " The existence of representatives of some
description may be traced in every page of our history, and is coeval with all law and government in England. What though they were occasionally laid aside; their
rights invaded. . . ." And he furthermore informs us
" wherever we find the slightest traces of the House of
Commons . . . there is no mention of its being a new institution, which is strong proof that it was an old one." [1]
Authorities ancient and modern are freely invoked. Burke's
" Thoughts on the Causes of the Present Discontent,"
Doctor Jebb, Fortescue, Coke and Blackstone are made to
support the radical contention, while a certain volume,
written in the reign of Queen Elizabeth, by Sir Thomas
Smith, Doctor of Laws, and entitled " De Republica an-
glorum," is quoted on his trial by Henry Yorke, as con-
firming explicitly his position in regard to political reform. [2]

From the forests of Germany in the first century to the
publication of Richmond's letter in the eighteenth, the cup-
board of history was swept bare. No crumb lay hidden
from the radical broom. The voting privileges, however, of

[1] Stuart, *Peace and Reform*, p. 86.

[2] " Atque ut concludam breviter, quicquid in centuriatis comitiis, aut
in tribunitiis, populus Romanus efficere potuisset id omne in comitiis
Anglicanis tanquam in coetu

I. Principem.

II. Populumque

representante, commode transigitur, interesse enim illo conventu
omnes intelligimur cujuscunque amplitudinis status aut dignitatis
princepsve, aut Plebs fuerit, sive per teipsum hoc fiat, sive per pro-
curatorem." From the trial of Henry Redhead, alias Henry Yorke,
State Trials, xxv, 1080.

our English ancestry are scarcely germane to this discussion. Indeed, the reward which is ours from their study, is inversely proportional to the time expended. The same might be said for those quixotic and *doctrinnaire* arguments in support of annual Parliaments and Universal Suffrage. In one case the evil of the Rotten Borough is to be remedied by the following plan: " Let a list be made out of the voters in every borough. And let it be ordered by Parliament that every borough not having a thousand voters shall, out of the inhabitants of the town or hundred gradually raise them to that number." [1] This accomplished, it is suggested that a return be made to the old Anglo-Saxon system of hundreds and tithings. " Let the presidents of ten tithings select the presidents of the hundred; the presidents of the hundred, the president of the thousand, and so on. Each division of ten thousand families could send two members to Parliament, the votes to be taken by the heads of tithings, and carried by them to the heads of hundreds, to be conveyed to the heads of thousands who, with the head of the ten thousand should declare the representatives elected." [2] If we follow out this scheme, the writer hopes that the peace and tranquillity of Alfred's reign may be restored. Frend, the deviser of this utopian dream, though a clear thinker on other subjects, is obsessed, as were so many of his contemporaries, with the idea of indirect elections. His plan contains nothing of merit, save perhaps the intimation that a right of referendum remained in the hands of the people.[3]

The proposal of Gerrald was even more fantastic. He recommended the division of the one hundred and twenty-five thousand males in England into twelve hundred and fifty primary assemblies. Ten primary assemblies made

[1] Frend, *Peace and Union*, p. 16.

[2] *Ibid.*, p. 20. [3] *Ibid.*, p. 22.

one secondary assembly. To this body every primary assembly was to send ten delegates. Each of the secondary
assemblies would send two deputies to a national convention, which would be in turn the source of many civil and
political blessings.[1]

Various divergent theories were held by other writers.[2]
All recognized, however, that the attainment of any reform
was more difficult than perfecting the details of a theoretical ideal. Two methods of obtaining their general end
were suggested. At first their hopes were set on a petitioning of Parliament. As it became more and more evident
that this method was useless, a national convention was demanded. Paine stoutly upheld the idea of a convention.
" I have no idea of petitioning for rights," he wrote;
" whatever the rights of the people are they have a right
to them, and none have a right to withhold them, or to
grant them. Government ought to be established on such
principles of justice as to exclude the occasion of all such
applications, for when they appear they are virtually ac-
cusations." [3] Boldness is what we need. " Instead then
of referring to Rotten Boroughs and absurd corporations
for addresses or hawking them about the country to be
signed by a few dependent tenants, the real and effectual
mode would be to come at once to the point, and to ascertain
the sense of the nation by electing a national convention." [4]
This convention is to be elected by universal suffrage—
one man, one vote. How it shall be convened, where it
shall meet, and who shall summon it, we are not told.

---

[1] Gerrald, *A Convention*, p. 112.

[2] Among these latter it is interesting to note that Major Cartwright
is the only one who mentions or approves of woman suffrage.

[3] Paine, *Address to Addressors, Works*, iii, 81.

[4] *Ibid.*, p. 87.

CHAPTER VI

Radicalism and the Economic Crisis

MONOPOLIES, LUXURY AND THE NEW INDUSTRIALISM AS
THE CAUSE. VAGUENESS OF THE PROPOSED REME-
DIES. THE INTIMATION OF THE MINIMUM WAGE

" The profit of the world is for all. The king himself
is served by the field." [1]

This sentence, the most lucid one in a long, rambling discourse on the troubles of the times, gives the keynote to the
economic demands of radicalism. Those demands were
all too often half-formed, inchoate, fragmentary. The
radical consciousness was but dimly aware of the omni-
present urgency of economic reform. The mirage of political equality, blurring the vision and distorting the per-
spective, danced constantly before its eyes; "ballot-box
influenza" had become an obsession, annual Parliaments
and universal suffrage ultimate and final goals, rather than
milestones on the dusty road of progress. Nevertheless,
the spirit of discontent was due mainly to economic distress. It was physical suffering and physical want, those
ever active stimuli of protesting humanity, which stirred
the emotions and steeled the determination of the British
radicals. For that reason, if for no other, any study of
radical agitation which casts economic opinion to one side

[1] Matthews, *Remarks on the Cause and Progress of the Scarcity
and Dearness of Cattle, Swine, Cheese,* etc., 1797, p. 205.

is without fair proportion and equitable balance.[1] It is, however, one of the most serious difficulties of the historian that this opinion so powerful, often determinative in its day, seldom leaves an adequate trace, either of its own expression or of its force in society. A thing of the hour, called out by the insistent needs of daily life, it lives only as long as the situation lasts. Once the crisis passes away, the whole incident is forgotten and its literature which is the historian's only clue, is thrown to the rubbish heap. Fortunately, however, in this instance it is not altogether the case. A few pamphlets, but enough to give us some inkling as to what the situation and opinion really were, have come down to us. They are not the least interesting material for the study of our period.

Monopolies, relentless and brutalizing, were assumed to be the source of the prevalent economic misery, and special opprobrium was cast by the radicals upon all who plotted to raise the price of foodstuffs. Denunciation of the corn dealers and the wholesale butchers are common. The wholesale butcher or " the carcass butcher," as he is called, is accused of attending all the chartered markets within fifty miles of London, although those markets were intended for the local community only. It is claimed that the London wholesalers go there, and buy up all the live stock, so that when it reaches the Smithfield market, the cutting or retail butcher finds to his sorrow that it is already sold, and that there is no longer competition as in the old days.[2] The wholesale butchers not only forestall the cattle; they actually buy the very farms. What right has a butcher

---

[1] Robinson, *The New History*, pp. 132 *et seq.*

[2] *Monopoly: The cutting butchers' last appeal to the legislature upon the high price of meat, by a Philanthropic Butcher,* London, 1795. This is replied to by the wholesale butchers by *Facts for the Consideration of the Public at Large.*

to be a farmer; or a farmer to be a butcher! If the butcher
cares for the plow, let him get a farm, but he should leave
his cleaver behind him.   It is not fair that he should carry
on both trades.   The law should stop these monopolies,
but if it won't, then the landlords ought to prevent their
tenants from butchering, and the magistrates who dispose
of the market stalls should see to it that the butchers are
kept at a distance.   Dwellers outside of London must join
in assisting their city brethren.   If they pledge themselves
not to buy of the farmer-butcher, much might be done,
and also, if the farmer-butcher were forbidden to sell every
fifth female calf for veal, there would be more cattle in the
kingdom.   No yearling swine should be killed, either.   As
it is now, the butchers, who care nothing for the country,
are greatly diminishing the supply of livestock by their
short-sighted and selfish methods.

The butchers are not the only offenders.   We are told
also of a butter monopoly.   "About twenty years ago the
obnoxious practice of contracting for dairies was but little
known."   Butter was sold fresh and at a reasonable rate.
Now, the great jobbers engross the butter supply in New-
gate and Leadenhall markets.   "Their practice is to ride
from dairy to dairy in the country, and to buy up all they
can; this means of engrossing such large quantities enables them to sell at two prices, for the dealers are compelled to apply to them first."   The bakers are not behindhand in sharp practice.   They adulterate their bread by
using salt, alum and soap.   And as for the brewers, they
are famous for their sly ways.   They put tobacco in their
beer, to whet the thirst; Spanish licorice is used for color-
ing; isinglass gives beer a translucent appearance, and
copperas makes it foam.

"Before the accursed spirit of monopoly destroyed the

little farmer, he had plenty of fowls, ducks, etc., very cheap, but the gentleman farmers disdain to breed anything but for their own table . . . the middle people are sinking into the state of the Neapolitan *lazzaroni*. It is a land for the rich, and it is a hell for the poor. Everything is committed upon the issue of money. I believe there are few days pass away in the public offices when some forlorn individual is not brought up to the bar of justice to receive punishment for his inability to pay dues enacted by the multifarious imposts of the legislature." [1]

The gentry, indeed, manipulate the law on their own behalf. John Thelwal assures his readers that the laws which regulate commerce are specially designed to aid the rich agriculturists. Such a law, he says, is that which prohibits the importation of foreign corn under fifty shillings a bushel; and even in this instance good wheat might be over fifty shillings a bushel, and yet the ports be closed to foreign commerce. For the officers only took the average, and since more poor corn was sold than good, the average was low. It might be fifty shillings, while good corn was fifty-three. Speculation also made the matter worse. On the Isle of Wight, he instances the case of a well-to-do farmer who bought up all the grain on the island and refused to sell it, and " to such a height are these speculations carried that corn on the Isle of Wight, in the summer of 1795, reached a price of from twenty to twenty-five pounds a load, standing on the ground, though in the memory of the oldest inhabitant of that island it was never twelve pounds before."

The gentry force the government to abet their class interests in other ways. Their puppets in the House of Commons facilitate the filching of the common land by

---

[1] Matthews, *Remarks, op. cit., passim.*

enclosure acts. The growth of large farms goes on apace. " The practice of enlarging and engrossing of farms, and especially that of depriving the peasantry of all landed property, have contributed greatly to increase the number of the poor." The landowners and farmers join several small farms together and thus take away the livelihood of many who formerly lived in independence. The peasantry are now beggared. " Formerly many of the lower sort of people occupied tenements of their own, with parcels of land about them, . . . but those small parcels of ground have been swallowed up in the contiguous farms and enclosures; the cottages themselves have been pulled down; the families who used to occupy them are crowded together in decayed farmhouses, with hardly ground enough about them for a cabbage garden." [1]

John Thelwal describes the process by which the wealthy landlord absorbs the small holding of his poor neighbor. Such a man is an " agricultural cannibal," cries Thelwal. He continues in his evil ways until perhaps he becomes the master of a county. His greedy voraciousness should be summarily checked. " If a gentleman (for such is the title with which we perversely dignify every two-legged being whom fortune has elevated above the common feelings of humanity) purchases a small estate, or takes the lease of any antiquated mansion, almost the first step he takes towards accomplishing his projected improvements is to level the surrounding cottages to the ground, and to drive the wretched inhabitants from the spot." Poverty

---

[1] David Davies, *The Case of the Laborers in Husbandry,* pp. 55, 56. The author of this book, the rector of Barkham, Berks, is a strange composite of sentimental philanthropy and rational radicalism. Combined with his thoughtful analysis of existing misery are to be found sundry observations on the improvidence and extravagance of the poor, etc.

is annoying and unpleasant to these sensitive gentlemen; cottages destroy the view; they are but "warts upon the landscape." And what right, anyway, have the poor to gather free fuel from the enclosed heath? "Shall low plebeians, vulgar, base-born hinds, born in the pale of matrimonial beggary, dare to violate the sacred fences of their masters? And when the sharp, biting winter freezes their joints and the scanty earnings of their industry will scarcely furnish them with so much food as may keep life and soul together, shall they presume to snatch a wretched stake from him who wallows in indulgence, to make a little fire in their crazy cabins?"[1]

Thomas Paine agreed with Thelwal in this matter. "Cultivation," he wrote, "is at least one of the greatest natural improvements ever made by human invention. It has given the created earth a ten-fold value, but the landed monopoly that began with it has produced a great evil. It has dispossessed more than one-half of the inhabitants of every nation of their natural inheritance, without providing for them as ought to have been done an indemnification for that loss, and has thereby created a species of poverty and wretchedness that did not exist before."[2]

Monopolies are not the sole cause of the prevalent distress. There is too much commerce and trade, anyway, we are assured, for the welfare of old England. Wealth results from commerce and trade, and wealth breeds new desires. The result is extravagance. Extravagance has boosted high the price of provisions. Economy is now a lost art. Merchants ape the manners and customs of the nobility. "In the metropolis and other large cities and

---

[1] Thelwal, *The Peripatetic,* i, 129 *et seq.*

[2] Paine, *Agrarian Justice, passim. Cf. supra,* p. 94, and *infra,* p. 152.

towns the shopkeeper who used to be well contented with
one dish of meat, one fire, etc., has now three or four times
as many. His wife has her card parties. She must be in
the present fashion, with no stays; petticoat seams pinned
to the cravat, and the arms coming out at the pocket-holes
—she must go to the play-house in winter, to watering
places in summer, and to Ashley's Amphitheatre in Autumn
—in his shop is seldom a serving woman to be seen, but
several well-powdered gentlemen to serve with all the
politeness required by the first female characters." [1]

This unwonted demand for luxury has forced prices up-
ward, and the chief gainers are speculators, landowners and
merchants. People on fixed incomes have a hard time of it,
but " laborers having nothing to subsist on but their daily
bread must ever be behindhand in advancing the price of
their labor." Inasmuch as the laborer fares so badly, the
price of his labor should be raised in proportion to the price
of provisions. It would be advisable, even, for the government to pass a law to that effect, for "if provisions continue
so dear that the poor people cannot procure a moderate
sufficiency to supply their necessary wants, discontent will
more and more take place, and hungry stomachs and thin
clothing will weaken attachment to the constitution." [2]

It is not only the merchants and large proprietors who
are condemned. The farmer also receives his meed of
criticism. A pamphlet published in Birmingham discloses
the fact that the farmer's love of luxury is the evil pro-

---

[1] *The Crying Frauds of the London Markets, Proving their Deadly
Influence upon Two Great Pillars of Life—Bread and Porter,* by the
author of *The Cutting Butchers' Appeal; cf. Remarks on the Present
Times, Exhibiting the Causes of the High Price of Provisions,* by
James McPhail, *passim.*

[2] *Ibid.,* p. 113. McPhail believed that a reform in morality was the
greatest need of Great Britain.

genitor of all disaster. " When we consider," begins the narrative, " the numberless wretched objects which everywhere present themselves to our view; men bowed down with scanty fare and hard labor—women covered with poverty and rags—children by shoals, bare-footed and bare-legged, gathering the void of brutes to procure substance—while we reflect on this and the numerous complaints assailing our ears on every side, we are naturally led to inquire what can be the cause of so much wickedness."

The writer then dismisses political corruption, taxation, the war, and the slackness of trade as reasons, and insists that the " dearness of provisions " is the determining factor. His explanation of that dearness is somewhat peculiar. " The possession of wealth," he says, " is generally displayed in pomposity and affected grandeur, consequently it is no easy matter to distinguish between the land holder and the land owner. To clip the aspiring wings of the former, the latter advance their rents proportionably to the price of grain, etc., so that the farmer is obliged to return to his soil. . . . Avarice is never satisfied, but often disappointed. Not profiting by this experience, the farmer, taking advantage of the times, has gone on advancing his grain." Then the process is repeated again and again. The silly farmer, according to our writer, no sooner raises his prices than the proprietor raises his rental, to teach him that he is only a farmer after all.

For this the silly farmer is responsible. If he does not mend his ways the government will yield to the demand of the poor, and will then give a bounty on grain. When that happens the farmer will be sorry. " His prancing hocking," his chaise and pair, will then be set aside. The authorities will lend a hand, the author thinks, and if a bounty is not feasible, why, the government can fix the price of wheat. Already, assize of bread in London deter-

mines one price. Why should not a local custom be made
national? At any rate, British manufacturers are no better
than those on the Continent, consequently better markets
will do us no good. We must have cheaper food.[1]

To summarize these prevalent theories of monopolies
and extravagance we cannot do better than to glance at a
certain popular pamphlet, the " Rights of Swine." " Hard
indeed must be the heart," it begins, " which is unaffected
with the present distress experienced by the poor in general
in this commercial kingdom." Many thousands of people
are starving, we are told, and why? Corn and grass provide directly, or indirectly, the chief food of mankind.
Trade and commerce affect neither corn nor grass. " Corn
grows, not in the loom, nor grass upon the anvil." The
reason must be sought elsewhere. " The wealthy and vul-
uptuous " raise the rents of houses and of land. "Hearken,
O ye poor of the land," the address continues, ". . . the
present want of bread among the poor of the land is not
owing to the want of grain in the world, nor I presume in
this land, but owing to the price of it being excessive
above the price of the laborer." The address then shows
how wages have fluctuated up and down while land rent
has always steadily increased in value. In the existing law
the poor have no protection against that sort of danger.
Game laws, riot acts, etc., protect the rich, but where is
there a law which protects the poor? " Open your eyes, O

[1] *A Letter Addressed to the Farmers on the High Price of Provisions,*
by H. of Walsall, Birmingham, 1796. The title states, "originally
designed for the Birmingham and Stafford Chronicle, but refused
insertion by them." The *Birmingham Chronicle* took note of this
pamphlet as follows: "Our old friend H., from Walsall, we esteem for
his head and heart, but we must avoid the insertion of anything which
tends to render the children of distress still more unhappy by magnifying the causes of their calamity."

ye poor of the land! In vain are your hands and your mouths open . . . Is it not monstrously provoking to be robbed by wholesale and relieved by retail! Look again, and you will see that public collections, subscriptions, and charities are nothing more than the appendages of corruption, extortion and oppression. . . . Say not, therefore, ye oppressed 'there is a famine, or a scarcity of provisions in the land.' It would be false. The land contains plenty; and if provisions were (as they ought to be) reduced to your wages, you would enjoy your unquestionable rights— a comfortable sufficiency." [1]

These monopolies crushed down the farm laborer to the status of a pauper; kept wages stationary; raised prices; controlled markets; ruined retailers; injured the fertility of the soil; and day by day brought Great Britain nearer and nearer to the verge of starvation. But while monopolies, with the attendant luxuries and extravagances which follow in their train were particularly execrated, the " pestiferous novelties " in agricultural and manufacturing methods by no means escaped the condemnation of the reformers.

One writer claimed that the new breed of sheep, fatter and larger than the old kind, was in a measure responsible for the high price of meat. " It is more than probable," he says, " that the great noise which has been made of late years about increasing the size of livestock is a species of quackery, which is a real loss to the nation. Small animals

---

[1] *State Trials,* xxiv, 745. For other denunciations of monopolies and extravagance, see Governor Pownall, *Consideration on the Scarcity of Corn and Bread, Cambridge,* 1795. By hair powder, starch, paste, and by upholsterers, paperhangers, bookbinders, etc., he tells us flour is extravagantly wasted. *Cf. On Monopoly and a Reform in Manners,* 1795; *The British Tocsin,* 2d ed., 1795; *Observations on the Present High Price of Corn,* Bristol, 1795; *Letter to Pitt on the Cause of the High Price of Provisions,* Hereford, 1795.

take on much more in proportion to their food than large
ones for obvious reasons. First, the surface of the small
animal is much more in proportion to their weight than
large ones, and as the fat is mostly laid on the surface, they
have consequently a larger space to lay it on. Second,
the muscular fibres of small animals are less tense than
those of large ones, and admit more easily of that proportion of the fat which is insinuated in the process of fatten-
ing with the interior vesicles of muscular flesh." [1]

The foe of large cattle denounced the horse also. He
estimated the number of horses in Great Britain at two
million. It took three acres to provide provender for a
horse. The horses, then, of the United Kingdom, needed
six million acres for their support. This idea that the
horse was largely responsible for the high price of provisions, is echoed by other writers, one author, indeed, demanding that it be made illegal for a vehicle to be drawn
by more than two horses. An exception is made in favor
of the king, who may be drawn *ad libitum.*

More frequently do we meet with criticisms of new
methods in manufacturing. We are told that " the uncertainty of labor conditions is the most vicious result of
these new innovations. Caprice of fashion causes by fits
and starts a great demand for one species of goods and a
cessation of demand for another; and thus workmen who
are to-day fully employed may be to-morrow in the streets
begging their bread." [2] The uncertainty of factory labor
is often attacked. So also is the new-fangled machinery
which displaced so rapidly old and valued industries. An
anonymous author in 1794 bitterly assails the new spinning machinery. " A wooden wheel, costing two shillings

[1] Alexander Dirom, *An Inquiry into the Corn Laws and Corn Trade,*
Edinburgh, 1796.

[2] Davies, *The Case of the Laborers, passim.*

for each person, with one reel, costing three shillings " provided the old plant, which could be used by the women of the family, who would thus not be exposed to the evil effects of working in a factory. It is a crime to take little girls away from home, and place them in a factory without protection, under the sway of some overseer. Aside from the evil influence of that sort of thing they will not learn the arts of housewifery. Since machinery has come into use women and children are idle. A woman cannot work in the fields; after her house work is done she has much leisure time. Is it not better to employ it in spinning than in idleness? Formerly a widow could get along when she was paid one penny a skein, but now that twenty girls do the work of two thousand women, the widow is made a pauper. Then, too, the new machine product is inferior. Hand-work wool is much better twisted, and cloth made from it lasts longer. What are the poor people going to do? Wool spinning, he states, is a national industry. It is not like the cotton industry in Manchester. There machinery is a good thing, for it does not supplant British labor, only East Indian. Winding silk, manufacturing netting for fishing boats, and other local industries exist in great number, but none is so generally practiced as the spinning of wool.[1]

A trenchant observer shows that there was some basis for these criticisms. In 1797, John Thelwal took a walking tour in the west of England. We quote from his notebook: "At Frome, cloth mill, women waiting for spare wool to be spun by hand 2½d. per pound; great work spin 2 lb. a day. Children in factory 1s. 6d. to 2s. 6d. per week.

---

[1] *Observation on the Detriment which is Supposed must Arise to the Family of every Cottage throughout the Kingdom from the Loss of Woolen Spinning by the Introduction of Machinery in that Work,* London, 1794.

Day, 14 hours. Pallid and miserable. Women who pick knots off work." [1]

Just how this situation was to be combated the radical party did not know, nor did it greatly care. Universal suffrage and annual Parliaments would find a way. The details of reform could safely be left to the future. A certain Catharine Phillips, however, was not satisfied with generalities, and we owe to her a carefully-outlined platform of eight specific, if somewhat peculiar, reforms. First, public granaries should be built. Second, tithes of all kinds should be abolished. Tithes Miss Phillips considered the most detrimental factor in the industrial situation. "It is a barbarous custom," she said. "They ought not to be tolerated in a Christian country. For one man to be allowed to take a tenth of the whole produce is shocking to humanity, for he has labored but very little—perhaps not at all, as many parishes are served by curates, at small expense to the rectors." Third, the number of dogs should be lessened. Fourth, the number of small farms should also be increased. Fifth, hair powder should no longer be used. Sixth, fishing ought to be encouraged, and on that account taxes should be taken from salt, and settlements should be made along the north of Scotland. Seventh, oxen should be used more generally in place of horses. They should also be equipped with collars, instead of yokes. Eighth, the barren and waste lands should be planted and cultivated at

[1] Cestre, *Thelwal*, p. 164. These jottings bear the ear-marks of truth. We may be still further assured of their trustworthiness if we take notice of Thelwal's approval of the healthy conditions which prevailed in certain newer and larger manufactories. Thelwal indeed, though a warm hearted and emotional man, was in many ways a stern realist, fairly immune to superficial sentimentalities. "Filth and rags but tolerably healthy" was his caustic description of one woolen manufactory.

the expense of the national government for the benefit of the entire community.[1]

Thomas Paine also brought forward a proposal to diminish economic misery. In 1797, he published his " Agrarian Justice." This little pamphlet was called forth by a sermon of Bishop Watson on the subject of God's beneficent intention in creating both rich and poor. Paine denied that God made men rich and poor. " He made only male and female and gave them the earth for their inheritance." Monopolization of the land has violated and not fulfilled God's will; and to make amends an inheritance tax ought to be laid on all landed property, the money thus collected to form a vast national fund. Every person in Great Britain upon reaching the age of twenty-one years, whether poor or rich, male or female, is to be paid from it the sum of fifteen pounds. " When a young couple begin the world," argues Paine, " the difference is exceeding great whether they begin with nothing or with fifteen pounds apiece. With this aid they could buy a cow and implements to cultivate a few acres of land; and instead of becoming a burden upon society, which is always the case where children are produced faster than they can be fed, they would be put in the way of becoming useful and profitable citizens." [2]

The diffuse though specific remedies of Catharine Phillips and the proposed inheritance tax of Paine's "Agrarian Justice," were trifling and half-way measures to Thomas Spence. He alone of all the British radicals un-

[1] Catharine Phillips, *Considerations on the Causes of the High Price of Grain, and other Articles of Provision for a Number of Years Past, and Propositions for Reducing them, with Occasional Remarks,* London, 1792.

[2] Paine, *Agrarian Justice,* 1797, *passim.* Conway, *Life of Paine,* ii, 251.

derstood in its full significance the economic basis of human society. " It is childish," he claimed, " to expect ever to see small farms again, or ever to see anything else than the utmost screwing and grinding of the poor till you quite overturn the present system of landed property." The landlords, he said, are " a warlike enemy quartered upon us for the purpose of raising contributions. William the Conqueror and his Normans were fools [compared] to them in the art of fleecing, and therefore anything short of the total destruction of the power of these Samsons will not do, and that must be accomplished not by simple shaving, which leaves the roots of new strength to grow again. No: we must scalp them, or else they will soon re- cover and pull our temple of liberty about our ears." [1]

The advisability of scalping the landlords did not appeal to the rank and file of the radicals. Poor Spence finally admitted that he was held up to the public as a fool and a madman, and that " the greater part think it would be best to treat me and my opinions with contempt.[2] These spe- cific reforms, indeed, created little stir. The truth was that the radicals were chiefly interested in political reform. Here and there, to be sure, desultory pamphlets would ap- pear urging economic innovations. There were many criti- cisms of the oat-devouring horse; and suggestions for state granaries were fairly numerous.[3] But there was no

---

[1] Spence, *The Restorer of Society to Its Natural State in a Series of Letters to a Fellow Citizen,* Letter V. In defence of this gory theory Spence says: " It is plain that if the lords of the Philistines had scalped Samson instead of shaving him, they might have saved both themselves and their temples."

[2] Spence, *The Trial of Thomas Spence,* p. 67, bound with *The Constitution of the Perfect Commonwealth,* 1798.

[3] E. S. Gray, *A Proposal for Supplying London with Bread.* In these granaries a huge supply of grain is to be stocked, and fortifica- tions are to be built around them. *Idem, A Letter to the Honorable*

common platform, no unified specific demand which, in
the world of economic thought, might compare with annual
Parliaments and universal suffrage. There was, indeed, a
widespread feeling that wages should be higher, but the
feeling had not crystallized into a definite plan.

A hint, a suggestion, however, of how this was to come
about we may gather from an advertisement which appeared in a Norwich paper: "Day Laborers." It read:
"At a numerous meeting of the day laborers in the little
parishes of Heacham, Snettishham and Sedgford, this
day, 5th November, in the parish of Heacham, in the
county of Norfolk, in order to take into consideration the
best and most peaceful mode of obtaining redress of all
the severe and peculiar hardships under which they have
so many years painfully suffered, the following resolutions were unanimously agreed to: 1st, that—*The laborer
is worthy of his hire,* and that the mode of lessening his
distress, as hath been lately the fashion, by selling him flour
under the market price, and thereby rendering him the object of a parish rate, is not only an indecent insult to his
lonely and humble situation, in itself [sufficiently mortify-
ing from his degrading dependence upon the caprice of his
employer], but a fallacious mode of relief, and every way
inadequate to a radical redress of the manifold distresses of
his calamitous state; 2nd, that the price of labor shall at
all times be proportioned to the price of wheat, and should
be invariably regulated by the average price of that necessity of life." The advertisement states further that this is
the only way by which the status of the laborer as a self-
respecting man may be maintained, and it invites assistance
and co-operation from all of his friends. If they will

*the Corn·Committee on the Importation of Rough Rice as a Supple-
ment of Wheaten flour,* London, 1796. This writer justifies granaries,
from Genesis, XLI.

write to Adam More, laborer, at Heacham, postage pre-
paid, they will receive further information concerning the
proposal.[1]

The intimation, in this advertisement, of a minimunm
wage may also be supplemented by the proposal of one
lone member of the House of Commons. Samuel Whitbread, contemptuously termed by Byron " The Demos-
thenes of vulgar vehemence," though a Whig member of
Parliament, had distinctly radical leanings. He frequently
acted independently of party, and particularly when his
humanitarian sympathies were aroused. In 1795 he
brought in a bill to revive an old act of Elizabeth's. This
act provided that justices of the peace might assess the
wages of laborers in husbandry. The law had been passed
to prevent laborers from striking for a higher wage, and
to that end had been amended and revised in the reign of
James I and George II.[2] Whitbread now proposed government action to keep wages from falling too low. He explained, in the House, that the act of Queen Elizabeth em-
powered justices of the peace to fix the maximum reward
of labor. His bill, he stated, only went so far as to em-
power them to fix the minimum.

In this measure Whitbread received practically no support. Fox addressed the House in one of his long, meaningless speeches, more filled with denunciation of the government than with feeling for the poor. A certain Mr.
Burden denied that the price of labor was inadequate to
the price of provisions; he knew of places where the laborers were able to accumulate money. And Dundas followed
in the same strain, with a few remarks anent the lateness
of the season, and the failure of the crops.[3] Whitbread's

---

[1] Young, *Annals*, xxv, 503.

[2] Hammond, *Village Laborers*, pp. 133 *et seq.*

[3] *Parliamentary Register*, liii, 648.

bill was negatived at its second reading without a division. Upwards of six score years were to pass ere the " wildcat " theory of Samuel Whitbread was to meet with the approbation of a British Parliament.

SECTION II

CHAPTER I

THE RADICAL SOCIETIES. THEIR GENERAL AIM AND PURPOSE

THE QUASI-RADICAL SOCIETIES REVIEWED. THE LONDON
CORRESPONDING SOCIETY AND ITS ALLIES. THEIR THREE-
FOLD PROPAGANDA: CORRESPONDENCE, PUBLICATIONS AND
PUBLIC MEETINGS

THE British radicals made little headway in putting
their theories into practice. Unforseen circumstances
played havoc with their plans. Prejudices, bitter and un-
yielding, blocked their progress, while a Tory government,
lynx-eyed and unrelenting, rendered their designs abortive.
Yet, despite this failure of organized radicalism, the story
of what was undertaken serves not only as a commentary
upon the radical movement, but likewise as a mirror in
which are reproduced the social conflicts, prejudices and en-
thusiasms of the British people.

In the history of this radical campaign a noteworthy
distinction exists between the radical leaders in theory and
the radical leaders in practice. Paine did not return to
England after 1791. To Godwin and Bentham the philosopher's chair was more congenial than the platform or the
committee-room. Mackintosh and Frend, however radical in theory, knew not how to hobnob with the common
people. Gerrald, it is true, was a prominent member of the
London Corresponding Society, but his deportation soon
cut him off from his associates; and Thelwal, though a
popular speaker, had but little weight as an organizer or

leader. Furthermore, existing conditions made radical representation in Parliament impossible. Thus no radical nucleus could assist in the formation of a party, or in the conduct of a campaign.

Yet both party and campaign there must be, and the solution was simple. Several radical clubs and debating societies had sprung up in Great Britain. Their number could be multiplied; uniform constitutions could be formulated; common purposes and actions settled upon. A convention of these societies might draw still closer the bonds of unity. And, indeed, an executive committee of this convention, secret if need be, might concentrate even more effectively the political pressure which these societies might bring to bear. It was hoped by these means that a powerful and unified force would dislodge, and perhaps cast aside, the dead weight of conservative authority and prestige. The plan was good in theory; in practice it proved ineffectual.

If we are to judge fairly and comprehensively the organized work of the British radicals, it is necessary for us to hasten over the career of certain societies which, for one reason or another, received more popular attention than their real influence warranted. "The Revolution Society," "The Society of the Friends of the People," and "The London Society for Constitutional Information," were of this character. Strictly speaking, the first two of these societies were not even radical. Their history, however, is so interwoven with that of radicalism that cognizance must be taken of them.

The Revolution Society may best be described in the words of its steward, who declares it composed of "all gentlemen who wished well to the principles of the revolution. To them a general invitation is issued to dine at a London tavern, where, for seven shillings and sixpence,

they may get as good a dinner and as much sherry, punch
and port as they liked, and leave, well contented with
their country." Quite innocuous were these old Whig *bon
vivants*. The revolution of 1688 was their excuse for
much wine and good fellowship. They assembled annually to recall with reverence and to applaud those noble
principles of freedom incorporated into the British Constitution in that year. In all the glory, laud and honor
offered these idealized concepts of liberty there was nothing revolutionary or militant. There was nothing revolutionary or militant about the society at all, save in the
name. The members were patriotic Englishmen; some of
them boasted that, through the crisis of the Regency Bill,
they had been more loyal to the king than the Whig Party,
and a bumper to King George never failed to conclude
their festivities.[1]

This society was based upon three principles of so-called
radicalism, the insistence upon which, in Dr. Price's sermon, so infuriated Burke. They were as follows: first,
that all civil and political authority is derived from the people; second, that abuse of power justifies resistance; third,
that rights of private judgment, liberty of conscience, trial
by jury, and freedom of election are ever to be held sacred
and inviolate. The events of 1789 in France were commonly interpreted in England as inspired by these same
ideals, and in consequence, as might have been expected, the
revolution in France found, at first, warm support in the
Revolution Society. This is indicated by its annual banquet
on November 4, 1789; for on that day, with Earl Stanhope
in the chair, Dr. Price made the following motion, that
" The Society for commemorating the Revolution in Great
Britain, disclaiming national partialities, and rejoicing in

[1] *A Letter to Edmund Burke by a member of the Revolution Society,
passim.*

every triumph of liberty and justice over arbitrary power,
offers to the National Assembly of France their congratulations on the revolution in that country, and on the pros-
pect it gives to the first two kingdoms of the world of a
common participation in the blessings of civil and religious
liberty." [1] To this congratulatory message the French National Assembly replied in equally felicitous terms. Much
mutual affection was displayed. Many were the verbal
courtesies exchanged; and in the meantime the opportunity
for an additional annual dinner in praise of liberty must
not be lost. The Revolution Society gladly embraced the
opportunity, and July fourteenth became only less hallowed
than November fourth.

No trouble arose in 1790. By 1791, however, bitterness
and animosity broke out beyond the power of a good dinner
to allay. Many of the more influential members began to
absent themselves from its feasts. Fox and Sheridan no
longer came. It was said that they feared the occurrence
of riots.[2] When the society met on July 14, 1791, twenty-
one toasts were drunk, including the " Rights of Man,"
the " Sovereignty of the People," " Ireland and her band
of Patriots," "George Washington and the liberty of North
America," " the Memory of Dr. Price, the Apostle of Liberty and the friend of Mankind," " the Memory of Hamp-
ton, Locke, Franklin," etc. Speeches were many and per-
fervid. A French visitor extolled the virtues of the society,
and the occasion was also enlivened by spirited songs.[3]

---

[1] *Letter to Burke by a member of the Revolution Society, op. cit.,
appendix.*

[2] London *Morning Post*, July 15, 1791.

[3] *The Gentleman's Magazine* for 1791, Part II, p. 678. One song
begins:

> " Not now the venial tribe shall raise
> The song of prostituted praise."

The withdrawal of the leaders, coupled with the course of events in France, caused the downfall of the society. It lingered on for some time, but became less and less conspicuous as the years passed by.[1]

More serious in purpose, but even less radical in tone, were the Friends of the People. This society was organized on the eleventh of April, 1792, to obtain Parliamentary reform. To this end a declaration was drawn up and one hundred and forty-seven gentlemen subscribed, including twenty members of the House of Commons. The initiation fee was placed at two and one-half guineas, with annual dues of the same amount. The aim of this society as officially announced was: first, to restore the freedom of election by an equitable representation of the people in Parliament; second, to restore to the people a more equal and more frequent exercise of their right of voting. With this purpose in view it was hoped that similar societies throughout the country might co-operate with the London group. The hope never materialized. Grey presented the petition of the society in Parliament, only to be greeted with scorn and derision.

Outside of London the society had no influence. It held aloof from other political societies, and with the more radical associations would have no dealings. The Friends of the People, with the passing of the decade, gradually sank into insignificance. After the treason trials of 1794, their sessions virtually ceased.[2]

---

[1] On August 20, 1791 a meeting of the society in the Thatched House Tavern subscribed fifty pounds for the diffusion of Paine's writings. The landlord thereupon refused the use of his premises for future occasions.

Extracts from the proceedings and correspondence of the Revolution Society are given in *The Annual Register* for 1792.

[2] Francis Place, in his *Scrap Book, British Museum Additional Manu-*

The London Constitutional Society was organized on a different basis. It was genuinely radical, and stood in much closer sympathy with the main current of radical opinion and action. This society owed its origin to the excitement of the Wilkes controversy. Originally intended as a vehicle for promoting constitutional knowledge and the traditional liberties of England, it was galvanized into new life by the quickened popular interests in political and social reform coincident with the French Revolution. The erratic Major Cartwright was chairman of this association; and, as he and his friends were viewed askance by Fox and other Parliamentary reformers in the House of Commons, no understanding existed between the Friends of the People and the London Constitutional Society. Indeed, for a time the latter body was the leading radical organization. Paine entrusted to it his " Rights of Man," and as agent for the distribution of that book the society was regarded with deep suspicion by all 'opponents of Paine. Overtures were made to it by the other radical clubs, and these overtures were welcomed. To all appearance the future was secure.

The society took a prominent part in popularizing radical theory. " The Rights of Man " was widely distributed besides other pamphlets, such as Paine's " Letter to Secretary Dundas," of which 8,962 copies were sent to local distributors to be scattered throughout the country.[1]

Nevertheless, soon after 1792 the society began to decline in both influence and membership. Internal dissension was largely responsible for this. Many members, in-

scripts, 27,808, p. 18, tells us that a few members met afterwards in a desultory fashion. For the treason trials, *vid. infra,* pp. 197 *et seq.*

[1] *State Trials,* xxv, 167.

deed, never approved of Paine, and some of them seceded
for that reason.[1]   The advisability of sending a delegate
to the Edinburgh Convention was likewise a source of
friction, and, although a delegate was finally sent, the disgruntled opposition soon deserted the society.[2]

A prolific correspondence also was carried on with other
clubs and societies.   The nature of this, cautious in spirit
if not in word, indicated an attitude indifferent and lukewarm toward more radical associations throughout Great
Britain.   But there was no room for middle-of-the-road
opinion after 1792, and from that year on the membership
of the London Constitutional Society rapidly diminished.
The bred-in-the-bone radical found a more effective out-
let for his work elsewhere.   The timid and more moderate
thought it wiser to withdraw.

To find sustained enthusiasm, we must look to certain
other clubs and associations, quite different in character
from the three already mentioned.   Societies recruited
from a more proletarian source: mechanics, craftsmen,
and the petty tradesfolk, existed throughout the island.
They were particularly strong in the great factory towns.

The genesis of the London Corresponding Society was
widely different from that of its more aristocratic neigh-
bors.   It may be traced to a conversation carried on by
Thomas Hardy, a London shoemaker, as early as 1791.
The first meeting was held on June 22, 1792, with a total

---

[1] The number of seceders was said to have been kept secret. *Public
Advertiser*, March 23, 1792.   Among them, however, was Grey. *Jordan's Parliamentary Journal*, January 4, 1793.

[2] The Constitutional Society refused to take any part in a future convention, according to the only member of the society in the House of
Commons, a Mr. Thompson. *The Senator* for 1794, p. 1249.

attendance of eight persons.[1]   By the second of February,
the muster roll included seventeen; a week later twenty-
five; and very shortly after this time, it was believed that
sufficient headway had been made to divulge the aims and
purposes of the society.   Encouraged by the endorsement
of the Duke of Richmond, a little printed statement was
issued, in which were incorporated his words as follows: " These facts are self-evident, and need no comment.   Let us look at this metropolis, and see that the
majority of its inhabitants have no vote.   It is the
view or intention of this society to collect the opinions of
all of the unrepresented part of the people as far as possible,
for they are certainly the persons aggrieved, and have the
greatest possible right to stand forward like men for their
privileges.   If they are united and firm, who are they that
dare oppose them in their determination? " [2]   This statement, issued February 13, 1793, was the first public announcement of the London Corresponding Society.

The society, its initial bow once made, proceeded to or-
ganize.   A committee on constitutions was appointed,
which began its work by announcing a tentative set of
eight rules.   The more important of these provided for
general meetings, unlimited membership, and a central
committee of correspondence to communicate with other
societies.   These rules, expanded and amended, became
the constitution of the London Corresponding Society.
The document is long, detailed and explicit.   Any individual proposed by two members might join, on affirming
his belief in the necessity of manhood suffrage.   For the
automatic and orderly growth of the society it was to be
divided into as many sections or divisions " as there shall

[1] *Place MSS.,* 27,808, p. 13.
[2] *Ibid.,* 27,811.

be thirty members to make up the number requisite for such division." Every division was to meet once a week, and every member was to pay a penny a week dues, while a central committee was to be formed, consisting of a delegate from each division.[1] To attend a meeting, tickets of admission were required, bearing the owner's name and that of the secretary.[2] In the general meetings, reports were presented from each division, followed by a debate on the question before the house. A typical meeting seems to have been that of the 6th of December, 1792. On that occasion there were put before the house several reports of interrupted meetings. A motion for the gratuitous admission of soldiers was withdrawn, and bail was raised for an arrested bill-sticker.[3]

The Beaufort Building in the Strand was for a long time the centre of the radical propaganda. The room of the central committee of the London Corresponding Society was fitted with benches and desks, after the manner of a school. The president's chair was at the end of the room, in a sort of pulpit raised three feet from the floor.[4] It was said that the meetings frequently became very crowded. In 1795, when there were seventy divisions of the society, there foregathered in this place a delegate and sub-delegate from each division. Visiting radicals were admitted to the floor, and it is small wonder that the stuffiness of the room aroused much complaint.

The work of this society and its allied associations was largely confined to three main channels. Through corres-

---

[1] *Place MSS.*, 27,813, p. 36.

[2] *Ibid.*, 27,814, p. 168.

[3] *Manuscript Journal* of the London Corresponding Society, *Place MSS.*, 27,812, vol. ii (the pages in this Journal are not numbered).

[4] *Place MSS.*, 27,808, p. 28.

pondence, through the publication and diffusion of radical petitions and tracts, and through public meetings, a thorough reform of society was sought. Without organization it was recognized that the widespread spirit of unrest throughout the nation would be of little avail. Local organization would not be sufficient. Closer cohesion must be had, and to this end an elaborate system of correspondence was initiated by the London Corresponding Society.

In London proper, overtures were first made to the earlier existent Constitutional Society. In March, 1792, was sent this modest request for mutual co-operation: "We shall accordingly be happy to enter into correspondence with your society, if it is not too much presumption to expect such an honor." [1] To this address the Constitutional Society replied in friendly fashion—more friendly, perhaps, than it intended, for the humbler Corresponding Society, emboldened by the reply, requested a closer affiliation.[2] At this the Constitutional Society balked, but consented to admit six members of the Corresponding Society to honorary membership. This partial alliance led to nothing. The Corresponding Society gradually tired of its supplicatory rôle, and finally, in 1794, wrote sharply to this effect: "The London Corresponding Society conceives that the moment is arrived when a full and explicit declaration is necessary from all the friends of freedom. . . . The Society for Constitutional Information is therefore required to determine whether or no they will be ready when called upon to act in conjunction with this and other societies." [3] The London Constitutional Society, however, had no intention of incriminating itself, and, although re-

---

[1] *Place MSS.*, 27,811.

[2] *Ibid.*, 22,814, p. 172.

[3] *State Trials*, xxiv, 562.

turning a conciliatory answer, refused to engage in co-operative action.

Outside of London, greater success was met with. As early as May, 1792, a general address was drawn up and distributed to the various reform associations of the country. A quick-fire exchange of letters between these societies at once began. Apparently the London Corresponding Society became the tacitly recognized head of this movement. Some organizations submitted themselves to its guidance. Others proffered aid. Some sent money, while from many sources came tales of disaster; we hear of defaulting treasurers, betrayal within and oppression without. Many complained that no attention was paid to their communications, frequently expressing their fear that the post-office would confiscate their missives.

Graphic accounts set forth conditions in widely separated localities.[1] The Derby correspondent wrote that the Militia Bill had met there with much opposition. " Two radical meetings have been held. Five hundred people were present, while the cavalry and the fifteenth infantry were under arms. I had a strong contention with Justice Murray," he writes. " He read the riot act and threatened to arrest me. The miners themselves are determined to reply to force by force." A parade then followed, in which an effigy of Pitt was carried, and the writer closes with these words: " Afterwards I attempted two meetings, but no sooner had I begun to address the people than an old Justice of the Peace ordered me to be arrested. The citi-

[1] For correspondence with Sheffield, Edinburgh, Birmingham, Newcastle, Bristol, Norwich and Hertford, see *State Trials*, xxiv, 406, 407, 410, 483, 484, 485, 486 respectively. For further information from Birmingham and Sheffield, see *Place MSS.*, 27,813, pp. 365 and 565. For the financial affairs of the Sheffield Society, and an abridged constitution; and also for correspondence with Norwich, Exeter, Portsmouth and Manchester, see *Place MSS.*, 27,815, p. 93.

zens present surrounded me, declaring that they would sooner die than allow me to be taken. Had I not interposed, the parson would have surely been thrown into the river." [1]

Fertile in expedients and ideas are some of these associations. Sometimes they even take the initiative. As an illustration, we find the friends of the people in Norwich calling on the London Society to join with them in procuring a smaller and more equitable division of all of the land of the country, as a reasonable means of both lowering prices, and providing employment. [2]

Although in this correspondence first place was accorded to clubs and societies, letters to and from individuals are frequently recorded. An editor was told to "pluck up courage; that the clergy and courtiers are not so numerous as they appear." [3] Resolutions and addresses to individuals were frequently accompanied by a personal appeal, carefully and respectfully worded. Such a one was sent to a certain Mr. Hollis, and signed by Thomas Hardy. " I trust you will pardon me," writes Hardy, " the freedom taken with you, sir, but I do assure you it proceeds from an ardent zeal to propagate the knowledge of our design to the friends of freedom, that they may have an opportunity of writing in promoting that important cause in which we are engaged. Any information from you tending to accelerate that grand design, would be cordially received." By letters of this kind, sent out as feelers, important data were gathered as to the number and, more important still, the names of possible converts or allies. [4]

---

[1] *Place MSS.*, 27,814, p. 156.

[2] *Public Advertiser*, May 26, 1792.

[3] *Place MSS.*, 27,814, p. 187.

[4] March 9, 1792, Hardy writes to Rev. Mr. Bryant, of Sheffield, and after some preliminary compliments, requests the addresses of Sheffield men. *Place MSS.*, 27,811.

Again, letters, printed and distributed very much as
handbills, were circulated with copies of the society's resolutions. They were sent apparently in accordance with a
regular system. First of all a man with suspected radical
sympathies would receive a letter reading: " Dear Sir:
Knowing you to be a friend of freedom, I take the liberty
of sending you a copy. . . ." If this communication met
with no reply, a second appeal was sent. It informed the
reader that the people seemed very happy in hugging their
delusions. " I shall not disturb their repose," continues the
writer, "nor trouble you with any more of our crude
thoughts until I have an answer from you." [1]

The society was not always so painstaking in its correspondence. It replied sharply to one correspondent, whose
address it had refused to receive, " Your statements are too
low and contemptuous." Or perhaps, on the other hand,
caution and moderation are advised, as may be seen in answer to a letter from a certain Martin in Turo, who wrote
" that the inhabitants are at a white heat in the republican
cause, and ready to strike at the root of the matter." [2]

The published writings of the London Corresponding
Society comprised addresses, petitions, and public appeals
of one sort or another. Their first address is dated May,
1791. After a preamble, stating the necessity of reform,
and relating the circumstances of the society's foundation,
the address pleads for popular support in these words:
" Inasmuch as every individual has a right to share in the
government, it behooves each and every citizen to keep a
watchful eye upon the government." [3]

[1] *Place MSS.*, 27,814, p. 185.

[2] *Ibid.*, 27,815. In the Manuscript Minutes of the society, the word
republican is scratched out, and the word sentimental substituted.

[3] *State Trials*, xxiv, 378.

This address " to the public " is followed shortly by a more elaborate one, " to the British nation." We are told that notoriously burdensome taxes exist in Great Britain; that the cause of this grievance lies in the corrupt composition and venal practices of the House of Commons; and that the Corresponding Society exists for the purpose of inquiring into and making public " the exact state of the present Parliamentary representation—for obtaining a peaceful but adequate remedy to this intolerable grievance, and for corresponding and co-operating with other societies, founded for the same object." [1] Further details dealing with the constitution of the society follow. The address concludes with an array of facts and figures to the effect that a majority of the House of Commons are returned by not more than one-thousandth part of the nation.[2] Later in the same year was issued an "Address to the inhabitants of Great Britain," and from time to time other addresses were issued, in purport and tenor differing but little from those we have already quoted.

Petitions of the society were sent to various men of prominence. Dundas, the arch enemy of radicalism, was the recipient of one of these. On the fourth of December, 1792, the society petitioned him in regard to certain illegal persecutions which they laid at his door. Margarot, with customary boldness, wrote: " I, therefore, in behalf of your fellow citizens, this day, call upon the king's ministers to protect and uphold us in the pursuit of our constitutional rights." He objected " to the saucy interference by usurped authority of men unnamed, working with threats upon the fears of uninformed publicans." [3]

---

[1] *State Trials,* xxiv, 380.   [2] *Ibid.,* p. 382.

[3] *Journal of the London Corresponding Society, Place MSS.,* 27,812, vol. ii.

The activities of the Corresponding Society met with little sympathy from men of high rank. That Dundas would regard their claims with a favorable eye was scarcely within the bounds of possibility. A different treatment might have been expected from Fox. Yet when the society requested him to present their petition to Parliament, the Whig leader replied quite coldly that he was willing to present their petition, but at the same time he confessed that " it might with more propriety be presented by some other member, as it was understood that a radical reform was contended for with universal suffrage, to which he had always been an avowed enemy." [1]

Notwithstanding this snubbing in aristocratic quarters, the society planned a petition to the king himself. In " An address to the King's Majesty," the petition ran, " we approach with reverence, but with firmness, to lay before you our grievances, in order that you may redress them." [2]

It was one thing to plan this petition, and quite another to get it before the eyes of King George. A deputation was sent to deliver it to the Secretary of State, so that it might reach the king through the regular channels. It never did,—it reached only the privy council. Another committee waited upon the Duke of Portland, and handed their document to his servant, who carried it to the ducal secretary. The servant brought back word that there would be no answer. He was then sent again by the delegates to inquire, apparently, whether the petition would be received. The reply this time was that mes-

---

[1] *Journal London Corresponding Society, Place MSS.,* 27,812.

[2] *Ibid.* Before the attempted presentation the petition was changed to read: " We approach you in the exercise of our constitutional right to lay before you the distresses of the people occasioned by the present war." This address was afterwards printed and distributed in London by order of the society.

sages could only be received in writing. Finally, the inquiry having been made in writing, the servant returned after a long interval, to announce that the Duke of Portland had gone out.[1]

Two other publications of the society are of particular interest to us. One of them is entitled, " The London Corresponding Society's Addresses and Publications; " the other, " The State of Representation in England and Wales." In the former, the fundamental ideals of the society are clearly set forth. " Numerous as our grievances are," we read, " reform one alone and the others will disappear. What we must have," it argues, is

> "An Honest Parliament,
> An Annual Parliament,
> A Parliament where each individual will have his
> representative.

Soon then we shall see our liberties restored, the press free, the laws simplified, judges unbiased, juries independent, needless places and pensions retrenched, immoderate salaries reduced, the public better served, taxes diminished, and the necessaries of life more within the reach of the poor." [2] And among other very happy results, this Utopian Parliament was confidently expected to secure the breaking-up of large farms, the depopulation of prisons and the reform of the English Poor Law.

The other pamphlet (and with this we close our consideration of the publications of the society, was the report of a committee of the Friends of the People. The report, revised, condensed and reprinted by the London Corresponding Society, and one of its offshoots, " The Reforming

[1] *Place MSS.*, 27,813, p. 365.

[2] *The London Corresponding Society's Addresses and Publications*, p. 15.

Society," was published May 14, 1795. By this time the Friends of the People had virtually disbanded. They had, however, laid bare in an exhaustive report the illogical inequalities of the state of British representation, and it was a clever move on the part of the London Corresponding Society thus to reproduce, for their own benefit, the conclusions of their more gifted, conservative neighbor. The report is a clean-cut statement which, without rhetoric, gives facts and figures to demonstrate the corruptions, delays and expense involved in electing the members of the House of Commons. No inference is drawn; no specific reform is demanded; the committee simply state the conditions as they find them, and conclude with a general statement which proves that seventeen boroughs, containing on the average under a hundred and fifty voters, return twenty-seven members, while 2,611 persons return 327 members. The total membership of the House was at this time 627. A majority, then, of 81 was returned by less than six thousand voters.

The London Corresponding Society, like other radical organizations, hoped to realize its aims through meetings as well as through correspondence and publications. Public meetings, apparently, did not take place early in its career but general meetings of the members were held, it is true, and to them the spies of the government found a ready admission. But no meeting for the public was held till the fourteenth of April, 1794. Not even this was called a public meeting of the society, but the fact that it was held in the open field between London and Hampstead, known as Chalk Farms, is indication that a more extensive gathering was looked for. The object of this meeting was to protest against the proceedings of the government in dispersing the British Convention. From two to three thousand people were said to have been present, and correspondence of great significance was made public.[1]

First, a communication from the London Corresponding Society to the Friends of the People was read. The Corresponding Society stated that " it earnestly solicits at this time the concurrence of the Friends of the People in assembling as speedily as the nature of the business will admit a convention of the Friends of Freedom. . . . The Friends of Reform are friends of peace . . . but they will not be alarmed by the threats of venal apostates. They will not draw back because they have seen some of their best friends doomed to die. . . . They will therefore look with confidence to the determination and to the co-operation of the Society of the Friends of the People in the attainment of an object which involves the dearest interests of society." [2] The answer of the Friends of the People was then read, assuring the Corresponding Society of their good will but at the same time declining to participate in the proposed convention. This refusal was received, save for a few hisses, in silence. The Friends of the People had, at any rate, been forced to show their hand.

After these letters, the society passed ten resolutions. Words of praise and comfort were spoken for the Edinburgh prisoners; the execution of Charles I and the expulsion of James II were referred to; the society announced its own determination to stand by the cause of freedom till the end; and ordered that 200,000 copies of the proceedings be published.[3]

---

[1] *State Trials*, xxiv, 22.   [2] *Ibid.*, xxiv, 735.

[3] The Chalk Farms meeting created little stir. *The Annual Register* does not mention it at all. The press gives but a curt notice. One excerpt only is particularly interesting. To quote *The Oracle and Public Advertiser*, May 20, 1794: " Citizens," said an orator addressing himself to the society, " a dagger is opposed to your views. The point is power; the handle property. Seize the handle and you can turn the point wherever you will."

In the following year the society held its largest meeting. On November twelfth a mass-meeting in Copenhagen Fields protested against the suppression of free speech by the Seditious Meetings Bill, and the continued suspension of the writ of *habeas corpus*. Francis Place, an eye-witness, tells us that "the number of people at the public meeting was certainly very large;" the Proceedings published by order of the society claim upwards of 150,000. This may be an exaggeration. There were, however, "three platforms, called tribunes, erected at what were supposed to be convenient distances. Each of these platforms was surrounded by a vast number of persons. So great, indeed, was the number, that not one-half of the spectators could get near enough to hear a single word of what was said by the speakers. . . . The purpose of the meeting was an address to the nation, a remonstrance to the king, and resolutions thought applicable to the alarming crisis." [1] In the history of freedom of speech this meeting has an important place. Much attention has accordingly been given to it by historians, and copious extracts from the proceedings are to be frequently met with. The same may be said of the other meetings of the society. The London Corresponding Society, as a defender of the rights of free speech, has had its full meed of attention, and that phase of its activity needs no further emphasis. A brief mention, however, of two meetings is of interest.

At the last public meeting of the society, held in June, 1795, in St. Mary-le-bone Fields, Regent's Park, among the resolutions passed we find, "that neither the Commons, nor the Lords, nor the King, nor the three combined can be considered as having the power to enslave the people, but that they may either separately or unitedly do such acts

[1] *Place MSS.*, 27,808, p. 39.

as would justify the resistance of the people."[1]   This was
the last meeting actually held after the passage of the
Treason and Sedition Bills.   A sporadic attempt was made
on July thirteenth, 1797, to hold another.   Notice of the
meeting was posted.   Then came a notice of the magistrates
forbidding it.   Conferences were held, with no result.   The
meeting was permitted to start.   Magistrates, stationed
with constables at the foot of every tribune, arrested the
speakers.[2]

These three campaign methods—correspondence, publications and public meetings—were the general means adopted
by the Corresponding Society.   Similar methods were
adopted by the other radical associations throughout the
nation.   Our information concerning them is far from full.
Yet we have sufficient data to conclude that the procedure
was not different from that outlined.

What was the strength of these societies?   In the *True
Briton* newspaper we are given Burke's estimate of the
number of pronounced radicals, or, as he called them,
Jacobins.   Burke believed that the total number of adults
of some standing in England approximated 400,000.   Of
these, he says one-fifth, or some 80,000, were Jacobins.
The *True Briton* states that this percentage was too large;[3]
the facts apparently would sustain its contention, and
as an indication of the correctness of the newspaper's
conclusion, we may be reasonably certain that the London
Corresponding Society had fewer members than was popularly believed.   The reputed number was upwards of five
thousand.   The minutes, however, which give us detailed information concerning the membership of the society at different times, tell another story.

[1] *Place MSS.*, 27,808, p. 64.   [2] *Ibid.*, p. 81.
[3] *The True Briton*, Monday, Jan. 30, 1797.

An effort was made early in the history of the organization to include all the societies outside of London in one
general national association.   This endeavor received a
set-back soon after its proposal, for we find that a motion
to send a letter to all the radical societies in the country,
inviting them to adopt our title " and to incorporate themselves with us," was negatived, on the ground that Tewks-
bury radicals had already declined such an offer.[1]   The
roll of the London Corresponding Society was accordingly
confined to London radicals, but this shows that the society at no time had more than two thousand members.[2]

The number of reformers incorporated in the other radical societies can only be surmised.   No reliance whatever
can be placed on the statement of the boastful Margarot.
that in Sheffield alone there were fifty thousand enrolled

[1] Journal London Corresponding Society, *Place MSS.*, 27,812.

[2] The first record that we have, shortly after the founding of the
society, details the number of men in each division.   At that time,
Thursday, October fourth, 1792, there were reported ten divisions, containing a membership of three hundred and eighty-seven.   Six weeks
from that date the number of divisions was fifteen.   In two more
weeks it had risen to twenty-seven, and on the fourth of April, 1792,
1328 signatures were on the muster roll.   During the opening year of
the French war, however, an actual decline occurred, for, with the
advent of the famous state trials, and the awakening radical enthusiasm of 1794, bringing as it did an increase of one hundred and
twenty-four in the month of July, the total number is only nine
hundred and seventy.   The next month a further increase took place.
A hundred and ninety-three new members were reported and, at a
general meeting of the society held in the same month, there were
present one thousand six hundred and forty-eight members.   This
is the largest actual count which we have.   At one of the public meetings of the society, nearly two thousand members were said to have
attended.   The society itself never officially claimed a larger membership.

radicals.[1] It is true that a Sheffield magistrate proclaimed
that there was in his town "a most horrid conspiracy
against state and church under the pretence of reform,"
and that various pikes, spears, and "cats" were there unearthed.   Nevertheless, to believe that there were fifty
thousand desperate radicals in and about Sheffield, when
London harbored but little over a thousand, is unthink-
able.   Magistrates, to be sure, were obsessed by the vision
of a red tide of anarchy.   The Rev. John Griffith, of Manchester, became tremendously excited over a suspected
"damning of Parliament," while Carles and Spence, two
magistrates of Birmingham, took great pride in ferreting
out malcontents.   In Norwich there was more cause for
alarm.   The city was said to have been a hot-bed of radicalism, and even the claim is made that the first intimation
of a general convention of the people came from Norwich.
Radicalism, indeed, must have been firmly entrenched there,
for in the city were some thirty different clubs.

London, Norwich and Edinburgh were the great centres
of the radical propaganda, yet the radical clubs in those
towns certainly contained no very large proportion of the
inhabitants, and it is not unfair to assume that in the country districts radicalism made less headway.   Burke's estimate of fifty thousand must be cut in half.   There is no
trustworthy evidence to show that more than one-tenth of
the adult male population was enrolled in the radical associations.

We may be equally certain that the financial backing of
these organizations was negligible.   Here again our only
detailed source of information is the minute book of
the London Corresponding Society, according to which,
the following provision was made for financial sup-

[1] *State Trials*, xxiii, 414.

port: " Each member shall pay to the section of his division one penny a week." [1] Averaging but little over a dollar a year for the individual, the society could hardly have been accused of affluence. Great difficulties were indeed encountered. On July nineteenth, 1792, we discover from the treasurer's books that the assets were nine pounds and five shillings. The liabilities at that time were six pounds, seven shillings and eleven pence.[2] This situation improved somewhat by the next year; when a mass-meeting was then debated, a total fund of over thirty pounds was on hand. During the following year the receipts of the treasurer show that between April ninth and June thirtieth, over sixty pounds was collected.[3] Taking this as an average quarter, the annual income of the society would appear to have been under two hundred pounds.[4]

[1] *State Trials*, xxiv, 380.

[2] *Journal of London Corresponding Society, Place MSS.*, 27,812.

[3] *Place MSS.*, 27,813, p. 365.

[4] *Place MSS.*, 27,808, p. 78.

Aid was received from outside sources for the legal expenses of defending indicted members. From Derby came four pounds four shillings. Portsmouth sent two subscriptions, and other towns aided. Erskine, also, in the trial of Hardy, gave his services free of charge, so that, for that trial the only expenses were seventeen shillings for subpoenaing witnesses. Frequently, however, the society was much put to it for money. Particularly was this true toward the end of its existence. Special circulars were sent to members urging a renewed generosity. This, however, availed but little, for by October, 1797, the receipts had dwindled to but little over thirty pounds. *Ibid.*, 27,815, p. 183.

CHAPTER II

THE BRITISH CONVENTION

ORIGIN, PROCEEDINGS AND DISPERSION. INNER PURPOSE OF
CONVENTION. THEORY OF THE GOVERNMENT SUB-
STANTIATED

WE have now outlined the major activities of organized
radicalism. Did it attempt other enterprises? And, if so,
were these endeavors legal, or illegal? Were they broached
merely as tentative suggestions, or were they in reality undertaken? We know that a convention of delegates did
actually convene at Edinburgh, November 29, 1793, for a
brief existence of fourteen days. What significance may
be attached to that meeting? What spirit animated its
leaders? Their plans, what were they? To this list of
questions no hard and fast answers may be made. A careful scanning, however, of diverse evidence, enables us to
conclude that the " British Convention," [1] not only in spirit
exceeded its ostensible purpose, but also in certain well-
defined emergencies proposed a direct violation of the law.

The first suggestion of an assembly of this nature came
from Scotland. As early as 1792 various democratic societies had been organized in the Northern Kingdom. Those
in Edinburgh united on July twenty-sixth of that year
under the title of " The Associated Friends of the People."
This association invited the various local radical clubs

---

[1] " The British Convention of Delegates of the People, associated
to obtain universal suffrage, and annual Parliaments," so the title ran.
State Trials, xxiii, 443.

in Scotland to a convention, to be held on December eleventh, 1792. That convention met; in it the Edinburgh delegates numbered one-third, and no resolutions of moment were passed. The meeting of this preliminary convention ended in two days.[1]

In the following April, the assembly, as yet purely Scottish, reconvened. The London Corresponding Society got wind of its meeting. On May thirteenth, Hardy wrote to Edinburgh requesting a union with the Edinburgh reformers,[2] and a correspondence ensued. In October, the Edinburgh societies requested their English brethren to join them in the convention. This letter was dated October fifth. " The delegates must reach Edinburgh," they wrote, " by the twenty-ninth of the month." On the twenty-fifth, Hardy replied that the London Corresponding Society would be represented by Gerrald and Margarot, who would shortly arrive in Edinburgh.[3]

The English delegates failed to reach Edinburgh by the end of October as planned. The convention of the Associated Friends of the People did not await the coming of their English guests, but on November first, 1793, adjourned, to meet again in 1794.[4] Immediately after adjournment, however, four English delegates arrived: Gerrald and Margarot, from the London Corresponding Society; Sinclair, from the London Constitutional Society; and M. C. Brown, from Sheffield.[5] A change of plan was now necessitated. The Scottish delegates were recalled. On the nineteenth of November, 1793, they joined their English brethren, and the session of the Associated Friends

[1] Mathieson, *Awakening of Scotland,* pp. 125, 127.

[2] *State Trials,* xxiv, 407.

[3] *Ibid.,* xxiv, 422.   [4] *Ibid.,* xxiii, **412.**

[5] Brown afterwards represented the Leeds Constitutional Society as well as the Sheffield group. *Ibid.,* xxiii, 440.

of the People was continued under the new name of the British Convention.[1] One hundred and fifty-three delegates attended the sessions, representing over forty local societies.[2] The object of the convention had been affirmed before the arrival of the English delegates, and its declared purpose was certainly made clear. "After prayers," the minutes tell us, "the convention proceeded to the further consideration of the motions, *etc.*, on the table relative to the explicit construction to be put on the two original resolutions of the Association, namely, 'a more equal representation of the people in the Common House of Parliament, and a shorter duration of Parliamentary delegation.'" And it was proposed "that there could and evidently would be but one sentiment in the house, that the explicit meaning of the first resolution was universal suffrage, and of the second annual elections, and that nothing short of these two could be adequate to the present universally corrupt state of the nation."[3]

The British convention, then, with this end ostensibly in view, busied itself for a few days in details of organization. The whole body of the convention was divided for morning sessions into small sections, so that individual debate might be furthered. On every day the general meeting was begun and ended with prayer. Subscriptions were taken up for expenses, and when somewhat meagre, renewed generosity was urged, particularly upon the visit-

---

[1] The term "British Convention" was not applied till November 23, (see Minutes of the Convention, *State Trials*, xxiii, 427).

[2] The number is over fifty, if we distinguish between the different clubs in the same town. *Ibid.*, xxiii, 391, 392 and 413.

[3] *State Trials*, xxiii, 401. This resolution was very solemnly passed. The delegates all arose and joined hands to indicate their approval.

ing spectators.[1]   Committees for visiting prisoners were
appointed; books and pamphlets were recommended to the
public.[2]   Many artless incidents marked the career of the
assemblage.   The speeches were spirited.   Citizen Gerrald
" compared the Constitution of 1688 to a dead horse," [3]
and "showed the insipidity of the titled gentlemen and the
propriety of the term citizen."   French phraseology was
adopted.   The meetings were called sittings, the delegates
citizens, and motions of more or less import were voted
upon.   On December tenth, the convention was officially
dispersed.   The high provost entered the hall and ordered
the delegates to depart.   They agreed to go upon a show
of force.   This the provost gave by placing his hand on
the arm of the presiding officer.   And thus the convention
ended.

Had the government taken no further action, history
would have scarcely chronicled this assemblage.   The
forced ending of the sessions, however, was but a preliminary step.

From the beginning this gathering had been regarded
with suspicion.   The word convention bore a far different connotation in 1793 from that held in the twentieth
century.   It had no general application at the earlier date,
nor was it a blanket term applied indiscriminately to the
festive reunions of commercial travelers or to the
gatherings of bibulous societies.   A convention was a
serious affair.   In France, whither the eyes of the civilized world were directed, a convention meant an as-

[1] *State Trials*, xxiii, 413.

[2] *Ibid.*, xxiii, 422. One publisher offered to give the Society one-half
of the proceeds if they would sell his book for him.

[3] The minutes say 1788, evidently misquoting him. *Ibid.*, xxiii, 438.

sembly of the people which, both *de jure* and *de facto,* was
the government of the nation. Furthermore, in America,
delegates representing radical clubs had composed a so-
called Continental Congress which had declared itself the
government of the country, and only five years previously
a Constitutional Convention had been held. Was a similar
attempt altogether improbable in Great Britain?

The authorities, with this possibility constantly in mind,
arrested several of the leading members of the convention
and tried them in the Scottish courts for sedition. William
Skirving, Maurice Margarot and Joseph Gerrald were
picked out as ringleaders. All three were found guilty and
sentenced to transportation for fourteen years beyond the
seas. What bearing have these trials upon our purpose? As
indicative of the "mossbacked" obscurantism of the Scottish
law they are valuable.[1] The unfairness of the trials, the
legal definition of sedition as stated by the bench, the stu-
pidity, ignorance and brutality of the judges, and the packed
jury, we must resolutely put to one side, and review the
trials simply and solely as evidence of the spirit and temper of the convention.

Taking up the indictment of Margarot as fairly representative of the attitude of the government, we find the
convention charged with holding meetings which, " though
held under the pretence of procuring a reform in Parliament, were evidently of a dangerous and destructive ten-
dency, with a deliberate and determined intention to disturb the peace of the community and to subvert the present
constitution of the country." [2]

---

[1] For an able exposition of the legal phases of the trials, see Cockburn, *Examination of the Trials for Sedition in Scotland, passim.*

[2] *State Trials,* xxiii, 609.

This indictment the crown proposed to substantiate in three ways: first, by deductions drawn from the general tenor of the meetings, such as the adoption of French phraseology, customs, etc.;[1] secondly, by an effort to demonstrate that universal suffrage and annual Parliaments were, in themselves, not only unconstitutional, but directly contributory to sedition; thirdly, by the specific charge that the accused proposed actual resistance to the law. The first and second of these ways of approach we may dismiss as too shadowy for discussion, but investigation proves the third more important. Margarot is directly charged with favoring the following motion, which the indictment alleges to have been passed by the convention, to wit: " This Convention, considering calamitous conse-quence of any act of legislature which may tend to deprive the whole or any part of the people of their undoubted right to meet . . . do hereby declare, before God and the world, that we shall follow the wholesome example of former times, by paying no regard to any act which shall militate against the constitution of our country, and shall continue to assemble and consider the best means by which we can accomplish a real representation of the people and annual election until compelled to desist by superior force. And we do resolve that the first notice given for the intro-duction of a convention bill, or any bill of a similar ten-dency to that passed in Ireland in the last session of Par-liament, or any bill for the suspension of the *habeas corpus* act; or the act for preventing wrongous imprisonment or

---

[1] Much significance was attributed to the use of the word " Tocsin." Lord Swinton, one of the judges, remarked, " This is a very ill chosen word. It is an instrument made use of by the people in France to assemble. It is borrowed from a place from which I would wish to borrow little." *Ibid.*, xxiii, 625. The defence tried to prove that the word was of Chinese, rather than of French origin.

against undue delays in trials in North Britain; or in case of invasion; or in the admission of any foreign troops whatever into Great Britain or Ireland; all or any of these calamitous circumstances shall be a signal to the different delegates to repair to such place as the secret committee shall appoint." [1]

Did Margarot make this motion, and was it adopted? At the outset it may be confessed that no positive proof exists that this particular motion was made or passed. The evidence presented at the trial was confined to the minutes and the testimony of the witnesses; and as Lord Cockburn, the historian, with one exception, well states: " A person anxious for the proof will obtain little satisfaction from either of these sources. The minutes, though apparently honest and even rashly open, are meagre, abrupt, desultory and confused, and read as if they had been jotted amid the noise and interruptions of each sitting. And the witnesses, instead of being required to explain fully, and in their own way, what the convention really aimed at, are chiefly examined on detached points." [2]

This summary rings true, save for one flaw, indicated in Lord Cockburn's use of the words " rashly open." It is strange that " rashly open minutes " should leave a blank space where certain important motions and important speeches should be inserted. Nevertheless we find that instances of this are both significant and numerous. On the eighth day's sitting, November twenty-seventh, 1793, the exact words of the minutes are: " The minutes being read, a motion was read and presented by Mr. Walter Hart, 2nded by Citizen Calder, that no notes be allowed to

[1] *State Trials*, xxiii, 611.
[2] Cockburn, *Trial for Sedition*, i, 223.

be taken but ———— " (here the minutes leave a blank space).[1]

On the thirteenth day's sitting we are told that " Citizen Margarot opposed the business as foreign to that for which we were met upon, and thought it unnecessary to attempt to lop off the branches while we were endeavoring to ———— " (here again we have the blank space).[2]

Still more eloquent are the minutes for November twenty-eighth. "Citizen Sinclair read the amendment upon Citizen Callender's motion, as agreed upon by the committee. And it was resolved, upon the motion of Cit. ———— that the House should resolve itself into a committee for its mature consideration. In the course of the conversation Citizen Brown gave an explanation of the *habeas corpus* act. After an excellent discussion of the question, pertinent remarks and amendments, the convention was resumed, and the whole as amended being read over, the members stood upon their feet and solemnly and unanimously passed the resolution as follows: ————." [3] (Who proposed this motion, and what it was, the "rashly open minutes " do not state.)

We know, however, from the minutes, that great alarm was occasioned by the Irish Convention Bill which broke up political meetings in Ireland. We know that one, Callender, moved that the appearance of such a bill in the House of Commons should be a signal for an immediate gathering of the delegates. We know that Margarot did not consider this motion definite enough and the convention

[1] *State Trials*, xxiii, 431. The only account of the proceedings of the convention which we have after November ninth was taken from "The Edinburgh Gazette." It was admitted to evidence by the government on the same basis as the minutes of the earlier proceedings.

[2] *Ibid.*, xxiii, 441.

[3] *Ibid.*, xxiii, 433.

supported him by voting an unanimous approval of the spirit of Callender's motion, while expressly disavowing its wording.[1] We are also aware that the formation of a more decisive resolution was referred to a committee and that a report of the committee was made. The report was unanimously approved,[2] but what it contained we can only surmise. The minutes are silent, and their silence is not without significance. They state, "It passed unanimously in the form of a declaration and resolution (*vide* end of this case)." The conclusion of that day's proceedings is marked in the minutes: "A secret committee was appointed to fix a place for the meeting of the convention under the circumstances mentioned in the preceding resolution."[3] Of the words of this motion we are left in ignorance, but immediately upon the passage of this unknown resolution, Gerrald congratulated the convention on its action, and then passionately denounced the Convention Bill in Ireland. He was followed in similar strain by Brown of Sheffield. Why should the resolution which they praised have been concealed?

The leaders of the convention must now have felt that the days of the assemblage were well-nigh spent. The second day after Margarot made his announcement of a secret committee, he spoke at some length of the enmity of certain influential people towards the convention. He also urged that preparations be made against dispersion. "We have already," he said, "appointed a secret committee for fixing a place of meeting on certain emergencies, and we ought to be equally well provided against the present case; for if we should happen to be dispersed to-night,

---

[1] *State Trials*, xxiii, 456.

[2] *Ibid.*, xxiii, 456.

[3] *Ibid.*, xxiii, 459.

how or where are we to rally again?"[1]   To confront this
situation Margarot proposed "that the moment of any illegal dispersion of the present convention shall be considered as a summons to the delegates to repair to the place of
meeting to be appointed for the convention of emergency,
and that the secret committee be directed, without delay,
to fix the place of meeting."[2]   This motion was passed.
The next morning Margarot was arrested, and the day of
his arrest saw the dispersion of the convention.

So much for the light thrown by the minutes.   The detailed examination of the witnesses, moreover, makes it
additionally clear that some action, at least, was taken by
the convention looking toward illegal activity in the future.
One, Cockburn, asknowledged that he had heard of a proposed session in case of a British Convention Bill, and
thought he had heard something similar concerning an
invasion of foreign troops.[3]   Cockburn was a member of
the convention.   Aitcheson, who was assistant secretary
of the convention, corroborated this testimony.   He furthermore said, "I came in one evening pretty late, and
Mr. Sinclair, or some person, had made a motion, and as
soon as I had taken my seat, Mr. Sinclair made a motion
that something that had been passed before should be
burned.   And I was surprised, and I got up and opposed
it, and it was seconded upon the ground that as everything
we had done before was open to the public, we should do
nothing secret, and therefore the motion was not carried."[4]   These recollections were to some extent corroborated by the brothers Rice, although both brothers were
much troubled by loss of memory.   Upon this testimony
alone Margarot was convicted of sedition.   The evidence,

[1] *State Trials*, xxiii, 464.   [2] *Ibid.*, xxiii, 465.
[3] *Ibid.*, xxiii, 647.   [4] *Ibid.*, xxiii, 654.

scanty for legal conviction, is none the less significant as indicative of the spirit animating the leaders of the convention. That Margarot was an active agent in proposing a new convention in certain emergencies seems reasonably clear. Just what those emergencies were we have no definite knowledge.

Further light is thrown on the proposed plans by certain English evidence, which does not appear in the Scotch trials. This evidence, found in the proceedings of the government against Thomas Hardy for high treason, and supplemented by sundry other inferences, would seem to bear out the government's contention that the proposed convention intended to usurp the function of Parliament. In the trials of the next year, it was proven that Margarot wrote to Hardy that a secret committee was to call together a new convention in certain cases. " Thus you see," writes Margarot, " we are providing against what may happen." Then he adds, " letters convey imperfectly, and with no great degree of safety, what we may wish to inform each other of." [1] The London Corresponding Society was apparently in active sympathy with the British Convention. In 1794, at a general meeting held in the Globe Tavern, an address was ratified. The preamble was long. In it the glorification of the Magna Carta, the disparagement of old Sarum, and the tyranny of the law, were equally elaborated. It ended with these words: " We must now choose at once either liberty or slavery for ourselves and our posterity. Will you wait till barracks are erected in every village, and till subsidized Hessians and Hanoverians are upon us? There is no redress for a nation circumstanced as we are, but in a fair, free and full representation

[1] *State Trials*, xxiv, 429.

of the people. We must have redress from our old laws, and not from the laws of plunderers, enemies and oppressors. You may ask, perhaps, by what means we are to seek redress. We answer that men in a state of civilized society are bound to seek redress of grievances from the law as long as any redress can be obtained by the laws. But our common Master, whom we serve, has taught us not to expect to gather grapes from thorns, nor figs from thistles."

And therefore the society resolved, " That during the ensuing session of Parliament the general committee of the society do meet daily for the purpose of watching the proceedings of Parliament and of the administration of the government of this country, and, resolved, that upon the first introduction of any bill or motion inimical to the liberty of the people, such as landing foreign troops in Great Britain or Ireland; for suspending the *habeas corpus* act; for proclaiming martial law; or for preventing the people from meeting in societies for constitutional information, or any other innovation of a similar nature; that on any of these emergencies the general committee shall issue summonses to the delegates of each division, and also to the secretaries of the different societies affiliated and corresponding with this society, forthwith to call a general convention of the people, to be held at such place and in such manner as shall be specified in the summons, for the purpose of taking such measures into consideration." [1]

The London Corresponding Society, indeed, had long been familiar with the idea of a convention. They had received, as early as 1793, a letter from a radical society in Stockport, which stated, apropos of the looked-for reform, " can we expect it from the present order of things?

[1] *State Trials*, xxiv, 445.

Would not the evil be done away with at once by the people assembled in convention? Does it appear probable that the odious laws of which we complain will be abolished by any other way?"[1] No sooner had the Edinburgh convention ended its sessions than another one was suggested. Not only was it proposed in the resolutions of the Correspond- ing Society at the Globe Tavern, but delegates were, in cer- tain places, actually chosen. " At a general meeting of the delegates of the United Societies at Norwich, held on the twenty-ninth of February, 1794, it was resolved that one or more delegates shall be sent to the next general convention, as called for by our London correspondents."[2] In Bristol, the constitutional society wrote to the London organization as follows: " We rejoice in your manly constitutional per- severance, and applaud with approval the resolution of forming another general convention."[3] This letter was dated the twenty-fourth of April, 1794.

Sheffield went even further. A preliminary meeting of delegates from Sheffield and the towns about, for the forth- coming convention, was planned there. It was decided, however, to delay the meeting until advice could be ob- tained from London.[4]

A new convention undoubtedly was to be organized. How much authority was it to have? Here we must rely on circumstantial evidence. Whether the Corresponding Society actually defined the powers which the talked-of convention was to hold we cannot tell. The minutes of the Society, at least that portion of them which was not muti-

[1] *The Second Report of the Secret Committee of the House of Commons. The Senator,* viii, 154.

[2] *Ibid.,* p. 208.

[3] *Ibid.,* p. 208.

[4] *Ibid.,* p. 210.

lated,[1] make no further mention of it. One speech and one pamphlet, however, are suggestive.

The speech was made by Barrère before the National Convention in France. Barrère was an honorary member of the London Constitutional Society. His speech was entered on the books of the Society in England, and furthermore, members of the English society were acquainted with him in Paris. Barrère's speech was on the topic of conventions. "A convention," he said, "differs from an ordinary legislature in this respect; a legislature is only a species of a superintending magistrate, a moderation of the powers of government. A convention is a perfect representative of the sovereign. . . . The powers of a convention must, from the very nature of the assembly, be unlimited with respect to every measure of the general safety, such as the execution of a tyranny." [2]

The pamphlet takes this same view. It was written in 1793 by Gerrald, and entitled, "A Convention, the Only Means of saving us from Ruin." After a long enumeration of social and political evils, Gerrald writes: "In this awful season of national calamity, I see no other recourse than interposition of the great body of the people themselves, electing deputies in whom they can confide, and imparting instruction which they must enjoin to be executed." [3]

In closing, then, it is worth while to note that, before the British convention met, the theory that the people might revolutionize society by electing delegates to a con-

---

[1] Hardy says: "The counsel for the prisoners very wisely cut the leaves out of the book . . . fearing lest by any accident the journal might fall into the hands of the government's sharks." This portion, one-quarter of the minute book, he said, contained only the names of prominent men. *Place MSS.*, 27,812, vol. ii.

[2] *Secrecy Committee, The Senator*, viii, 89.

[3] Gerrald, *A Convention, op. cit.*, p. 85.

vention was at least familiar to the leaders of the convention, and the fact that this method of action was the only
one emphasized by the " Rights of Man," places its significance in yet bolder relief.

Indeed, the conclusion is inevitable that the convention
had no intention of simply petitioning Parliament. The
British radicals knew full well the futility of that procedure. Lord Erskine, the contemporary jurist, was wrong
when he assured the jury in the Hardy trial that the government's theory of the convention planning to assume
and maintain by force all the functions of the State which
was the charge imputed to it was not within the compass
of human belief.[1] Lord Cockburn, the modern historian,
also was wrong in describing the British Convention as
bent solely on Parliamentary reform.[2]

---

[1] *State Trials*, xxiv, 940.

[2] Cockburn says, " Now I have repeatedly discussed the subject many
years after its prejudices were over, with persons of intelligence and
candor, and acquainted with the utmost secrets of the convention, and
I have never heard one of them give any account other than this, that
universal suffrage and annual parliaments were really its sole objects."
Cockburn, *Examination of the Trials for Sedition*, i, 224.

They acted foolishly, Cockburn further implies, in copying French
ways. He holds them guiltless of all else.

CHAPTER III

The Societies Accused of Treason

THE PREVALENT SPIRIT OF UNREST, AND THE RADICAL SOCIETIES. THE QUESTION OF TREASONABLE PRACTICE

THE Government, actuated by the belief that the radical clubs meditated an armed rebellion, arrested several of their leaders on the charge of high treason. Was the government justified in that belief? It has been held by the majority of English historians that the radical societies throughout Great Britain, matured no general and comprehensive designs of rebellion. The Cambridge Modern History coolly dismisses the point with the statement that " Pitt evidently misjudged the problem that was before him," [1] while other histories of more weight acknowledge the existence of political agitation, more or less illegal, but emphatically deny that any plans for an armed revolt were carried forward.[2]

A hurried survey of the sources would substantiate this view. So full of excitement and alarm was the decade between 1789-1799, that credence was given to a vast number of imaginary designs, such as the so-called " Pop-gun Plot." And as a matter of fact the government did show unseemly nervousness; political meetings were dispersed and radical associations disbanded. In some cases, also,

[1] *Cambridge Modern History*, viii, 761.
[2] May, *Constitutional History of England*, ii, 31.

men were tried for high treason on absurd evidence. The
most marked instance of this was the trial in April, 1794,
of Walker, an eminent Manchester merchant. The testimony of the crown rested entirely upon one man—a dis-
reputable individual whom Erskine proved to be both
drunkard and knave. In this case the innocence of the defendant was finally admitted by the counsel for the crown.[1]

Nor did the more important trials later in the year 1794
indicate, upon the surface, a more serious situation. The
government attempted to repeat its Scottish triumph in England, and in consequence we find that on Monday, October
6, 1794, the grand jury returned a true bill against Thomas
Hardy, John Horne Tooke, and ten other radical leaders,
not, this time, on the charge of sedition, but on that of
high treason. Three only of these twelve men were brought
to trial—Hardy, Tooke and Thelwal. All three were acquitted, and the government, despairing of success, discon-
tinued the proceedings against the others.

Judging from the outcome of these trials only, one would
be led to conclude that the government was laboring under
a complete misapprehension of the aims and purposes of
the radical clubs. Even a casual reading of the trials
would further that interpretation. The trial of Hardy
alone comprises some 1,208 pages of closely-printed matter.
It took the crown no less than a week to present its case,
and a very disorderly, unconvincing and protracted presentation it was.[2] A close scanning, however, of this testimony, discloses to us, almost concealed by the flotsam and
jetsam of irrelevant theory and hypothesis, many serious
and incriminating facts. Furthermore, the prisoner was

[1] *State Trials,* xxiii, 1164.

[2] Lord Brougham in *Historical Sketches of the Statesmen of the
Reign of George* III, ii, 60, says that the attorney-general was fond of
entangling himself in his own evidence.

represented by the incomparable Erskine, who played havoc with the evidence of the crown by very clever cross questioning, and glossed over, with little attention, evidence, the significance of which the crown had not the wit to emphasize. He won the case for the defence against a stupid, pointless attack, enmeshed in the toils of its own wordiness.[1]

It is natural, then, that the historian, in reviewing the sources, should conclude that the alarm manifested by the government, was without foundation. A more careful analysis, however, yields different results. Although it is true that Thomas Hardy and John Horne Tooke were acquitted, it must not be forgotten that evidence not legally sufficient for conviction may yet establish a strong historic presumption of guilt. And also, it is constantly necessary to differentiate between the naked facts as proven, and the eloquence of Erskine, who could, all too easily, " make the worse appear the better reason."

As a matter of fact, the evidence produced at this trial, added to that gathered at other trials, not so widely known, together with that from the two Parliamentary reports on seditious practices, and the newspapers and other sources, indicate rather strongly that certain members of the radical societies were determined, not only to equip themselves with weapons, but also to band themselves together for a definite armed uprising. This evidence may be classified under two heads:

I Evidence of seditious spirit;

II Evidence of seditious practice.

As to the seditious spirit, there can be no question but that a general spirit of unrest pervaded Great Britain toward the end of the eighteenth century. All classes were

---

[1] Brougham tells us that Erskine so fascinated a jury that it was impossible for them to keep their eyes away from him. Brougham, *op. cit.*, iii, 318.

keenly alive to this. " The suspicious novelties " of the radicals were viciously anathematized by the conservatives and sturdily defended by their own upholders and abettors. An energetic campaign began. It was carried on by many and various means. The question then naturally arises, to what extent were the defenders of the old order and the advocates of the new willing to go? Was the campaign one of argument alone? Did forced restraint on the one hand, and insurrection on the other, play any part in the dispute, and if so, to what extent?

From the thundering denouncement of pulpit and bench to the formation of military companies for the suppression of radicalism, the conservative opposition ran its natural course. A vivid illustration of reactionary spirit is afforded by the speech of a recorder at Old Bailey Sessions who, when sentencing a boy of eleven to death, dwelt upon the probable immorality resulting from the introduction of " the modern system of politics." [1]   Publicans were threatened with the loss of their licenses should they permit radical speeches to be made. The Loyalist Association of Portsmouth resolved, " that it be recommended to the magistrates to caution all victuallers and publicans of this borough, against suffering any meetings of a seditious tendency at their houses, under pain of not having their licenses removed." [2]   An address to the 158 victuallers and loyal innkeepers and publicans of Manchester and Southford, states, " Continue, my brave countrymen, to stigmatize sympathy for slaughter and sedition, and let the indignation of your hearts declare against those democratic tyrants who would enslave the freedom of your glorious constitution. . . . They are monsters, as you have found

[1] *The Sun,* Jan. 14, 1793.
[2] *The Star,* Dec. 22, 1792.

them, and ought to be driven from the haunts of men." [1]
Clerks, servants and understrappers, were induced to sign
loyalist declarations.   Church-and-king riots, if not actively
instigated, were at least passively encouraged by officialdom.   The riots in Birmingham in 1791 were of this
nature, as also that in Manchester in 1792 which resulted
in an attack on the office of the Manchester *Herald*.[2] Large
numbers of associations were formed for the destruction
of the hydra-headed monster, Jacobinism, and for the
same purpose the machinery of government was actively
invoked.

What reply were the radicals to make?   So intense
with divergent feeling was society of the period that it is
not easy to judge.[3]   Indeed, many of the incidents which
attracted popular interest, give no proof at all of the real
intentions of the radicals.   No little sword play was indulged in by the press.   " The True Briton," in an article
entitled " Strong Spirit of the Reformers," states : " While
an umbrella was held over Mr. Fox's head in Old Palace
yard last Monday, one of the mob, irritated by such distinction, cried out ' equality.'   But the Patriot went on,"
exclaims the *True Briton,* " while his friends abided the
pelting of the furious storm." [4]   Boisterousness upon the
street, then as now, seemed a favorite pastime.   Pitt him-

[1] *The Observer and Sunday Advertiser,* Sept. 23, 1792.

[2] *Morning Chronicle,* Jan. 1, 1793; *Morning Post,* July 18, 1791;
Laprade, *England and the French Revolution,* pp. 44-51, has a full ac-
count of this riot in Birmingham.   For the riot in Manchester, see
Morning Chronicle, Jan. 1, 1793.

[3] Cockburn, *Trials for Sedition,* ii, p. 23, gives a vivid account of
this thing.   The recollections of R. Potter, M. P., offered another clue ;
London Despatch and *People's Political and Social Reformer,* Feb. 26,
1834.   *Place MSS., op. cit.,* 27, 816, p. 439.

[4] *The True Briton,* April 10, 1797.

self was pelted in St. James Park by angry spectators,[1] while Admiral Gardiner, the opponent of Fox, was also roughly handled.[2] Nervous excitement pervaded all classes. Religious fanaticism, clothed in garbled prophecy, there was in abundance. One poor prophet organized a pilgrimage to Jerusalem,[3] while a certain female, assuming the title of " Britannia, or the Genius of England," announced that she was commissioned to warn their Majesties of the impending fate of the country.[4]

Many popular disturbances were due to the high cost of living. The poor suffered greatly, and indeed all classes of society recognized that something must be done. No one was better aware of the deplorable condition of the country than Arthur Young. According to his testimony " the situation is very alarming." [5] So likewise thought the best informed of his friends. Mr. Simmonds wrote to him in 1795 that " complaints of the dearness of the necessities of life seem to pervade the entire island, and I fear that the necessities may be still dearer. If we are forced to persist in this war, and how we are to get out of it is difficult to see, the middle class of people, to which you and I belong, must be driven down to the lower." [6]

Discontent among the working classes was reflected ere long in serious riots, especially during the trying year 1795. In Leicester a wagonload of corn was seized and carried to a churchyard. Officers attempted to rescue it. The riot act was read, but the hungry people at length were

---

[1] *Oracle and Public Advertiser,* Dec. 18, 1795.

[2] *Gazetteer,* June 8, 1796.

[3] *Oracle and Public Advertiser,* Jan. 22, 1796.

[4] *Morning Chronicle,* Jan. 22, 1796.

[5] *Reports of Committees,* ix, 79.

[6] *Correspondence of Arthur Young, Additional MSS., British Museum,* 35,127, vol. ii.

permitted to divide the corn among themselves. The mob, still not content, assailed the soldiers with brick-bats and stones. The soldiers fired upon them, killing three and maiming eight.[1] The poor people in Chichester forced a farmer to unload his provisions. Placed in jail, they were rescued by a large mob. Lives were lost at Lewis in an anti-high-price riot, by a charge of light cavalry on the people. In Pontefracte the unfortunate remarks of a corn dealer brought the popular wrath down upon his head. Reported as saying that he hoped the day would arrive when people would not be so saucy at to eat wheaten bread he was personally assaulted, and his wagons appropriated.[2] Two thousand people in Wiltshire engaged in a demonstration against the farmers and millers. In Carlisle a committee of the people confiscated all private grain and placed it on sale in the town hall at popular prices. Women were particularly active in these demonstrations. At Bath they prevented a ship from sailing laden with grain, and one, Sarah Rogers, was the leader in a cheap butter campaign.[3]

There was a great difference of opinion as to how this distress should be met. In Manchester, in November, 1795, premiums were given to farmers for bringing their crops to market.[4] Shortly after this, in February, 1796, the borough reeve, clergy and other prominent citizens, pledged themselves by way of example to reduce by one-third the quantity of flour which they would consume.[5] Such measures were merely palliative. The situation grew worse. By special police order the public houses were

[1] *Oracle and Advertiser*, Aug. 10, 1795.
[2] *Ibid.*
[3] Hammond, *op. cit.*, p. 121.
[4] Axon, *Manchester*, p. 121.
[5] Reilly, *Manchester*, p. 287.

closed early, and other strenuous methods were adopted. Despite this proclamation, on July twenty-ninth, a riot broke out in the potato market over a question of weights and measures. The mob was driven away by the soldiers. It reassembled the next morning and, pouncing upon several loads of meal, threw them away. Toward the end of 1796 pies and puddings ceased to be seen in Manchester, and so acute became the shortage of wheat in the city that the farmers were assisted by the soldiers in threshing their fall supply.

London suffered equally with the rest of the country. Official recognition of the suffering was made by the authorities. Twice during 1795 the sum of a thousand pounds was voted for the temporary purchase of grain. An effort even was made to abolish the corporation dinners of London for a whole year. This sacrifice the city fathers could not bring themselves to make. They agreed to suspend them, however, until the first of October, 1795. The attitude of the press varied greatly. The quasi-radical *Morning Post* said, as early as 1791, " It is ridiculous to talk of revolution in this country, for it wants none. The bishops are not overfed, nor are the curates starving. The dependents upon the civil list of nearly one million pounds live on, and as for the sinecures of Church and State, while the poor manufacturer and peasant is obliged to eat his black bread in a darkened room, it is for the honor and dignity of the country that we encourage them." [1] The *Oracle and Advertiser* of July 11, 1795, describes with great care a certain print which exhibited " a large tree with innumerable branches." From these by way of fruit are suspended loaves of bread, different joints of meat, heads of cabbage, and a bottle with " gin " inscribed

[1] *Morning Post,* July 7, 1791.

upon it.   Under this several men are sitting, with their mouths wide open.   These words are printed on the label: " If you don't fall I must rise."   The ministers and other persons seen at some distance were diverting themselves with the misery of the scene.[1]   Even the conservative press admitted the seriousness of the crisis.   It advised self-denial of pastry, and likewise the purchase of bread by the state.   It even demanded a law which would prevent bakers from selling loaves on the same day on which they were baked, on the theory that five stale loaves equal four fresh ones.[2]

Direct instances of a seditious spirit on the part of the radical societies greet us on every hand.   Margarot, the exiled secretary of the Corresponding Society, wrote in March, 1794, to his friends in Norwich: " This morning ten ships of war have left Spithead for the Channel, and it is reported that the Brest fleet is out; rumor always magnifying things, says there are seventy sail of French at sea; if so, there must be a number of transports among them, and a descent may probably be the consequence—for God's sake, my worthy friends, do not relax in the cause of freedom." [3]   As early as the 28th of November, 1792, we find a letter written by a military officer stationed at Sheffield.   Replying to an inquiry from Pitt concerning the disposition of the people of Sheffield, he tells of the rejoicing of the people at French victories.   A procession was held, where a French flag was raised, and also a picture on top of a pole which portrayed Burke and Dundas stabbing Liberty.   A poem was read containing the refrain, " Let

[1] *Oracle and Public Advertiser,* July 11, 1795.
[2] *The London Times,* July 16, 1795.
[3] *Secrecy Committee, The Senator,* viii, 198.

us like Frenchmen live, or else like Frenchmen die." The
officer writes further that, although perfect peace was preserved, a debating society in the town was saving money
to buy firearms and to corrupt the soldiery.[1]

In 1794, " The Tragedy of Charles I " was enacted in an
Edinburgh theatre. In the course of the play the actors
sang " God Save the King." An uproar straightway arose.
The crowded audience jeered and hissed and, finally with
one accord, gave voice to the revolutionary air, " Maggy
Linder." An officer of the garrison, to compel a respect-
ful reception of the national anthem, summoned his soldiers. The result was a riot attended by bloodshed.[2] The
strife was renewed at the following comedy; a crowd gathered outside the theatre; and bludgeons were freely used.[3]
Another theatrical performance of an even more significant character took place the same year in London. This
was an amateur entertainment given by one of the local
branches of the London Corresponding Society, an association organized for a " reform in Parliament." The
play bore upon its face full evidence of disloyalty. The
title-sheet of the production was as follows:

For the Benefit of John Bull
Given at
The Federated Theatre in Equality Square
A New & Entertaining Farce Entitled
Le Guillotine
or
George's Head in a Basket.

[1] Tomline, *Life of Pitt,* iii, 459. A foot-note states this letter was
found among Pitt's papers.

[2] *Oracle and Public Advertiser,* April 18. A similar riot took place
in Rochester; another one in Lynn. Thelwal, *An Appeal to Popular
Opinion,* p. 481.

[3] *Oracle and Public Advertiser,* April 19, 1794.

Dramatis Personæ:

Numpy the Third, by Mr. Gwelf (being the last time of his appearance in that character); Prince of Leeks, by Mr. Gwelf, Jr., . . . Banditti, Assassins, Cutthroats, Wholesale Dealers in Blood, etc.

Between the acts a new song, entitled "Twenty More, Kill Them," by Bobadil Brunswick. Tight Rope Dancing from the Lamp posts, by Messrs. Canterbury, York and Durham. . . . . In the course of which will be sung in full chorus, "Ca-Ira" and "Bob Shave Great George our . . . ," the whole to conclude with the grand decapitation of Placemen, Pensioners, and German leeches.[1]

At Sheffield the popular societies were numerically strong. They were likewise bold and enterprising, for, under the leadership of a popular agitator, known as Red-Head York, they held a mass-meeting. This was in April, 1794. It was an open-air event, and York was the orator of the day. To hear the proceedings no less than eight thousand people assembled. During the course of his speech, in a reference to the throne and Church, York made the following announcement: "The day is at length arrived when fanaticism and superstition, deprived of their tinsel trappings, and exposed with their natural ugliness to the view of mankind, shall slink scowling back to the cave of obscurity." And also his hearers are advised "to march in a body to London; to demand redress for their grievances;" while for a peroration to this philippic are these significant words: "Should conditions not improve the people will send the five hundred gentlemen in St. Stephen's Chapel about their business."[2] It is true that at his trial in 1795 many of the witnesses for the defence denied that these words were uttered; the fact of their utterance, how-

---

[1] *State Trials*, xxiv, 682.   [2] *Ibid.*, xxv, 1037.

ever, was established not only by the testimony of many
reputable citizens, but also by their appearance in the
pamphlet published under the auspices of the Sheffield
Society.

Many riotous demonstrations against the government
took place throughout the nation. One of them was held
in 1792 in Dundee. Fox and other defenders of the Society
made light of this event, declaring that it was nothing more
than the act of a few schoolboys. From the evidence of a
Scottish member of Parliament who witnessed the occurrence it was a more serious affair. The riot lasted from
Friday to Tuesday, and was participated in by a mob of
five hundred, consisting of men from sixteen to sixty years
of age. A liberty pole was planted, and various diversions
of a French type indulged in.[1] Another riot occurred on
Easter Monday in Manchester where a public assembly
met in answer to a hand-bill. Opposed to it was a mob.
The reformers were said to have fired, obeying a man
whom they called captain.[2]

If these political disturbances are considered in connection with the numerous food riots previously reviewed; if
we keep in mind at the same time the popular indignation at
the inequalities of the criminal law as evinced by various
demonstrations, such as that which took place before New-
gate on the fourteenth of July, 1794,[3] we can scarcely
doubt that the temper of the people could easily have been
fanned into a flame of revolt.[4]

We pass now from the discussion of seditious spirit, on

[1] Jordan, *Parliamentary Journal*, Dec. 17, 1793.
[2] *Oracle and Public Advertiser*, April 25, 1794.
[3] *The World*, July 15, 1794.
[4] Further evidence of this may be had from the *Place MSS.*, 27,817,
p. 4, and *Oracle and Public Advertiser*, May 16, 1794.

the part of the members of radical clubs, to that of seditious practice. Of this there is proof, both circumstantial and direct.

First of all, a common understanding apparently existed between the Society of United Irishmen and the English radical clubs. The United Irishmen rebelled in the year 1798; therefore, if any co-operation with them existed on the part of the societies of England, it is evidence not to be lightly discarded. That there was a mutual understanding is suggested by three facts:

(1) O'Connor, a member of the Irish Directory, or the Central Committee of the United Irishmen, came to England in 1798. He was entertained there by the London Corresponding Society, and sailed for France in the company of John Binns, a member of the London Association.

(2) Two delegates from the Society of United Irishmen, namely, Hamilton Rowan and Simon Butler, attended the meeting of the Edinburgh Convention in 1794.[2]

(3) A correspondent of the London Corresponding Society met Lord Edward Fitzgerald in Chester, and inquired of him " How things were going in Ireland; " while for his own part, he assured Fitzgerald that great success was being met with in England in winning over the Scottish Regiments.[3]

Secondly, armed insurrection was encouraged. The government produced at the *State Trials* a letter written by one Davidson. This man was an influential member of a society in Sheffield. In his letter he offered to prepare and ship to Norwich as many pikes as were required,[4]

---

[1] *Reports from Committees,* x, 795.

[2] *Report of the Secrecy Committee of House of Commons, The Senator,* viii, 102.

[3] *Correspondence of Castereagh,* i, 206.

[4] *State Trials,* xxiv, 588.

while at the home of an officer of the Norwich Society was
discovered a letter stating that the French fleet would soon
be under way, and that Norwich must be prepared to rise
in arms at that happy event.   Indeed, the London Corresponding Society itself directly advocated armed resistance.
In the instructions of the Society to its delegates are found
these words : " You are to call on our fellow citizens to be
ready with us to pursue our common object to the scaf-
fold, or rather (if our enemies are desperate enough to bar
up every avenue of inquiry of discussion) to the field." [1]

Upon the loyalty of the army and navy everything depended.   The effort of the radicals to undermine that
loyalty was perhaps the most serious charge that could
have been laid at their door.   Popular discontent assisted
them greatly in this attempt.   The French war was detested.   So also was conscription.   In Scotland, in 1794,
certain of the Fencibles, or the militia of Glasgow, refused
to obey their officers.   Troops from neighboring towns
were summoned ; five companies and two cannon were sent
to Edinburgh, and the malcontents were arrested.   The
infuriated populace attempted a rescue,[2] but without success.   Two officers accompanied the prisoners out of town.
Returning, they were knocked down by a mob and sought
refuge in a nearby house.   The mob broke down the
windows and would have seized the officers had not the
military arrived in season.[3]

In the Highlands the greatest difficulty was met with
in obtaining recruits.   The radical press claimed that the
" mode of raising volunteers in the Highlands is to threaten

---

[1] *Report of the Committee of Secrecy of the House of Commons.
Report from Committees*, x, 809.   From the written instructions of
John Gale Jones deputized to visit the societies in Birmingham.

[2] *Courier*, Dec. 22, 1794.

[3] *Morning Chronicle*, Dec. 24, 1794.

the farmers that their leases will not be renewed unless the son enlists." [1]   All over Scotland opposition to the army was bitter.   In Dumfries some fifty or sixty muti-neers rescued a number of confined men but were chased by two officers whom, in turn, they surrounded and threatened; a show of pistols brought the mutineers to their senses. [2]   This Scottish unrest culminated in the widespread disturbances which greeted the promulgation of the Militia Act.   The country was greatly aroused throughout the autumn of 1797.   In Glasgow the utmost confusion and disorder reigned.   In a letter to the *Morning Chronicle* it was stated that " The Duke of Montrose has been driven by the people from his seat in the vicinity of Dumbarton, and has found shelter from violence in this city.   In consequence of this outrage his Grace has been obliged to send off from hence a troop of dragoons to escort the Duchess and her family hither.   Our foot and cavalry volunteers have received word to hold themselves in readi-ness at a moment's notice, and are constantly under the necessity of appearing in uniform.   The country people are unanimous in refusing to be balloted for.   To such lengths have they gone in some places . . . that they have torn to pieces the rolls, and have chased the deputies to their homes." [3]   Other Scotch towns received the news of the Militia Act in much the same way.   In Eccles six or seven hundred men and women—the latter with aprons full of stones—compelled the farmers to sign a declaration of resistance, while at Jedburg another riot took place. [4]

Dumbartonshire was not behindhand in this display of mob violence.   In the village of Eastern Kilpatricks a mob

[1] *Morning Chronicle*, Jan. 15, 1795.

[2] *Oracle and Advertiser*, July 23, 1795.

[3] *Morning Chronicle*, Aug. 31, 1797.

[4] *Ibid.*, August 29, 1797.

of three hundred prevented the execution of the Militia
Act. Soldiers were summoned from Glasgow. The riot
act was read, and upon the refusal of the mob to disperse,
ten of their leaders were seized and imprisoned. In Edinburgh the enforcement of the act met with resistance. The
soldiers were stoned, one being mortally wounded. The
mob was fired on, and eight or nine were killed and many
wounded. Among those killed was a woman who beat a
drum. On the same day in Selkirk a crowd of young men,
estimated in numbers from six to seven hundred, compelled
a constable to surrender the lists of recruits. These they
burned before the church door. The chief magistrate,
threatened with a ducking, forbore interference.[1]

Despite this opposition, however, a rigid enforcement of
the act was insisted upon. Rioters were severely punished
by transportation and by imprisonment, while many people were compelled to give security for their good behavior.

The societies in Scotland took an active part in promoting disaffection among the soldiers. A favorite method
of accomplishing the desired result was the circulation of
pamphlets and letters. One of these, taken from a soldier,
after making a bitter denunciation of the French war, and
advising the army to take no part in it, continued as follows: " You cannot be compelled to go! leave not your
country! Assert your independence! Your countrymen
look up to you as their protector and guardian, and will in
turn lift up their arms to assist you." [2] In this propaganda,
Downie, an official of the Edinburgh societies, was impli-
cated. Several soldiers swore upon the witness stand that
they had read papers advising a mutiny.[3] These men

[1] *Morning Chronicle*, Sept. 5, 1797.

[2] *State Trials*, xxiv, 100.

[3] *State Trials*, xxiv, 96, 97. For other mutinies, see the *Annual Register* for 1795, pp. 24, 27.

were members of the fencible regiment stationed in Edinburgh.

In England the war was nearly as unpopular. The forced seizure of men for military service, popularly known as " crimping," met with an indignant opposition. The position of a recruiting sergeant was perilous. Sometimes the recruiting station would be attacked. It was said that twelve thousand men had participated in one of these onslaughts. The windows of Pitt's house were broken; bonfires were lit, and the recruiting house attacked. Only by the reading of the riot act and the calling forth of the horse-guards was the tumult quelled.[1] On one occasion the trick of a recruiting sergeant in presenting a coin to a young lad for the ostensible purpose of procuring some merchandise, coupled with the prompt seizure of the boy for taking the king's shilling, resulted in the hasty gathering of some two thousand people. The crimp was hustled about, placed under a pump, thoroughly beaten, and slit through the ears.[2] Not only were the recruiting officers attacked, but deserters were befriended, and an open conflict took place in the streets of London between a mob defending a number of deserters from the Sixtieth Foot, and an armed force which tried to capture them.[3]

[1] *Oracle and Advertiser,* July 15, 1795.

[2] *Ibid.,* April 17, 1795. A favorite device for procuring recruits apparently was to entice the intended victim into a house of prostitution. Brayley, *History of London and Middlesex,* p. 559. Also *The Courier,* July 19, 1794. Reprinted in a tract of the London Corresponding Society, entitled, *Reformers not Rioters.* See also *Oracle and Advertiser* for July 27, 1795. *Ibid.,* Jan. 14, 1795.

[3] *London Chronicle,* April 6, 1797. Of course the more reputable of the citizens of London did not participate in any physical resistance to the government. Nevertheless, they also protested in orderly fashion against the war. This was done to some extent by the London corporations. We find that Aldgate as a ward, officially resolved neither to serve in the new militia, if balloted for, nor to pay the fine

Outside of London the situation was the same. In Bristol, Bath, Oxford and Norwich, mutinies either occurred or were feared. Bristol was in a state of especial alarm, owing to the assembly of the colliers at Kingswood for the purpose of redressing some grievance.[1] Wiltshire and Leicester witnessed disturbances also. There was trouble in Yarmouth, and also in Portsmouth,[2] while at Newcastle-on-Tyne volunteers for the war were viciously assaulted.[3]

This state of affairs gave a tempting opportunity to the radical societies. Both in England and in Scotland radical hand-bills were actively circulated. In vain did the government try to stop this practice. At Oxford and Norwich a soldier or non-commissioned officer who would provide evidence for the conviction of one of his fellows was offered a bonus of three days' pay.[4] At Maidstone, two years later, we find as much as two guineas offered for the conviction of anyone placing treasonable hand-bills in the hands of soldiers. One, Richard Fuller, was convicted of this practice. In his possession were discovered two or three highly inflammatory posters. In one of them the soldiers are urged " to put on the uniform of liberty." " You have sixpence per day for clothes, food, and expenses," the address tells them, " and out of this you are to find all things necessary for the existence of man; even the common heritage of nature, personal liberty, is not

prescribed by the act. Similar action was taken by Cripplegate ward. Both the middle class and the poorer folk of London detested the war and the necessity of serving in the army. *Oracle and Public Advertiser*, August 29, 1794.

[1] *London Packet,* or New Lloyds *Evening Post,* March 23, 1795.

[2] *The True Briton,* August 13, 1796; *ibid.,* August 27, 1796.

[3] *Morning Chronicle,* July 30, 1795. The Pitt men were guilty of this outrage. One of the volunteers was said to have been trampled to death by them.

[4] *Ibid.,* May 28, 1797.

yours; you are tied up like dogs; the lash sharpened with cruel knots lays bare your bones; the spike runs through the sole of your foot and makes the suspended wretch writhe and howl with agony—these are the rewards of your loyalty, and these the blessings which attend the service of a king." [1]

Henry Fellows, who was convicted of the same offence, was employed by the Corresponding Society.[2] Two papers were found in his possession. One was an exhortation to the army, urging the soldiers to mutiny. In it a few grievances are enumerated,—among them poor pay, and inefficient, brutal officers,—whereupon the hand-bill exclaims. " these, comrades, are a few of our grievances, and but a few. What shall we do? The tyranny which is falsely called discipline prevents us from acting like other men. We cannot join in a petition for that which common honesty would freely have given long ago. We have only two choices: either to submit to the present imposition, or to demand the treatment proper for men." [3] The other was a communication to the secretary of the London Corresponding Society, reporting on the progress made.[4] The marines at Chatham were urged to mutiny. Another man, named Rhodes, also connected with the radical societies, was caught at Maidstone sticking up treasonable posters; he was said at the time to have been employed by two

---

[1] *Report of the Committee of Secrecy Relative to Seditious Societies,* 1799. *Reports from Committees,* 1775-1801, x, 809. Fuller, a shoemaker, was tried at Old Bailey. There was no defence, save illiteracy. *Old Bailey Session Papers,* 1797, p. 447.

[2] *True Briton,* May 25, 1797.

[3] *Reports from Committees,* x, 810.

[4] *Reports from Committees,* x, 810. The handbill states still further that " the regiments which send you this are willing to do their part," and it concludes with the admonition: " BE SOBER! BE READY !"

strangers who were members of the London Corresponding Society.[1]

More distressing still to the government was the fact that the fleet could not be relied upon. With the details of the famous mutiny at the Nore history has been long familiar, but few historians seem to have suspected that the mutineers had any connection with the London Corresponding Society. Yet a contemporaneous newspaper tells us that " as one of the Gravesend passenger boats passed the mutineer Lancaster, several passengers proclaiming themselves members of the London Corresponding Society, gave three cheers, which so enraged the others that a pitched battle was fought." Other evidence goes to show that Williams, one of the leaders of the mutiny, was a prominent speaker at a London debating society.[2] Indeed, if the *True Briton,* the organ of the administration, is to be trusted, Smart, a mutineer on the Grampus, admitted at his court martial that he was a member of the Corresponding Society.[3] Another mutineer was said to have belonged to a radical society in London,[4] while Joyce, one of the ringleaders of the mutiny, had formerly, in the village of Kirkentulloch in West Scotland, been a leader in the radical cause.[5]

Fatal as the outcome of the grand mutiny at the Nore was, the idea of a naval revolt lingered on. The second report of the Committee of Secrecy, issued in 1799, states that Tomms, a marine, on the ship Diomede, planned to shoot the officers and take the vessel from Sheerness to a

[1] *The True Briton,* May 26, 1797.
[2] *London Chronicle,* June 19, 1797.
[3] *The True Briton,* July 15, 1797.
[4] *Ibid.,* July 28, 1797.
[5] *London Chronicle,* May 25, 1797.

foreign port. An oath was taken to this effect. Tomms was a member of a corresponding society in Nottingham.[1]

There can be no doubt but that certain members of the radical clubs actually planned an armed revolt. We have already seen how Davidson, a Sheffield man, offered to supply pikes to the associated clubs at Norwich. We know from other sources that pikes were actually manufactured in Sheffield for members of the local societies. William Gammage, a blacksmith in Sheffield, swore that he in person had manufactured many pikes. Joseph Eyr, a carpenter, testified that he had made pike handles, while Widdison, another carpenter, fashioned a dozen pike handles, and Hill, a smith, made ten dozen or more pike heads of fine steel.[2] The pike is described as a fine steel rod, pointed and fluted as a bayonet, which, when affixed to a stout ashen stick four feet in length, made an effective weapon.

The " night cat," of which a model was made, was a reproduction of the calthrop of classical times. It could be used only against charges of cavalry or dragoons. Although simple in construction, it was most ingeniously calculated to throw into confusion a charging body of horsemen. Four light-weight iron or steel bars, two or three feet in length, were selected. These bars were so welded together in the middle that the eight points, sharpened to an edge, projected out in opposite directions.

[1] *Second Report of the Committee of Secrecy,* Appendix, p. 21, in *Reports of Committees, op. cit.,* x, 819. The evidence of a connection between the societies and the naval mutinies, is sufficiently clear, and what is more serious, from the government's standpoint, the London populace stood as willingly behind the naval mutineers as it did behind the deserters from the army. For we learn that two naval officers met openly one of the mutineers on the Strand; they collared him; he knocked one down and escaped from the other. The crowd made no effort to assist the officers. *London Chronicle,* June 22, 1797.

[2] *State Trials.* xxiv, 665.

When hurled to the ground before oncoming horses, one end would be impaled in the ground, while the other, projecting outward, provided for a time an unsurmountable obstacle. The calthrop or " night cat " was, indeed, a portable, inexpensive and effective weapon.

In London, the focal point of the radical propaganda, many had procured weapons. The wealthier members of the London Corresponding Society bought muskets and organized " The Lambeth Association." This body drilled regularly and even possessed a uniform. Its ostensible purpose, as set forth in the constitution, was to preserve order and to repel invasions.[1] It hired a drill master and met at different private houses for drill. Among the members there was some talk of action upon the introduction of Hessians into England.

It was known that arrangements had been made with the Sheffield sympathizers to ship pikes from that town to London to augment the London supply. Hodson, a witness in Hardy's trial, gave evidence that the members of the society were advised to buy arms, and testified still further that the following manuscript had been given him to print in the form of a hand-bill: " The Ins tell us that we are in danger of invasion from the French. The Outs tell us that we are in danger from the Hessians and Hanoverians. In either case we should arm ourselves, get arms and learn how to use them.[2] The Lord Mayor of London was perhaps not far wrong when he announced in the House of Commons that in London the authorities were resting on the top of a volcano.

So far, although proving that certain individuals both in thought and in deed meditated rebellion, and although

[1] *State Trials*, xxiv, 694.

[2] *Ibid.*, xxiv, 837.

implicating to some extent the radical associations, we have
not established the fact that any plot, widespread and
concisely planned, existed.   Such a plot, in embryo at least,
did exist.   All southern Scotland was involved.   This conspiracy centred at Edinburgh, and the radical societies
throughout southern Scotland provided the necessary organization.   Some of these societies displayed great activity, as did that in Paisley, for on May 23, 1794, Dundas
wrote to Pitt that Paisley was in readiness to revolt, and
that for many weeks the Friends of the People had been
arming.[1]   In other localities preparations lagged.   But
whether zealous or lukewarm, all the societies were in close
touch with the central body in Edinburgh, which had been
long noted for its reforming proclivities.   It was here that
the radicals had met in convention.   It was here that a
larger number of artisans were gathered than in any other
part of Scotland.   Among these men, many of whom were
unemployed, the seeds of rebellion found a fruitful soil.
The dispersing of the Edinburgh Convention, with the
consequent suppression of free speech, together with the
industrial depression, drove many of these men into the
ranks of the radical societies.

   After the dispersion of the British Convention, the
Friends of the People in Edinburgh kept up their organization.   Their chief executive agent was a committee, called
the Committee of Union; and an inner committee, that of
Ways and Means, chosen therefrom, served as the real
centre of authority for the affiliated societies.   The conspiracy, the details of which we are about to elaborate, was
broached in this inner committee.   Whether they were ever
formally adopted by the chief committee we do not know.
The charge was vigorously denied by two or three members

[1] *Secrecy Committee, The Senator*, viii, 225.

How much reliance can be placed upon their denial is difficult to state.   It is certain that these very men tacitly or openly permitted the plans to mature.[1]

The conspiracy was a complete failure, but more because it was discovered prematurely than because it lacked dimensions and seriousness.   It was planned that seven events should take place simultaneously.   They were:

  1. The capture of the Lord Chief Justice Clerk, and all government officials at their homes.

  2. The firing of the excise house for the purpose of ambuscading the military.

  3. The capture of the castle while the soldiers were fighting the flames, or in ambuscade.

  4. The seizure of the bank with its contents.

  5. An order to be given to all farmers of the neighborhood to keep their food supply at the disposal of the rioters.

  6. All gentlemen within three miles to be commanded not to leave their homes under penalty of death.

  7. A petition to be sent to the king to end the French war or take the consequences.[2]

This conspiracy, with its various ramifications, was nipped in the bud by the authorities.   It was discovered by an accident.   In a letter to Pitt, Dundas reported the disclosures, which finally brought to light the whole affair. This letter, written on May 19, 1794, tells us, that when the goods and chattels of a certain bankrupt were lieged, various pikes and battle axes were discovered in the house where he lived.[3]   The owner of the house refused to ac-

---

[1] Bonthone, one of the inner committee, acknowledged that he assisted Fairley, the agent of the society, in preparing the west counties of Scotland for the proposed rising.

[2] *State Trials,* xxiv, 38.

[3] *Secrecy Committee, The Senator,* viii, 229.

count for them. Thereupon the authorities searched the
houses of two blacksmiths, friends and intimates of the
owner. In them also were found pikes and battle axes.
One of these two blacksmiths fled from the city, the other
insisted that the weapons were intended for purposes of
defense alone. Unfortunately for him, his apprentice
swore that his master said, " the battle axes are for gate
ornaments." These three men then, the first by his silence,
the second by his flight, the third by his contradictory statements, aroused the government's suspicion.

Wholesale arrests were made, including the nine members of the Committee of Union. Seven of them turned
State Evidence, and on their testimony, Downie and Watt,
the other members, were convicted of high treason. By
the testimony of these men not only is the conspiracy dis-
closed in its main features, as already described, but even
the method is made clear by which they were to be perfected. The allied societies, through the country districts,
were to be kept constantly informed of the determination
of the central body at Edinburgh, by means of messengers.
Such a messenger was the lad Fairley. From him, despite
his canny secretiveness, important information was ex-
torted. Leaving Edinburgh ostensibly to visit his sister in
Glasgow, Fairley spent two weeks upon the journey, visited
twenty-six towns, and remained with his sister a portion
of an afternoon. Furthermore, he received from Downie,
the treasurer of the Edinburgh Association, traveling
money. Why he should have been given this, Fairley could
not explain.[1] In every one of these twenty-six localities
Fairley called upon the leaders of the Patriotic Societies,
including among them two surgeons and a dissenting minister. One of the surgeons, Doctor Forrest of Stirling, con-

---

[1] *State Trials*, xxiv, 106-9.

fessed with much reluctance, combined with a convenient loss of memory, that the words "arms" and "French Invasion" were mentioned during his conversation with Fairley. He likewise acknowledged that the picture of a pike was drawn, which should serve as a model for pikes to be made in Edinburgh.[1] Indeed, a blacksmith, swore upon the witness stand, that a man named Watt, a member of the Committee of Union, had ordered him to manufacture five dozen pikes. William Brown, another smith, was commissioned to prepare fifteen pikes.[2] These weapons, in both cases, were to be paid for by Downie, who, according to the testimony of Margaret Whitecross, a servant in his employment, kept a pike secreted in his own home.[3] In Watt's home, as a matter of fact, twelve pikes fitted upon poles were discovered, and in the smithy of Orrocks, Middleton and Lockhart, two or three were unearthed.[4]

At the time these disclosures were made it was evident that the crisis in Edinburgh was fast approaching. Shortly before its discovery men of the better station in life, as well as the timid ones, gradually withdrew from the societies. Of the former type was Bonthone, an Edinburgh teacher, who had been an enthusiastic member of the Friends of the People and one of the committee of ways and means. When, however, Bonthone became aware of the proposed plans which have been described, he withdrew, and none too soon, for within a week or two his former colleagues were placed under arrest.[5]

---

[1] *State Trials*, xxiv, 113-115.

[2] *Ibid.*, xxiv, 93.   [3] *Ibid.*, xxiv, 88.

[4] *Ibid.*, xxiv, 85.

[5] Watt's confession was sent sealed to the sheriff the night before his execution. Further details of this plot were given in the *Oracle and Courier*, Nov. 6, 1794.

It is little to be wondered at that the Society for Political Information in Norwich wrote the London Corresponding Society, and requested the Society in London " to come closer to the main question. It is only desired to know whether the generality of the societies mean to rest satisfied with the Duke of Richmond's plan only; or whether it is their private design to rip up monarchy by the roots, and place democracy in its stead." [1]

[1] *Secrecy Committee, The Senator,* viii, 157.

CHAPTER IV

The Suppression of Radicalism

THE PROSECUTION OF THE INDIVIDUAL. TRIALS FOR SEDI-
TIOUS WORDS AND PUBLICATIONS. ORGANIZED RADICAL-
ISM UNDER THE BAN. THE TWO ACTS. THEIR PROGRESS
THROUGH PARLIAMENT. THE PASSING OF THE LONDON
CORRESPONDING SOCIETY

WHATEVER faults may be laid at the door of Pitt's administration, it cannot be accused of half-way measures
in the suppression of radicalism. From 1792 to 1799 a
series of coercive acts, rigidly enforced, crushed most effectively the incipient growth of a radical party.

The first hint of suppression came in 1792. It was in the
form of a proclamation against " wicked seditious writings
printed, published and industriously dispersed." The government forthwith endeavored to stamp out the incipient
growth of radical opinion by the use of judicial machinery. From 1792, for ten years or more, indictments
brought by the crown against individual offenders for the
dissemination of seditious ideas followed one another in
quick succession. Several of these trials have become
famous landmarks in the history of the liberty of the press
and of freedom of speech, as, for instance, the trial of
Thomas Paine in England, and of Thomas Muir in Scotland. Paine's trial in particular has been quoted from
freely; and, indeed it was a memorable one. Erskine,
as counsel for the defence, never appeared to better advan-

tage.   The great lawyer, devoting himself to principles
alone, made a comprehensive, masterful, impassioned but
yet dignified defence.   Freedom to criticise and condemn,
Erskine upheld as the foundation stone of liberty.   English
history, he maintained, demonstrates that this right had
long since been won, and the proof thereof may be deduced
from Paley, Locke, Milton, Hume, Harrington and even
the great Burke.   Specially effective are these noble words
of Milton:

" To the pure all things are pure; not only meats and
drinks, but all kind of knowledge, whether of good or evil;
the knowledge cannot defile, nor consequently the books,
if the will and conscience be not defiled.

" Truth and understanding are not such wares as to be
monopolized and traded in by tickets, and statutes, and
standards.   We must not think to make a staple commodity
of all the knowledge in the land, to mark and license it
like our broadcloth and our wool-packs." [1]

Historians of our own day, asserted Erskine, even those
who stanchly defend the monarchical theory of the state,
feel no less strongly than did Milton this necessity of
defending liberty of speech.   And in this connection, he
cites Hume to the effect that " The spirit of the people
must frequently be roused, in order to curb the ambition
of the Court. . . . Nothing is so effectual to this purpose
as the liberty of the press, by which all the learning, wit,
and genius of the nation, may be employed on the side of
freedom; and everyone be animated to its defence.   As
long, therefore, as the republican part of our government
can maintain itself against the monarchical, it will naturally be careful to keep the press open, as of importance to
its own preservation." [2]

[1] Milton, *Prose Works*, Birch edition, 1753: *State Trials*, xxii, 439.
[2] Hume, *Essays*, edit. 1809, i, 12; *State Trials*, xxii, 442.

Where is there anyone who would suppress Hume, contended Erskine; he, like Milton, is immune—nay, more,—there are men who have written with ten times the freedom of Paine that have been unmolested, and for illustration Erskine quotes from the sermon of an eminent clergyman, a Mr. Cappe, of York. This sermon, preached during the American war of independence, is full worthy of record, for combined with a fearless denunciation of English misgovernment is to be found this graceful benediction to the new America: " It may be in the purposes of Providence, on yon western shores, to raise the bulwark of a purer reformation than ever Britain patronized; to found a less burthensome, more auspicious, stable, and incorruptible government than ever Britain has enjoyed; and to establish there a system of law more just and simple in its principles, less intricate, dubious, and dilatory in its proceedings, more mild and equitable in its sanctions, more easy and more certain in its execution; wherein no man can err through ignorance of what concerns him, or want justice through poverty or weakness, or escape it by legal artifice, or civil privileges, of interposing power; wherein the rule of conduct shall not be hidden or disguised in the language of principles and customs that died with the barbarism which gave them birth; wherein hasty formulas shall not dissipate the reverence that is due to the tribunals and transactions of justice; wherein obsolete prescripts shall not pervert, nor entangle, nor impede the administration of it, nor in any instance expose it to derision or to disregard; wherein misrepresentation shall have no share in deciding upon right and truth; and under which no man shall grow great by the wages of chicanery, or thrive by the quarrels that are ruinous to his employers." [1]

[1] *State Trials*, xxii, 460.

Even the apostle of conservatism, Edmund Burke, once defined a free government, Erskine maintained, as one where the people, " and not I, are the natural, lawful, and competent judges."[1] Paine himself demands nothing more than the fulfilment of this principle. Indeed, Erskine affirms: " These are the sentiments of the author of the ' Rights of Man,' and a writing can never be seditious in the sense of the English law, which states that the government leans on the universal will for its support."

In Edinburgh, in the following year, in the trial for sedition of Thomas Muir, a twenty-six-year old Scottish reformer, the accusation was that Muir had circulated dangerous books, among them Paine's " Rights of Man," and Volney's " Dialogue betwixt governors and governed." The extract from Volney, in the indictment, runs as follows:

" Civil Governors: 'The law enacts that ye be submissive.'

People: ' The law is the general will. . . .'

Civil Governors: ' You be a rebellious people.'

People: 'A nation cannot revolt; tyrants are the only rebels. . . .'

Whereupon the ecclesiastical governor said: ' There now is but one resource left: the people are superstitious; we must frighten them with the name of God and of religion.'

Priests: ' Our dearly beloved brethren, our children, God has appointed us to govern you.'

People: ' Produce to us your heavenly powers.'

Priests: ' You must have faith. Reason will lead you astray.'

People: ' Do you govern, then, without reason?'

Priests: ' God ordains peace; religion prescribes obedience.'

---

[1] Burke, *Letter to the Sheriffs of Bristol*, works edit. 1808, iii, 183; *State Trials*, xxii, 436.

People: ' Peace presupposes justice.   Obedience has the right to know the law it bows to.'

Priests: ' Man is only born into this world to suffer.'

People: ' Do you then set us the example.'

Priests: ' Will you live without God and without kings.'

People: ' We will live without tyrants and without imposters.' " [1]

Furthermore, it was asserted, on the testimony of a servant girl, that these words were read by Muir in his father's dining-room before his mother, sister, and various other folk whom the servant did not know.   Muir, however, acknowledged that he approved of this book, and even that he upheld certain of the principles of Mr. Paine.   He denied that he wholly approved of Paine, but nevertheless he appeared quite unashamed of his conduct.   Furthermore, he had visited France, a circumstance not mentioned in the indictment, but made much of at the trial.[2]

Here was sufficient evidence, and at any rate the authorities were predetermined upon their course of action. They packed the jury with members of the loyalist association, and Lord Braxton, who presided, was even reported as having said to one of his acquaintances: " Come awa', Maester Horner, come awa', and help us to hang ane of thae daamed scoondrels."

The jury found Muir guilty, and he was sentenced by

---

[1] *State Trials*, xxii, 123.   This dialogue was evidently widely known, for we find it printed and bound with other dialogues and letters more characteristically British in tone, *vide Letter from Ralph Hodge to his cousin, Thomas Bull.*

[2] A modern historian regards his foreign trip as very suspicious.   He quotes a letter to Henry Dundas from his nephew Robert, to the effect that Muir was an emissary from France, and he regards Muir's defense that he went to Paris on the representation of certain English radicals to plead for the life of the French king as scarcely credible. Ross, *William Pitt and the Great War*, p. 176.

the court to transportation for fourteen years.   That this punishment was meted out to a man for recommending Paine to his barber is at least significant.   Even more so is the fact that a British judge should close his charge to the jury as follows: " Mr. Muir might have known that *no attention* could be paid (by parliament) to such a rabble (the petitioners for reform).   *What right had they to representation?*   He could have told them that the parliament would never *listen* to their petition.   How could they think of it?   *A Government in every country should be just like a corporation; and, in this country, it is made up of the landed interest,* which alone has a right to be represented.   As for the rabble, who have nothing but personal property, *what hold has the nation on them?*   What security for the payment of their taxes?   They may pack up all their property on their backs, and leave the country in the twinkling of an eye.   But landed property cannot be removed." [1]

One other trial claims our attention.   In the summer of 1793, William Winterbotham, a Baptist minister, was indicted on the charge of uttering seditious words in a sermon   Winterbotham, like all good dissenters, was accustomed to celebrate the anniversary of the revolution of 1688 by preaching a thanksgiving sermon.   The watchful Tories, on the *qui vive* at these occasions, stationed, in 1792, several representatives in the Baptist meeting-house

---

[1] " This language is so outrageous that it might be ascribed to inaccuracy or hostility in the reporter, were it not that this is the same in all the reports, even those by the most ardent party friends; and though severely commented on in Parliament, *it was never disclaimed.* Howell says (vol. xxiii, p. 117, *note*), that he compiled his *State Trials* out of *all* the reports, which, however, did not suffer materially, and were ' *in no instance contradictory.*' The truth is, such passages were those by which their Lordships thought that they were best performing their duty, and they were always the most emphatically delivered." This note is taken directly from Cockburn, *op. cit.,* i, 177.

at Plymouth. These reporters for Toryism told a frightful tale. The first witness for the crown deposed that
Winterbotham not only approved of the revolution in
France, but also said that it had opened the eyes of Britons,
and in the reported words of the witness: " He then spoke
of the method of taxation in England, and said a tax-
gatherer will come into your house, and demand your property out of your pocket, without satisfying you to what
purpose the money is to be applied—he said that was not
liberty for a Briton—every man had a right in a land of
liberty to know how his money was to be applied.—He
then spoke of the expenses of the late armaments—said he
disapproved of three of them,—and said they were man-
oeuvres for ministers to make up their accounts;—said
then, how are your streets crowded with poor, your poor
houses with vagrants, and your gaols with thieves—it is
all owing to your oppressive taxes.—He then said he had
often heard people talk what a happy land they lived in,
and what a mild government they laboured under; but
that it was no such thing;—he was much astonished at their
quietness; and added, it is high time you should stand forward to defend your rights.—He then said he was sorry
to see justice so abused—said no magistrate or justice had
any right to hold his office, unless he obeyed his trust, not
even his majesty, if he did not see the laws duly observed,
he had no more right to the throne than a Stuart; and he
concluded by saying, he hoped we should soon see better
times." [1]

This witness, however, was not over intelligent upon his
cross-examination, as the following colloquy indicates:
" You have told us Mr. Winterbotham said his majesty,
if he did not see the laws duly observed, had no more

[1] *State Trials*, xxii, 828.

right to the throne than a Stuart; what did you understand by a Stuart—I understood he meant by a Stewart, some officer under the crown;—I considered it in the light of a gentleman's steward. You thought Mr. Winterbotham meant some officer under the crown like a gentleman's steward?—Yes; I took very little notice of it, and did not think much about it. You took but little notice, and paid but little attention then to what was meant?—No; I paid very little attention to what his meaning was about the Stewards." [1]

Other witnesses for the prosecution, avoiding pit-falls of definition, agreed that incriminating words had been delivered. For the defence, on the contrary, many reputable citizens testified that the minister never said that the French revolution would open the eyes of Britons. Members of his congregation indignantly denied also that their pastor mentioned oppressive taxation, or that he used the word oppressive in any connection. Indeed, one sturdy dissenter affirmed that Winterbotham's sermon was far from militant, for if he had "endeavored," the witness asserted, "to inflame the minds of his hearers it would have been impossible for such language to have escaped my notice."

Winterbotham was found guilty by a jury; promptly tried for another sermon, he was found guilty again, and for the two offences he was sentenced by Kenyon, the Lord Chief Justice of England, to two years in prison and a fine of two hundred pounds. [2]

The radical movement, however, continued to grow The Edinburgh Convention met, and the possibility of a convention of national magnitude was in the air. Sterner measures were deemed necessary and, on the twelfth of May, 1794, the papers and books of the London Corres-

---

[1] *State Trials*, xxii, 830.   [2] *Ibid.*, 907.

ponding Society were seized. A special Parliamentary committee was appointed, which straightway reported that the radical societies had acted illegally, and were meditating treason.[1] Two days after the seizure of the books and papers, Pitt moved in the House of Commons the suspension of the Habeas Corpus Act till February 1, 1795.

In introducing this bill for the suspension of the writ of *habeas corpus,* Pitt stated his belief that " a plan has been digested and acted upon; and at this moment is in forwardness towards its execution; the object of which is nothing less than to assemble a pretended convention of the people for the purpose of assuming to itself the character of a general representation of the nation, superceding in the first place the representative capacity of this House, and arrogating in the next place the legislative power of the country at large." [1]

The debate which followed was long. Typical of the Whig opposition was the speech of Mr. Lambton. He disapproved heartily of radical societies. He knew nothing about them at all, but he was quite sure that every Englishman would unite in suppressing riots which might occur. He also was convinced that the existing laws were sufficient for any crisis which might arise. Mr. Young replied for the government by instancing Cicero's suppression of Cataline, and emphasizing the secret nature of the radical societies, which made it impossible to fight them in the open.[2] Speeches were made by Gray, Channing, Dundas, Fox and Pitt, and a vote was taken. It stood 146 to 28 for the suspension.[3]

The trials of the radical leaders for high treason now

[1] *The Senator,* 1794, p. 1173.
[2] *Ibid.*, p. 1206.   [3] *Ibid.*, p. 1250.

commenced.   Public interest grew to a fever heat during
their progress.   Demonstrations, even somewhat comparable to those at the acquittal of the seven bishops, greeted
the verdict "not guilty."   Despite a very heavy November
rain, it was said that when the Hardy verdict was given
the crowds around Old Bailey almost prevented access to
the building, and the horse guards and the city militia had
to be summoned.[1]   Hardy tried to escape quietly, but he
found it impossible, and his friends, with great rejoicing,
drew him in a carriage through all the town, taking particular care to visit the Tory sections.[2]

A similar greeting was given to Tooke.   Even the jurymen who acquitted him were huzzaed with great vigor,[3]
while the Sheffield witnesses on their return to their native
town were wildly acclaimed.   Gammage and Moody were
met a half-mile outside of Sheffield by a great procession.
A silk flag was carried, emblematic of the liberty of the
press; transparencies, with the names of the jurors; flam-
beaux, and a coach decorated on one side with a painting
of the sun, and on the other with a figure of liberty.[4]

As for Erskine, the famous lawyer, his popularity knew
no bounds.   He had defended the prisoners free of charge[5]
with a whole-hearted devotion which had much overtaxed
his strength, and this the populace knew.   Consequently it
is little wonder that, when leaving the court, the horses

---

[1] *The Times*, Nov. 5, 1794.

[2] *The Courier*, Nov. 6, 1794.

[3] *Ibid.*, Nov. 24, 1794.   [4] *Ibid.*, Dec. 27, 1794.

[5] Erskine wrote to the Corresponding Society: " The situation of the
unfortunate prisoners entitles them to enjoy every degree of tender-
ness and attention, and their inability to render me any professional
compensation does not remove them at a great distance from me.   In
point of form, they must apply to the court to assign me as their
counsel, which I shall undoubtedly accept.   I am, gentlemen, your most
humble servant, T. Erskine." (*Place MSS.*, 27, 813.)

were taken from his carriage, while the crowd which drew it home shouted, " Erskine forever." [1]

In the midst of the popular applause following the verdict of the Hardy jury, Sheridan urged that Pitt's measure, suspending the *habeas corpus,* be repealed. Not only was his effort fruitless, but Pitt succeeded in still further prolonging its suspension to July 1, 1794. The ministry on this occasion was supported by a vote of 239 to 53.

Nor was the government yet content. A golden opportunity gave it still further excuse for yet more stringent measures. On October 29, 1794, the King in his state coach passed through Saint James Park to open Parliament. As the royal procession went by, it was greeted with a succession of groans and hisses, the bystanders crying out continually, " No Pitt! No war! Bread! bread! Peace! Down with George! " [2] On the way one of the windows of the king's coach was broken. Apparently no stone was thrown, nor was any missile found. The hole in the window, very small and circular, looked like a bullet hole. This hypothesis, however, was impossible, for there was no musket report, and no damage aside from the broken glass.

The attack on the king created wide excitement. The theory of the government was that an assassination had been planned by means of a poisoned arrow, blown through a blow-pipe. Several members of the Corresponding Society were arrested. Nothing could be proven against them,[3] but an excited Parliament nevertheless readily

---

[1] *Oracle and Public Advertiser,* Nov. 24, 1794.

[2] *Place MSS.,* 27,808, p. 48.

[3] P. T. Lemaitre, one of the prominent members of the Corresponding Society, stated that the entire plot was a device of Pitt's, for the purpose of stirring up opinion against radicalism. To back up this opinion, he narrates a very circumstantial story with many ramifications,

passed further measures of repression. On November 4,
1794, " The Seditious Meetings Bill " was introduced
into Parliament. This bill, sweeping in character, had
two main features. The first dealt with public meetings;
no meeting could be held in Great Britain in accordance
with its provisions, of more than fifty persons, unless on
the application of seven householders. That application
once made, announcements of the proposed meeting were
sent to the magistrates, any one of whom could end the
meeting if he considered that seditious expressions had
been voiced there. The second proviso related to public
lectures, and was aimed particularly at Thelwal. It provided that houses where lectures were to be held, for which
an admittance fee was to be charged, must be licensed by
two magistrates. Failure to comply with the first of the
two main provisos of this bill was to be regarded as a
felony, for which the penalty was death; violation of the
second was punishable by a heavy fine.

Another act, enlarging and more clearly defining the
scope of high treason, was introduced at the same time.
This bill was entitled, " An Act for the Safety and Preservation of His Majesty's Person and Government against
Treasonable and Seditious Practices and Attempts."

These two bills were popularly known as the two acts.
Their progress through Parliament was closely watched.
and hotly debated. A compendium of the debates, resolutions, petitions and public meetings held in regard to them,
published in the year 1796, comprises some 828 pages,[1] and
a glance through it vividly demonstrates the high pitch of
public excitement which these measures provoked.

which include the malicious schemings of a watchmaker named Upton.
Upton was a spy in the employ of the government. P. T. Lemaitre,
*Some Remarks Respecting the Supposed Origin of Popgun Plot, Place
MSS.*, 28, 808, p. 121.

[1] *The History of the Two Acts.*

The latter of the two bills, an Act for the Safety and Preservation of his Majesty's Person, was introduced in the Lords on October thirtieth. The Duke of Bedford and the Earl of Lauderdale vigorously fought its passage. The former urged that there were laws enough in existence; if enforced they would prove satisfactory.[1] The Earl of Lauderdale in vain pointed out the excessive power given to the judiciary by this measure. The bill passed the House of Lords on November thirteenth, by a vote of sixty-six to seven. The debate on the Seditious Meetings bill in the Lords began December ninth. Bedford and Lauderdale were again the principal protestants. Said Bedford, " The present measure is liable to be abused grossly, shamefully, and, I am afraid, with impunity. I do not wish to enter into any invective against characters of the magistrates, but it is not to be concealed that many of those to whom so large a power is to be given by the present bill are corrupt and interested men. . . . The present bill is chiefly calculated to restrain the lower orders, and it' will become this House to recollect the relative situation in which they stand to that class of society. . . . They can do without us; we cannot do without them. . . . What has been the treatment of people in this country ? They have submitted to a disastrous and calamitous war with patience and resignation. Disastrous and calamitous it must be admitted by every man, and a waste of blood and treasure . . . and how were they induced to submit in patience, and to bear its evils without repining? They were told that it was a war carried on for the sake of liberty, and for the preservation of their free constitution." [2] There were not many, however, who agreed with Bedford. The bill received the sanction of the Lords on December fourteenth, by a vote of one hundred and eight to eighteen.

[1] *Parliamentary Register*, xliii, 106.   [2] *Ibid.*, 186.

The first mention of the two acts in the House of Commons was on November ninth. Every inch of their progress was vigorously contested, and they were not passed until December third. The Whig minority,—all that was left of it,—fully realized the import of the bills. So, too, did the country. Petitions for, and against, the measures poured in on Parliament from every hand.[1] Opposition, however, to the bills, made but little impression on the government. Upon the third reading the ayes were two hundred and sixty-six, the noes fifty-one.

Erskine and Fox were particularly prominent in opposing these projects. Erskine pointed out, in regard to the Seditious Meetings Bill, that "no such act had been dreamed of in the reign of King William, or in the two rebellions which raged in the subsequent reigns." He said that "even the act of Charles II, urged as a precedent, did not go the length of the present bill; it only allowed magistrates to interfere when an overt act of tumult took place, or to require security if danger to the peace was apprehended. But it never prohibited a meeting to be held; it did not forbid voluntary communication, but prohibited tumultuous petitionings. This bill prohibits petitionings upon grievances which already exist."[2] It was a ridiculous measure Erskine insisted, arbitrary, illegal and useless, and to prove that it was so, he instanced hypothetical cases which might arise, where it would work grievous injury.

Charles James Fox, in the debates on the two acts, was at his best. Never a painstaking logician, nor even a consistent thinker, Fox, in the clear, bold and courageous statement of opinion, knew no superior. The bills, he said,

---

[1] *Parliamentary Register*, xliii, 440, 441, 442, 474, 477, 480, 495, *etc.*

[2] *Ibid.*, 207.

were "an attack on the liberty of the country," and a "subversion of the constitution." "If I am asked how they are to be resisted in the present instance, I will say by peaceful means; by petitions; by remonstrance; but if they are once passed into law, and I am then asked how they are to be resisted, I will then answer that it is no longer a question of morality, but of prudence." [1]

Upon the Tory side a flood of oratory was let loose. Sir William Poultny insisted that "no assembly, no meeting of the people could be held in America without the presence of the magistrates," and that the precautions called for by the bills were indeed necessary to preserve freedom of discussion.[2] Mr. Wilberforce, of anti-slavery fame, "saw reason on the whole for thanking the ministers who brought in the bill." He thought it necessary to preserve the great mass of people from political infection.[3] Lord Mornington drew with much feeling many parallels between Republicanism in England and in France, while Wyndham, Dundas and Pitt spoke more soberly, and at greater length on behalf of the proposal. The bill then became a law.

A storm of protest greeted these coercive measures. Throughout 1794, 1795 and 1796, petitions poured into London. Many of the London parishes also took action. A meeting of Cheap Ward, said to have been very numerous, voted five to one against the bills.[4] Similar action was taken by Saint James Ward. In Southwark, amid great excitement, a meeting of denunciation was held. Five hundred persons were gathered within a hall, and as many stood without. Someone moved that only electors

[1] *Parliamentary Register.*

[2] *Ibid.,* cv, 122.   [3] *Ibid.,* cv, 133.

[4] *Oracle and Advertiser,* Nov. 21, 1795.

should vote. The motion was carried, and the electors censured the government by a large majority.[1] A meeting of the Lord Mayor, aldermen and liverymen in Common Hall was held at the same time. In the midst of tremendous uproar resolutions were carried against the two acts.[2]

Petitions against the war and the ministry abounded. An address from Middlesex implored Pitt to adopt the most decisive measures for obtaining a speedy and honorable peace. From Norfolk and Herford came petitions to the same effect. A petition in Warwick occasioned the gathering of a tremendous crowd. Gentlemen seceding from this crowd drew up a counter petition.[3] An anti-war meeting in Kent was largely attended,[4] and on one day petitions were reported from Edinburgh, Nottingham, and Surrey.[5] Canterbury and Rochester also held meetings.[6]

The Tory newspapers took careful cognizance of this unrest. They particularly watched the doings of the radicals in London. A meeting in the Common Hall of the city of London was summoned by the Lord Mayor to hear the king's answer to an address of protest. The king refused to receive the address. A motion was made protesting against the refusal, and the mayor unwilling to put the motion was violently hissed.[7] Another meeting at the Palace Yard, Westminster, was said to have con-

---

[1] *Oracle and Advertiser*, Nov. 25, 1795.

[2] A crowd outside the hall cheered or hissed the departing aldermen as they voted for, or against, the protest. *Oracle and Advertiser*, Nov. 21, 1795.

[3] *True Briton*, June 8, 1797.

[4] *Chronicle*, April 19, 1797.

[5] *Ibid.*, April 6, 1797.   [6] *Ibid.*, May 3, 1797.

[7] *Ibid.*, April 13, 1797. The mayor attempted to stop a discussion. He was forced to give way.

sisted of "a motley crowd," which assembled from "a
neighboring public house." [1]

The declarations of the loyalists, on the other hand, are
impressive in their constant and reiterated approval of all
acts of coercion. The Loyalist Association of Norwich
paraded on the king's birthday. A boy on horseback led
the procession, supported by figures representing the army
and navy, and bearing a banner which represented an
angel carrying a crown. [2] Nearly every parish had its
loyalist association. One hundred and forty citizens in the
parish of Doddington and its hamlets expressed "their determination to choke with their utmost vigilance, the dissemination of principles inimical to the British constitution." [3] And so numerous, indeed, are these petitions, that
suspicion is sometimes thrown on their sincerity. We are
told of "jail birds that sing 'God Save the King' in
chorus, and sign a declaration of loyalty," [4] and an interesting recipe for making a parish loyalist association is
given us. "Take the rector, church warden, overseers and
sidesmen to the vestry. Put the rector in the chair, and
then call the meeting numerous and respectable. Take the
attachment to our happy constitution, king, lords and commons, and the blessings of each in equal quantity. To
which add the glorious revolution of 1688. Mix well with
these riots, tumults, insurrections, seditious writings, an-

[1] *True Briton*, April 4, 1797.

[2] *Norwich Gazette*, May 23, 1795.

[3] *British Museum, Place MSS.*, 35, 670, pp. 371, 372; *Hardwick Papers,
cccxxii, Cambridgeshire Militia Correspondence*. This toast was given
at a corporation dinner in West England: "May the tree of liberty be
transplanted from France to hell, and eternally bear as fruit the souls
of all republicans." (*Morning Chronicle*, July 22, 1794.) For an address of the Glasgow Merchants, see *ibid.*, Jan. 10, 1793.

[4] *Advertiser*, March 3, 1793.

archy, confusion, equality, neighboring nations, and specious mask of reform, republicans, levellers." [1]

No stone was left unturned by the adherents of the old
order.   Wherever a radical petition saw the light of day, it
was followed, if possible, by a counter petition.   A careful
scrutiny was kept on all quarters.   Said the *True Briton*:
" What are the respectable inhabitants of Westminster
about that they do not set on foot a counter petition to that
carried by the mob of Irish bricklayers and day laborers on
Monday, in Palace Yard.   It is surely proper that at such
times as this the real sentiment of the respectable part of
the community should not be misrepresented." [2]   Such
pleas, however, hardly sufficed.   Despite the best endeavors
of the Tories, the number of petitions against the bills rose
to ninety-seven, while in their behalf but sixty-five were
mustered.   Furthermore, while the Tories had to their
credit somewhat under thirty thousand signatures, the petitions against the bills were signed by over one hundred
and thirty thousand.[3]   The ministry did not worry over
these petitions.   What though a huge majority of the nation was opposed to the two acts, did not an influential
minority uphold the hand of the government?   Was not
the church, the aristocracy, the landed and commercial
interests solidly arrayed in their support? [4]   Nor was this
all.   Pitt gauged the situation aright.   He realized that patriotism was a trump card which he could always play.
His newspaper ally, the *True Briton,* in explaining the anti-

---

[1] *Gazette,* February 27, 1796.

[2] *True Briton,* August 6, 1797.

[3] *History of the Two Acts,* pp. 826, 827.

[4] The petitions for the acts quite generally were written in the name
of *the gentlemen, clergy, freeholders, and others.*   Many petitions from
purely clerical sources were submitted in behalf of the two acts.   None
are recorded against them.

administration sentiment in the nation, contended that
" the agents of the Gallican party are busily employed in
convening partial meetings of the people in the different
parts of the country, for the purpose of compelling the
king to dismiss his present ministers forever, and in consequence to assign . . . all places of trust and emolument to
their worthy patrons.[1]

This suggestion, even if devoid of truth, was not devoid
of influence. The bills once made law, the great bulk of
moderately-minded citizens acquiesced apparently in the
action of the government—if not from rational, at least
from patriotic motives.

The story of the London Corresponding Society, from
the treason trials in 1794 till its final disappearance in
1798, is one of constant repression and growing weakness.
The suspension of the Habeas Corpus Act enabled the
government to arrest and hold on suspicion its leading
members. These men, if their own story be accredited,
endured very harsh treatment. Their story was gathered
by the indefatigable Francis Place, in a general narrative
of persons committed under suspicion. The testimony
John Oxade gives is typical. Oxade, by profession a
master bookbinder, was apprehended so quietly that his
family did not know for a time what had become of him.
One day in prison Oxade noticed a plumber mending a
drain. Through his help, the first news of his arrest was
spread abroad. Oxade tells us, that " the aristocratic governor kept me a close prisoner in a solitary cell, upon bread
and water. Although no charge was made against me, yet
at the time my father, with competent witnesses, came to
demand a copy of my indictment, he told them that he

[1] *True Briton*, April 10, 1797.

knew nothing at all about me."[1]　" Among the other regulations," he said, " was that of shaving the prisoners twice
a week. . . . We strongly objected to it, on account of the
rough manner of performing it. We therefore agreed with
the head turnkey that he should perform it, and that we
should make him a compliment for his trouble."[2] The
turnkey by this arrangement made between three and four
pounds a week.

Great difficulty was experienced by the prisoners in seeing their kith and kin. Oxade wrote that they secured the
favor " of seeing their friends from the Privy Council,
only to discover that the hour set for such visits was the
same as that apportioned for the convicts to receive their
visitors. No difference was made between the treatment
which the political prisoners received, and that meted out
to the convicts, and he then describes how he and his
father were separated by two iron gates, between which
sentries were stationed.[3] The sanitary conditions of the
prisons and the indecencies to which the members of the
Society were subjected, were described with more gusto
than good taste, and when we are told that they were classified in the same category with the mutineers of the Nore,
the treatment accorded to these suspects only becomes the
more ruthless.[4]

In the meanwhile, the political prisoners exiled to Australia endured hardships equally distressing. Nor did
community of interest prevent the exiles from quarreling
with one another. Margarot, the representative of the
London Corresponding Society, apparently became over
friendly with the captain of the transport, and this the
other exiles disliked. They tell us that they do not intend

[1] *Place MSS.*, 27, 809, p. 207.　　[2] *Ibid.*, p. 220.
[3] *Ibid.*, p. 230.　　[4] *Ibid.*, p. 243.

"to give a detailed account of their personal suffering, but the sacred regard to justice which they owe to their country, and that invaluable honor attached to their condition calls on them to declare that Mr. Margarot was an accessory to the wrongs which they suffered." [1]   Mr. Margarot is then informed that he must no longer " pollute the immortal cause of liberty " by attempting to associate with them, for he knows well, so the narrative runs, that " he stands rejected and expelled from their society."   This quarrel continued for several years, for the voluble Margarot wrote in 1796 that Gerrald arrived, and was seduced from him by his enemy, Palmer.   And he then implies that Palmer, by improper practices, filched from Gerrald's daughter most of his property. [2]

The London Corresponding Society, its leaders arrested and imprisoned, its meetings prohibited, and its publications sequestered, soon fell a prey to internal dissensions. A harmonious spirit had pervaded the society in the midst of early vicissitudes, and there is little evidence of any friction within its membership, judging from the minutes, till 1793.   In that year the arbitrary power of the central committee met with some criticism.   One Godfrey, representing a small division, objected in vain to the central committee petitioning in the name of the society without a referendum, [3] and a general poll of the entire society was taken April 27, 1795, to determine the authority which the central committee might exercise.

No very serious trouble, however, made its appearance before 1797.   A schism came in that year, from which the

---

[1] " Epitome of a Narrative of the Sufferings of Palmer and Skirving during a voyage to New South Wales in 1794, on board the transport Surprise," *Place MSS.*, 27, 816, p. 3.

[2] Margarot to L. Goddard, *Place MSS.*, 27, 816, p. 110.

[3] *Ibid.*, 27, 812, Journal of the Society.

much harrassed and already greatly weakened society never recovered. This discord was caused by the proposed holding of public meetings in defiance of the law. The wiser men in the society opposed the holding of illegal meetings. They were also anxious to raise the dues to one shilling a week, and at the same time they were not willing to spend any money, save for necessities, till the debt was paid. The majority, however, determined to hold a public meeting, and as a result, Place and Ashley resigned in disgust.[1] They were not the only ones who left. On August 3, 1797, a letter was read from twenty-one men who, because of the proposed public meeting, withdrew. The seceders assured the society that their action was determined by a difference, not in principle, but in method.[2] The parent society must have seen them depart with a heavy heart.

The career of the London Corresponding Society, indeed, was about over. In vain did it attempt to encourage the waverer by this printed appeal: " Fly then to the standards you have deserted. Let not the men who have braved the vengeance of apostates, and all the rage of association grandeur, be unworthy of their trophies—perseverance will give you everything—and while every village lifts its feeble head and looks to be fostered by you—deny it not—rally to your division." [3] In vain, too, was a plan to defeat the purpose of the Sedition Bill.[4] The membership still continued to fall off, and ere long, so completely had the executive machinery broken down, that some of the divisions were quite in ignorance of what was taking

[1] *Place MSS.*, 27, 808, p. 80.

[2] *Ibid.*, 27, 815, vol. 5, p. 165.   [3] *Ibid.*, p. 154.

[4] *Ibid.*, 27, 808, p. 68. While on a mission in behalf of this plan, Binn, an agent of the Society, was tried for high treason. In the indictment he was charged with advocating resistance by force of arms. (*State Trials*, xxvi, 640, 641.)

place in the others.   We know little of the activities of the
society at this time.   No pamphlets were published by it
in this year.   Had there been funds to pay for any, other
obstacles might have proven insurmountable.   Abuse and
satire were the only remaining weapons as the following
broadside demonstrates.

" A Creed
for all Good and Loyal Subjects who go to
St. Paul's.
on 19th. Dec., 1797.

"I believe in God as by law established—in Billy Pitt, Heaven
commissioned Chancellor of the Exchequer; Promoter of all
court intrigues, visible and invisible; *creator and master* of
laws and commons whose politics are pure and morals un-
tainted; and Secretary Harry Dundas, the only beloved of
Billy Pitt, beloved before all women, man of men, head of
heads, minister of ministers, beloved not hated, being of one
opinion with his patron, by whom all ministers are made; who
for us men and our taxation came out of Scotland and talked
much in the house of integrity and was appointed East India
Comptroller under Billy Pitt, and went into Scotland, and
was there burned in effigy; and the third day he came back
again (according to the newspapers) and ascended into office
and sitteth on the right hand of his patron, to judge both loyal
and disloyal, whose folly shall have no end—and I believe
that murder, rapine, plunder and burning are the true and
proper means of conciliating the affections of the inhabitants
of Ireland, whom I believe to be the natural slaves of the
British Cabinet; and I believe in the House of Boroughs, the
legal representatives of the people, elected by one hundred and
sixty-two persons, either peers, sinecure placemen or immediate servants of the K—g, who can do no wrong—and I
believe in Ge—ge the T—D, Lord and giver of places, who,
together with Billy Pitt, is worshiped and glorified, who spoke
by a proclamation; and I believe in paper money and national

bankruptcy as outward and visible signs of the nation's prosperity; and I look for the remission of taxes not till the resur-
rection of the dead, and I look for better government in the
world to come." [1]

On the nineteenth of April, 1798, the end came. In the
Queen of Bohemia Tavern, the general committee, if we accept its explanation, was discussing a proposed offer of the
services of the society to the government, in case of invasion. While engaged in this patriotic debate, the entire
committee was apprehended and bundled off to prison.[2]
The London Corresponding Society now disappears from
history. A few of the more irreconcilable members
were unwilling to cease their agitation, and in the same
year, 1798, they were organized by O'Quigley, a representative of the United Irishmen, into a new organization
known as the United Englishmen. A brotherhood of
United Scotchmen also was founded, and it was expected
that it would co-operate with the United Englishmen.
The disappearance of the London Corresponding Society,
however, brings to an end our review of British Radicalism, 1791-1797.

[1] This broadside is bound in a volume compiled by Francis Place. It
is catalogued in Place's handwriting, under the caption, *Corresponding
Society's Publications.* The volume is one of a series in the Place
collection in the private library of Professor E. R. A. Seligman,
Columbia University.

[2] *Place MSS.*, 27, 808, p. 90.

CONCLUSION

WE are assured by an eminent contemporaneous historian that the "Reflections" of Edmund Burke will be forever the political book of prophecy for the English nation.[1] This statement reflects the prevalent estimate of Burke's book, an estimate which, strange as it may seem, has been rendered well-nigh unanimous. Nevertheless, a dissenting opinion is not without rational foundation. Nay, more, if our conclusion is to be drawn from the first section of this treatise, such dissent is inevitable. Not without timidity should one approach the sacred fane of Edmund Burke. Warned by the admonition of a recent editor that only those of riper years may grasp the true inwardness of the great philosopher, the author has been especially watchful of the indiscreet sentence and unguarded word. And yet, to comment upon Burke at all throughout the body of this work has seemed superfluous. The accumulated weight of radical argument which we have hurled at the conservative defences, is sufficiently conclusive to demonstrate their weakness and instability.

Certain inferences and conclusions, however, may be drawn from the contention between Burke and his enemies. A preliminary survey of the social conditions of England, both economic and political, is not calculated to arouse any impetuous enthusiasm for the defenders of the *status quo;* and an intensive study of contemporary opinion arouses less. The sordid revelation of misery, want and crime, on the one hand, and of chicanery, fraud and corruption on

[1] Rose, *William Pitt and the National Revival*, p. 556.

the other, transforms suspicion into certainty and luke-
warmness into condemnation. Wollstonecraft suspected
that Burke's reasoning powers were undermined, and it is
charitable to accept her explanation, since palliation for the
conclusions of Burke on the French Revolution there is none.
Yet Burke has been all but glorified by the mystic glamour
which tradition so superbly casts about her heroes, and a
taboo holy and sacrosanct is attached to his book. This
taboo, like many another, is but a taboo in theory, for the
constitution of modern England can hardly be said to re-
semble the idealized political structure which Burke pic-
tured as perfection. The Lloyd-George budget, with its
taxation of the unearned increment, attests but scant respect
for property as a God-inspired pillar of the commonwealth.
The impending denationalization of the Welsh establishment, and the present-day weakening of the ecclesiastical
control of education betokens as little awe of the Anglican
Church. Furthermore, with the practical elimination of
the House of Lords accomplished, and the extension of suffrage to all adults without distinction of sex imminent, the
corporation-controlled government of England, which
Burke loved so well, may be looked for in vain. Modern
England, apparently, is neglecting her political book of
proverbs.

The admirer of Burke is prone to hail with great enthusiasm the noble principles and generalizations which crowd
the " Reflections," and this is done with some show of
justice. Many of the generalizations are well written, and
a few undoubtedly are worthy of respect. To analyze and
discuss abstract principles, however, is a dangerous procedure, for the scholastic pitfalls of philosophy are many
and well concealed. We do deny the conclusions of Edmund
Burke, but we make no claim to controvert the abstrac-
tions of the Burkian philosophy. They may be admirable,

but it is perhaps as well to regard them with suspicion, and as an illustration in point we would quote from J. Holland Rose's scholarly biography of Pitt. Mr. Rose writes that we are apt to be impressed by the remarks of Paine " until we contrast them with the majestic period wherein Burke depicts human society as a venerable and mysterious whole bequeathed by the wisdom of our fore-fathers. An admirer of Burke [he tells us] cannot but quote the following passage in full: ' Our political system is placed in a just correspondence and symmetry with the order of the world, and with the mode of existence decreed to a permanent body composed of transitory parts; wherein by the disposition of a stupendous wisdom, moulding to-gether the great mysterious incorporation of the human race, the whole, at one time, is never old, or middle-aged, or young, but in a condition of unchangeable constancy, moves on through the varied tenour of perpetual decay, fall, renovation and progression. Thus by preserving the method of nature in the conduct of the state, in what we improve we are never wholly new; in what we retain we are never wholly obsolete.' " [1] The friends of Burke must admit that the meaning and intent of this passage is not particularly lucid. Yet the conservatism of the time stands or falls with Burke. It is true that Hannah Moore and John Reeves serve a useful purpose as illustrative of a certain attitude toward life, but the inconsequential preach-ments of the one, and the musty Bourbonism of the other, from the standpoint of a rational synthesis may be brushed aside. There remains only the author of the " Reflections."

Radical theory was by no means free from error. The majority of the radicals were frequently led astray by two natural, but perhaps inevitable, blunders; for in avoiding the Scylla of vague emotionalism they were drawn into

[1] Rose, *William Pitt and the Great War*, p. 19.

the Charybdis of exaggerated detail and over-refined minu-
tiae. The " Rights of Man " may well serve to illustrate
these two tendencies. In the first part there is a passionate
defence of humanity. But humanity is a large term: it
was one of the weaknesses of eighteenth-century radicalism
that it phrased its aspirations in the large and vague for-
mulae of natural law and universals. If the rationalism
which Paine advocated was to realize its larger dreams it
must be directed into straight and definite channels. The
dogmas of a Condorcet follow after the vision of a Rousseau. So also is the wide sweep of Paine's idealism to be
compressed into specific and exact demands. Consequently
he wrote a second part to the " Rights of Man," and in it
we may easily catch the drift of the author's mind. The
reaction from Rousseau had set in, and it was healthy, but
its effect was too powerful, too far-reaching. Clearness
of thought and preciseness of definition does not necessitate
a homeopathic division of the national income so that one
may determine the exact number of officials that the state
may employ at an annual salary of seventy-five pounds per
man; yet that is the kind of blunder which Paine continually makes. His very anxiety to be precise defeats his own
purpose, and in consequence at first glance his pamphlets
often appear artificial and bizarre.

This unfortunate elaboration of detail is particularly
true of those pamphleteers who bring forward their own
individual panaceas for political corruption. Indeed, it is
a characteristic failing of almost all eighteenth-century
radicals. A notable exception is afforded by Mary Wollstonecraft. The individual development of this woman's
revolutionary thought took a form at once more original
and more daring than her vindication of humanity.
Paine, " the Rousseau of English democracy," contended sturdily for an ideal which stretched back to the

time of the Pharaohs. Wollstonecraft, as good a fighter
and as uncompromising, fought for a new ideal, hitherto
unformulated and perhaps undreamed. But her intelligence and her audacity were far above the rank and file of
her associates, and she fought alone.

A more serious criticism of British radicalism is its
failure to comprehend the significance of economic fact.
Poverty, with its ever-present attendants,—insufficiency of
food and over-taxation of the body,—then as now was the
common enemy which humanity must face. To this fact
the radical leaders were oblivious. They touched economic
problems, it is true; they advocated this economic reform
and that economic reform; but there was not one man to
say that the enemy is poverty, and that poverty is caused
first by the waste of human power in unintelligent production; secondly, by the inequitable distribution of opportuni-
ties. Not only was there no one to say this, but there
was none, save possibly Spence and Godwin, even to inquire into the cause of those three brutalizing burdens
which bear down mankind—low wages, long hours, and
irregular work.

The early activities of the radical associations were well
calculated to accomplish their aim. Converts to the cause
must be won, and pressure must be brought to bear upon
the authorities. The leaders of the radical clubs were
aware of this necessity, and in the main faced it with determination and skill. The idea of a convention was feasible; any gathering of delegates elected from a great number of widely-scattered clubs would, at least, be quite as
representative of the people as the five hundred squires
assembled at Westminster. But the London Corresponding
Society erred in sending delegates to Edinburgh. A larger
and more representative meeting would have been a fairer
test of radical strength. The temptation to send delegates,

however, was a strong one, and so unfortunately the impetuosity of Margarot and Gerrald destroyed all possibility, if not all hope, of an effective convention genuinely British.

With the collapse of the Edinburgh undertaking a distinct cleavage appeared in radical societies, for while certain members undoubtedly looked forward to an armed insurrection, others refused to abandon their old methods of peaceable propaganda. The wiser radicals belonged to the latter number, among them Hardy, the secretary of the London Corresponding Society, Place, Ashfield and other prominent members. They were not only aware of the younger Pitt's intelligence, but also of his determination. Pitt comprehended clearly the problem which confronted him. However possible moderate reform might have been in 1789 or 1790, it was not possible in 1793. Radicalism, if it was not to triumph, must be crushed. Pitt chose to crush it, and he did so effectively. Meanwhile the irreconcilables, underestimating the strength of the government, continued to devise their revolutionary schemes. Of necescity, however, their plans were discussed with the greatest secrecy, and history finds but little to chronicle.

Nevertheless, although their theories may have been chimerical and quixotic, their activities ill-advised and premature, the British radicals; both opportunists and irreconcilables; were rebels, and at times rebellion is justifiable. What though their rebellion was unsuccessful, it was at least a premonitory rumble of disaster to that serene and cushioned security so characteristic of entrenched privilege in England.

BIBLIOGRAPHY

I. PRIMARY SOURCES

Certain of the better known historical sources of our period as, for instance, the Dropmore papers, with their wealth of diplomatic correspondence, are, for the purpose of this dissertation, well-nigh useless. On the other hand, an abundance of material of especial merit is to be found. First, of course, is the invaluable Place collection of original manuscripts, which contains the minutes of the London Corresponding Society; letters to and from its officials, together with many rare pamphlets and broadsides. Second only to the Place manuscripts are the newspaper files for the seven years under discussion. Not only do they contain incidents and occurrences which escaped the attention of the "Annual Register," but also in them may be studied the spirit and temper of the times, more realistically reflected than in any other source. Finally, the pamphlet literature of the period is unusually rich in both quantity and quality. A majority of these pamphlets, to be sure, are of purely transitory interest. The law of the survival of the fittest has no application in the pamphlet world, for those tracts and broadsides which relate to industrial and economic discussion are among the more difficult to obtain. Indeed, if it were not for Professor E. R. A. Seligman, of Columbia University, many of these pamphlets might have been lost altogether. In his library in New York City is perhaps the finest private collection of this type of literature in the world, for in it are several publications not to be found even in the British Museum. Professor Seligman's library has been very kindly thrown open to the author, who has found there many sources elsewhere unavailable.

Address of the British Convention assembled at Edinburgh, London, 1793.

Address to the Electors of Southwark by an Elector, London, 1795.

An Act for the safety and preservation of his majesty's person and government, and an Act for more effectually preventing seditious meetings, 1796.

Akin, John, Food for National Penitence, 1793.

Anderson, J., Observations on the Effect of the Coal Duty, 1792.

Annual Register, 1790-1798.

Antipolemus, or the Plea of Reason, Religion and Humanity against War, 1794.

Barbauld, A. L., The Reason for National Penitence, 1794.

Barlow, Joel, Advice to Privileged Orders or Europe, 1792.

—— History of England, 1794.

Belsham, W., The Reign of George III, 1796.

—— Remarks on the Nature and Necessity of a Parliamentary Reform, 1793.

Bentham, J., Works, 1843.

Bentley, Richard, Considerations upon the State of Public Affairs, 1790.

Bicheno, John, The Overthrow of Papal Tyranny in France, 1795.

Bill of Rights, 1795.

Bill for Regulating the Sale of Corn by Weight, in a Letter from a Farmer, London, 1797.

Boothby, B., Observations on Appeal from the New to the Old Whigs, 1792.

Bowles, John, Two Letters addressed to a British Merchant, London, 1796.

Bowles, John, The Retrospect, 1798.

Brissot's Ghost, Edinburgh, 1794.

British Tocsin, or the Proofs of National Ruin.

Burke, Edmund, Works, Payne's Edition, 1892.

—— Réflections on the French Revolution, 1790. (Burke, works, Payne edition, vol. ii.)

—— An Appeal from the New to the Old Whigs, 1791.

—— A Letter to a Noble Lord, Feb. 24, 1796.

—— A Letter addressed to a Member of Parliament on the proposals for peace with the Regicide Directory of France, 1797.

Callender, J. T., The Political Progress of Britain, 1792.

Cartwright, J., A Letter to the Duke of Newcastle, 1792.

Castlereagh (Lord), Correspondence of, 1853.

Chatfield, J., Report on the Treason and Sedition Bills, London, 1795.

Cobbett, Political Works, 1835.

Colquhoun, P., The Police of the Metropolis, 4th ed., 1797.

Collection of Addresses to the National Convention of France, 1793.

Considerations on the Present Crisis of Affairs as it Respects the West India Colonies, London, 1795.

Crisis Stated, London, 1793.

Crutwell, A Tour of the whole Island of Great Britain, 1801.

Crying Frauds of the London Market, by the author of the Cutting Butchers' Appeal, 1795.

Curry, James, Commercial and Political Tract on the Interests of Great Britain, 1795.

Dalrymple, A., Parliamentary Reforms, 1792.

Davies, D., The case of the labourers in Husbandry, 1795.

Dirom, Alexander, An Inquiry into the Corn Laws and Corn Trade, Edinburgh, 1796.

Dyer, G., The Complaints of the Poor People of England, 2d ed., 1793.

Eden, Frederick, The State of the Poor, 3 vols., 1797.

Erskine, T., The causes and consequences of the Present War with France, 1797.

—— Speech at the Trial of T. Williams, 1797.

Equality as Consistent with the British Constitution, 1792.

Errors of Mr. Pitt's Administration, by a Gentleman, London, 1793.

Europe in Danger, 1794.

Extenuation of the Conduct of the French Revolutionists, 1792.

Facts, Reflections and Queries, submitted to the consideration of the Associated Friends of the People, Edinburgh, 1792.

Faulkner, C., Merits of Pitt's Administration, London, 1796.

Fitzwilliam, A Letter to the Earl of Carlisle, London, 1795.

—— A Second Letter to the Earl of Carlisle, Dublin, 1795.

Flower of the Jacobins, 1793.

Fox, Charles James, Letter to the Electors of Westminster, 1793.

—— Speeches in the House of Commons, 1815.

Fox, William, An Explanation of Mr. Paine's Writings.

Free Communings, or a last attempt to cure the Lunatics suffering from the French disease, Edinburgh, 1793.

Frend, William, Peace and Union Recommended, Cambridge, 1793.

—— Proceedings in the University of Cambridge, London, 1795.

—— Scarcity of Bread, 1795.

—— Thoughts on Subscriptions to Religious Tests, 1788.

Gabell, Henry, On the Expediency of Altering and Amending the Regulations Recommended by Parliament for Reducing the High Cost of Provisions, 1796.

Gerrald, Joseph, A Convention the Only Means of Saving Us from Ruin, London, 1793.

Gifford, J., Reasons against National Despondency, London, 1797.

—— A Letter to Thomas Erskine on the Causes and Consequences of the French War.

Glimpse through the Gloom, in a Candid Discussion of the Policy of Peace, London, 1794.

Godwin, W., Political Justice, 1793.

Gray, D. S., A Proposal for Supplying London with Bread, London, 1798.

Grenville, A Serious Lecture for the Last Day, London, 1798.

Gulf of Ruin, or a Quick Reform, Which will you Chuse? London, 1895.

Hawkesbury (Lord), A Discourse on the Establishment of a National and Constitutional Force in England, 1794.

Hill, George, The Present Happiness of Great Britain, 1792.

Hills, Robert, The Causes of the Present High Prices of Coals, 1814.

Hinton, J., Vindication of the Dissenters, 1792.

History of the Two Acts, 1796.

Hoadley (Bishop), A Refutation of Arguments on the Test and Corporation Acts, 1790.

Hobhouse, B., Heresy—a Treatise, 1792.

Hodgson, W., The Commonwealth of Reason, 1795.

Hodson, S., An Address on the Present Scarcity and High Price of Provisions, 1795.

Holt, D., Vindication of the Printer of the Newark " Herald," 1794.

Horsley, S., Speeches in Parliament, Dundee, 1813.

Hog's Wash. (D. I. Eaton, editor).

Houldbrooke, Short Address to the People of Scotland on the State of Trade, 1792.

Howell, T. B., State Trials from the Earliest Times to the Present, 1817.

Important Defence of the Established Church, Dublin, 1797.

Jones, A., State of the Country, 1794.

Jones, J. G., The Substance of a Speech, on March Second, 1795.

King or no King, 1791.

La Grice, C. V., Prize Declamation on Cromwell, Cambridge, 1795.

Letter addressed to a Farmer in Birmingham on the High Price of Provisions, by H. of Walsal, 1796.

Letter from a Farmer on the Bill for the Regulation of the Sale of Corn, 1797.

Letter from a Friend of the People, or the Last Words and Dying Advice of a Weaver to his Children, Glasgow, 1792.

Letters on Political Liberty addressed to a member of the British House of Commons, 1789.

Letter to the Reformers, Dorchester, 1798.

Letter to the Right Honourable Edmund Burke by a member of the Revolution Society, 1790.

Liberty and Equality, 1792.

Lofft, C., Remarks on a letter of Edmund Burke, concerning the French Revolution, London, 1790.

London Corresponding Society, Addresses and Resolutions, 1794.

—— Meeting of, London, Oct. 26, 1795.

—— Principles and Views, 1796.

—— Proceedings, 1795.

—— Summary of Duties and Citizenship, 1795.

McPhail, J., Remarks on the Causes of the High Prices of Provisions, 1795.

Mackintosh, J., Vindiciae Gallicae, 1791.

Malthus, T. R., Essay on Population, 1798.
—— Investigation of the High Price of Living, 1800.
Manners and Customs of the People of Bull-land, by Old Hubert, 1795.
Mathews, J., Remarks on the Cause, Progress, Scarcity and Dearness of Cattle, Swine, Cheese, etc., 1797.
Miracle, The, An Antidote against French Poison.
Monopoly, The Cutting Butchers' Last Appeal to the Legislature on the High Price of Meat, by a Philanthropic Butcher, 1795.
More, Hannah, Works, London, 1818.
Morgan, W., Facts addressed to the Serious Attention of the People of Great Britain, 1796.
Newspapers and Magazines:
　　Courier;
　　Gazetteer or New Daily Advertiser;
　　London Chronicle;
　　London Packet or Lloyd's Evening Post;
　　Morning Chronicle;
　　Morning Herald;
　　Observer and Sunday Advertiser;
　　Oracle and Public Advertiser;
　　Star;
　　Sun;
　　Telegram;
　　Times;
　　True Briton;
　　World.
(Magazines)
　　Analytical Review;
　　Bee, or Literary Weekly Intelligencer;
　　British Critic;
　　Critical Review;
　　Gentleman's Magazine;
　　Monthly Review.
Observations on the Present High Price of Corn, Bristol, 1795.
Observations on the Detriment which is supposed must arise to the Farmers of every cottage throughout the kingdom from the loss of Woolen Spinning by the introduction of Machinery, 1794.
Observations on the Trial of James Coigley, 1798.
On the Necessity of Altering the Regulations recommended to Parliament for reducing the present high price of Corn, 1796.
One pennyworth of truth from Thomas Bull to his Brother, John, 1792.
One pennyworth more, or a second Letter from Thomas Bull to his Brother John, 1792.
Parliamentary Debates:
　　Parliamentary Debates (Woodfall).

Parliamentary Journal (Jordan).

Parliamentary Register (Debrett).

The Senator, or Clarendon's Parliamentary Chronicle.

Parliamentary Journals: Journal of the House of Lords; Journal of the House of Commons, 1791-1797.

Parliamentary Reports: Reports from Committees, 1774-1802, IX.

Committee on the Assize of Bread. First Report, 10th of Feb., 1800. Second Report, 6th of March, 1800, ibid.

Committee on the high price of Corn, first report, 16th of Nov., 1795; second report, 8th Dec., 1795; third report, 9th and 23rd Dec., 1795; fourth report, 8th of March, 1796; fifth report, 18th of March, 1796.

Committee on the high price of Provisions, first report, 24th of Nov., 1800.

Committee on improving cultivation of waste, unenclosed and uncultivated land, 23rd Nov., 1795.

Parliamentary Reports: Reports from Committees, X.

Committee of the House of Commons on Seditious Societies, and on the State of Ireland, 23d of July, 1799.

Paine, T., Works, Conway Edition, 1892.

Address to Addressors, 1792.

Agrarian Justice, 1797.

Rights of Man, First Part, 1791.

Rights of Man, Second Part, 1792.

Parr, S., Works, 1828.

Patriot, The, or Republican Government, Edinburgh, 1793.

Phillips, C., Considerations on the causes of the High Price of Grain, and other articles of Provisions, 1792.

Pigott's Political Dictionary, published by Citizen Lee.

Plain Caution to every honest Englishman.

Place, F., Additional MSS., British Museum, 27,811-27,817.

Price, R., Appeal to the Public on the subject of the National Debt, 1772.

——— Discourse on the Love of our Country, 1789.

Priestley, J. Essay on the first principles of Government, 1771.

——— Lectures on History and General Policy, 1826.

Prophecies of Richard Brother, 1795.

Publication of the Glasgow Constitutional Association, 1793.

Questions for the People of Scotland, 1793.

Ranby, J., Doubts on the Abolition of the Slave Trade, 1790.

Reeves, J., Thoughts on the English Government, 1795.

Reflections on the present state of the British Nation, by British Common Sense, 1791.

Reform or Ruin, Take your Choice, 1798.

Report on the Proceedings of the Committee of the Sugar Refiners, for the purpose of affecting a reduction in the high price of sugar, 1792.

Revolutionary Society, Correspondence of, 1792.

Richmond (Duke of), Rights of Englishmen, 1794.

Rights of Swine, Stockport, 1794.

Shaw, S., Tour of the West of England, 1788.

Sinclair, J., Address on the improvement of British Wool, 1791.

—— The Statistical Account of Scotland, drawn up from the communication of the Ministers of the different Parishes, Edinburgh, 1793-1796.

Society of the Friends of the People, Proceedings, 1792.

Somerville, T., Observations on the Constitution and present state of Great Britain, 1793.

Spence, T., Constitution of the Perfect Commonwealth, 1793.

—— The Meridian Sun of Liberty, 1796.

State of Affairs in Great Britain and France, by a Farmer, Newark, 1792.

State Trials, see Howell.

Stokes, A., Desultory observations, 1792.

Stuart, D., Peace and Reform, 1794.

Thelwal, J., An Appeal to Popular Opinion on Kidnapping and Murder, including a Narrative of the late Atrocious Proceedings at Yarmouth, 1796.

—— Farewell address to the Tribune Readers, Peripatetic, 1793.

—— Peripatetic, 1793.

—— Prospectus of a Course of Lectures to be given every Monday, Wednesday and Friday during the ensuing Lent, in strict conformity with the restrictions of Mr. Pitt's Convention Act, 1794.

—— The rights of Nature against the usurpation of Establishments, 1796.

—— Sober Reflections on a Seditious and Inflammatory Letter of Burke to a Noble Lord, 1796.

—— Strike but Here, 1796.

Thoughts on the Causes of present Failures, 1793.

Trapp, J., Crimes of the Kings of France, 1791.

Van Sittart, N., Reflections on the propriety of the immediate conclusion of Peace, 1794.

Waddington, S. F., Remarks on Mr. Burke's two Letters, 1796.

Warning to Tyrants.

Wilks, M., Origin and Stability of the French Revolution, 1791.

Wollstonecraft, Mary, Vindication of the Rights of Man, 1790.

—— Vindication of the Rights of Woman, 1792.

Wyville, C., A Letter to Mr. Pitt, York, 1793.

Young, A., Annals of Agriculture and other useful Arts, 1791-97.

—— The example of France a warning to England, 1793.

—— Correspondence, British Museum Additional MSS., 35,127.

II. SECONDARY SOURCES.

Adler, Georg, Der ältere englische Sozialismus und Thomas Spence, Leipzig, 1904.

——— Der englische individualistische Radikalismus im 18. Jahrhundert und William Godwin, Leipzig, 1904.

Aiken, L., Memoir of Dr. Aiken, 1823.

Amherst, William, History of Catholic Emancipation, 1886.

Axon, W. E., The Annals of Manchester, 1886.

Baines, Edward, History of Cotton Manufacture in Great Britain, 1835.

Baines, Thomas, History of the Commerce and Town of Liverpool, 1852.

Bogue and Bennett, History of the Dissenters, 1812.

Brayley, E. W., London and Middlesex, 1810.

Brougham, (Lord), Historical Sketches of the Statesmen in the time of George III, 1839.

Campbell, John, Lives of the Lord Chancellors, 1845

Cartwright, F. D., Life and Correspondence of Major Cartwright, London, 1826.

Cestre, C., John Thelwal, a Pioneer of Democracy, 1906.

Chapman, S. J., Lancashire Cotton Industry, 1904.

Cockburn, H., Examination of the Trials for Sedition in Scotland, Edinburgh, 1888.

——— Memorials of his own Time, Edinburgh, 1775.

Conway, M. D., Life of Thomas Paine, New York, 1892.

Cooke, J. W., History of Party, 1841.

Cunningham, W., Growth of English Industry and Commerce, Cambridge, 1892.

Curtler, W. H. R., Short History of British Agriculture, 1909.

Davidson, J., Land for the Landless, London, 1896.

Dechesne, L., L'evolution économique et sociale de l'industrie de la laine en Angleterre, 1900.

Galloway, R. L., History of Coal Mining, 1882.

Gilchrist, A., Life of William Blake, 1907.

Glascow, Past and Present, illustrated from Guild Court Records, 1884.

Graham, H. G., The Social Life of Scotland in the 18th Century, 1900.

Graham, J. A., Memoir of J. H. Tooke, 1828.

Hammond, J. L. and Barbara, The Village Labourer, 1911.

Hasbach, W., History of the English Agricultural Laborer, 1908.

Hutton, W., History of Birmingham, 1819.

Jevons, W. S., The Coal Question, 1866.

Johnson, A. H., Disappearance of the Small Landowner, 1909.

Kent, C. B. R., The English Radicals, 1899.

Laprade, W. T., England and the French Revolution, John Hopkins Studies, 1909.

Levy, H., Monopoly and Competition, 1911.

Mackintosh, J., History of Civilization in Scotland, 1896.

Massay, W., History of England during the Reign of George III, 1860.

Mathieson, W. L., The Awakening in Scotland, 1747-1797 Glasgow, 1910.

May, T. E., The Constitutional History of England since the Accession of George III, 1899.

Morgan, W., Memoirs of the Life of Richard Price, 1815.

Nicholls, G., History of the English Poor Law.

Porrit, E., The unreformed House of Commons, Cambridge, 1903.

Porter, G. R., Progress of the Nation, 1847.

Prentice, A., Historical Sketches and Personal Recollections of Manchester, 1792-1832, 1852.

Rauschenbusch-Clough, E. R., Mary Wollstonecraft, 1898.

Reilly, J., History of Manchester, 1865.

Roberts, W., Memoirs of Hannah More, 1833.

Robinson, J. H., The New History, 1912.

Rose, J. Holland, William Pitt and the Great War, 1911.

——— William Pitt and the National Revival, 1911.

Russell, L. J., Memoirs and Correspondence of Charles James Fox, 1853.

Sanford, H., Thomas Poole and his Friends, 1888.

Scrivenor, H., History of the Iron Trade, 1854.

Smith, E., William Cobbett : a Biography, 1878.

Stanhope, P. H., Life of William Pitt, 1867.

Stephen, J. F., History of the Criminal Law of England, 1883.

Stephens, A., Memoirs of J. H. Tooke, 1813.

Stoughton, J., Religion of England under Queen Anne and the Georges, 1878.

Taylor, H. C., The decline of Landowning Farmers in England, Madison, Wis., 1904.

Taylor, G. R. S., Mary Wollstonecraft, a study in Economics and Romance, 1911.

Thorpe, T. E., Joseph Priestly, 1906.

Todd, C. B., Life and Letters of Joel Barlow, New York, 1806.

Tomline, G. P., Life of Mr. Pitt, 1811.

Tooke, T., History of Prices and of Circulation, 1838.

Tyler, M. C., The Literary Strivings of Joel Barlow, New York, 1895.

Ure, A., The Cotton Manufacture of Great Britain, 1861.

Wallas, G., Life of Francis Place, 1898.

Ward, B., The dawn of the Catholic Revival in England, 1909.

Watson, R., Anecdotes of the Life of the Bishop of Llandaff, 1816.

Webb, S. and B., History of Trade Unionism, 1894.

Yates, J., Memoirs of Dr. Priestley, 1860.